STABILITY OF INTERNATIONAL STOCK MARKETS

STABILITY OF INTERNATIONAL STOCK MARKETS

NIDAL RASHID SABRI

Nova Science Publishers, Inc.
New York

For permission to use material from this book please contact us:
Telephone 631-231-7269; Fax 631-231-8175
Web Site: http://www.novapublishers.com

Library of Congress Cataloging-in-Publication Data

Sabri, Nidal Richard.
Stability of international stock markets / Nidal Richard Sabri.
p. cm.
ISBN 13: 978-1-60021-743-2
ISBN 10: 1-60021-743-5
1. Stock echanges. 2. International finance. I. Title
HG4551.S23 2006
332.64'2 – dc22

2007016544

Published by Nova Science Publishers, Inc. ✢ New York

CONTENTS

ABOUT THE AUTHOR

Nidal Rashid Sabri is a Professor and the Dean of Faculty of Commerce and Economics at Birzeit University, Palestine. He served as Director of the MBA program at the same University, received his doctoral degree from the University of Northern Colorado, USA. He served as a consultant on several missions with UN Organizations including; UNDP, United Nations Industrial Development Organization, United Nations Conference on Trade and Development (UNCTAD), United Nations Center for Human Settlements, and International Labor Organization (ILO). He also served as a visiting scholar in the research department of the International Monetary Fund.

He published many academic papers in various Journals including: *Research in International Business and Finance, Advances in Financial Economics, International Journal of Business, Review of Accounting and Finance, Journal of Multinational Financial Management, International Journal of Commerce & Management, International Management, Small Business Economics, International Review of Comparative Public Policy, Finance India, Journal of International Accounting, Auditing and Taxation, Middle East Business Review, and Management Accountant.* He is also, an author of about twenty books including *Financial Institutions, Income Taxation, and Budgeting.* He also served as an editor for the *International Financial Systems & Stock Volatility* (Elsevier Science publisher).

PREFACE

Today, we find the world stock market is expanding significantly as expressed by the number of institutions, instruments, products and trading volume; thus tending to be more mature than ever, but risky, changeable, and volatile. In addition, it is working in a different environment and under new features. The new features have materialized and emerged in the last two decades, which may be summarized as follows: Various market crises occurred in the last two decades, including international, regional, and national financial crises, such as stock crises in 1987, and 1989, 1994-1995 in Latin America stock market, 1997 in Asian stock markets. In addition, there is an increase in the role of international and regional corporate associations and commissions, on national laws of securities trading. There is also an increase in the role of international and regional stock exchanges associations on national stock exchanges, such as the role of World Federation of Exchanges, and the IOSCO.

On the other side, there are new developments in the environment of stock trading, such as the increasing number of firms listed in multiple international markets, the increasing number of cross- listed national corporations in international stock exchanges, and the increasing size of international public offerings. In addition, there is an increase in the share of the non-residents trading in the world stock markets, introducing new instruments known as derivatives and indexed stock products and funds in new markets including emerging markets, based on underling-listed shares. Increases equity portfolio flows cross the world stock markets. Increasing in the size of cross border stock trading transactions, initiating the alternative trading systems known as ATSs for stock trading as substitute or a complementary vehicle to the traditional stock exchanges.

In addition, there is an increase in the value and importance of the world stock markets as expressed by a percentage of the GDP of the respected economies, as well as measured by number of securities, market capitalization, and the traded value. Other conditions have emerged such as increasing international linkages between the world stock price indices, emerging a phenomenon of volatility transmission between pairs, regional and world stock markets, as well as across segments of financial systems, which produces the contagion crisis. Using internet in stock trading, including: investment advising, accessing market information, monitoring portfolios of securities, and getting prices quotes, which changed the environment of stock trading decisions. Changing the floor trading to a screen-based trading in the majority of the world stock exchanges, and automating the stock trading transactions, reducing the settlement period of stock trading, and imposing the related laws to prevent insider trading.

The above recent developments created new conditions for financial markets in general and for the stock markets in particular. Accordingly, there is a need, to examine this issue, and to discuss various related aspects of stability, efficiency, and liquidity of stock markets in the new emerging global context. This is the aim of this research book, it will cover new related laws, procedures, and practices incorporated into the world stock markets. It includes both developed and emerging economies, civil and common laws. English origin, French origin, German origin, and Scandinavian origin, and will cover all geographic regions including South and Northern America, East, and West Europe, South Asia, Australia, and Middle East countries.

It covers financial trading and legal aspects, as associated with the stock market efficiency and stability in a global concept. It aims to trace and point out the recent developments that occurred in the world stock markets in the last decade, including trends toward integration, liberalization, and globalization. To discuss the issue of market stability and efficiency in light of the new emerging environment of stock market trading. To indicate the most recent changes in the related laws and practices which have a direct effect on the stock trading stability. In addition, to offer a comprehensive view covering the international stock markets practices and their possible risk existing in the world today.

The findings of this book are based on legal aspects of the majority of the world jurisdictions, and the majority of the existing and new introduced practices to the world stock markets including the role of international commissions, and organizations in this regard. Examination of the stock market efficiency and stability presented in the sixth and seventh chapters is built on empirical investigations, opinions surveys of stock markets experts, and state of arts of the related studies, official reports, and suggested recommendations and best practices. Finally, this book is a modest attempt to help in preventing the next stock market crisis, or to understand how to deal with, in order to shorten the period of decline, shortening the period of recovery, and to reduce the effect of the irrational trading during unstable trading.

Chapter 1

FINANCIAL MARKETS

INTRODUCTION

The financial system is the most significant factor for the development of the world economy in both developed and emerging countries. It is considered as the engine of driving cash flows among concerning parties, including lenders, borrowers and investors. Various financial institutions, markets, and instruments produce the needed cash flow mechanism and channels at the national economy level as well as at the regional and world economy levels. The world financial market is expanding significantly considering the number of institutions, instruments, products, capitalization value, number of securities, and volume and value of trading, which existed at the beginning of the twenty -one century. The changes in this industry are moving so rapidly due to applying internet, communications and technology and introducing new innovative products and instruments. The financial system includes financial institutions as well as financial markets. In spite of the fact that both parts are integrated; to carry out the functions of money and capital flows among the different segments of the world economy, they are varied in their merits, mechanism, and functions. Thus this research book is devoted for financial markets rather financial institutions.

This chapter discusses different aspects of the financial markets in general, in order to indicate the location and the relationship between stock markets and other types of financial markets. The financial markets are moving and changing fast in operation mechanism and in the trading environment in the world economy. Recently, new countries emerged and added significantly, to the world financial markets, such as the joining of new various financial markets initiated and developed so fast in the last two decades including China, Russia, Eastern Europe, and other emerging economies. It also witnessed significant changes in liberalization, integration, and in introducing new products and instruments, based on underling major issues of both equities and fixed income securities. Accordingly, this chapter is devoted to summarize functions, classifications, and types of financial markets in general as existing today in the world economy. While the following chapters will be devoted to the world stock markets, in order to explore and discuss the related issues of stock trading stability, to improve and strengthen the world stock markets, and to enhance the relevant practices, and identifying the relevant laws and environment, thus to assure a liquid, efficient and a stable global environment of stock trading.

THE IMPORTANCE OF FINANCIAL MARKETS

The role of financial markets has been increasing significantly as expressed by several indicators including numbers and types of traded products, number of listed securities, the market capitalization of the listed securities, and the trading volume of financial markets. The size, value, and the importance of financial markets including a variety of products and markets such as the stock markets, the bond markets, currencies' markets, options and futures markets of equities and bonds which are increasing in both developed and emerging countries. For example, the domestic stock market capitalization exceeded 100% of the respected national values of GDPs in many countries, such as in case of NYSE, Hong Kong, Swiss, Luxembourg, London, Taiwan, TSX (Canada), Malaysia, JSE, Santiago, Australian, and Singapore exchanges. In case of Swiss it exceeds 200% of GDP, and in Hong Kong it exceeds 500% of their GDP in 2004, as shown in Table 1-1. However, the value of stock markets in the majority of emerging countries is still moderate, but improved in the last decade (WFE, 2006 based on IMF statistics).

Table 1-1. Significance of selected stock markets to their national economies (Percentages of domestic market capitalization to national GDP value in 2004)

Stock Exchanges	% of GDP
Hong Kong Exchange	527.7%
Swiss Exchange	210.3%
Singapore Exchange	196.9%
Luxembourg SE	143.3%
NYSE	108.3%
Santiago SE	114.1%
TSX Group- Canada	109.8%
Australian SE	118.8%
Bursa Malaysia	154.2%
Taiwan SE Corp.	124.2%
JSE	181.3%
London SE	127.4%

Source: WFE, 2006 based on IMF statistics.

Many economists consider the development of the financial market as a positive mark, and thus may lead to the development of the whole economy. In addition, the correlation between the economic growth of a country and its level of stock market development has been extensively examined in both emerging and developed countries. It is now a generally accepted concept that the development of a financial market may reflect positively on the economy growth of that country. This concept is also reported by various empirical studies, which have found that the development of stock markets is an important factor for the economic development and reported a significant correlation between both indicators for present and future expectations (Levine 1991, Levine and Zervos, 1996; Demirguc- Kunt, and Levine, 1996). In addition, some evidences concluded that more liquid and active stock markets might put a pressure on firms to increase their capital productivity. For example, the

US has a capital productivity of 60% higher than Germany which has less active stock market, as reported by 1996 McKinsey Global study (IFC, 1998, p.19).

FUNCTIONS OF FINANCIAL MARKETS

The financial markets have various functions and play a critical role in the national, regional, and world economy. Broadly speaking, the main function of the financial markets is to offer various mechanisms and vehicles to trade the financial instruments, currencies, and securities, to process the cash flow between the concerned parties, and to operate the capital accumulation that may be transferred to business projects and job opportunities. In addition, many other services and functions are offered by financial markets in both developed and emerging economies. In more details, the following are examples of the services and functions that may be found in the world financial markets:

Table 1-2. Types of traded products in the world stock markets in 2001

	% of the total
Stocks	95%
Corporate bonds	88%
Warrants	83%
Government bonds	76%
Convertible bonds	74%
Options stock markets	60%
Future stock market	55%
Mutual funds	43%
Exchange traded funds (ETFs)	43%
Money market instruments	29%
Other instruments and securities	25%

Source: WFE Trading Survey, 2003.

First: A place for trading and stating prices: The financial market is a place to trade financial securities between agents who need money such as investors and borrowers, and those who have excess cash as savers and lenders. Financial markets produce the efficient place for financial intermediaries, and other concerned parties who need to execute their trading, and exchange funds and financial instruments based on stated right prices. The stated prices are determined by the mechanism of the efficient financial market. The financial markets may trade in one item such as in the case of stock exchanges in the majority of the emerging countries, while others trade in a variety of products besides stocks in one place including government and corporate bonds, options and futures instruments, exchange traded funds, and money instruments. However, there are some financial markets trading in one or more types of financial instruments such as those trading only in future and options of equities. Currencies and other money market instruments may also trade in the same stock exchange or in specialized exchanges. Generally, the majority of the world stock exchanges have shares, bonds, warranties, futures and options securities as presented in Table 1-2.

Second: Accumulation of investments: Financial exchanges offer the right vehicle to accumulate investments in both developed and emerging economies. They offer the relevant environment for attracting and implementing investments, and thus developing the related economies. The total world accumulated funds channeled by stock exchanges including capital raised by new issues and already issued shares reached about $ 262 billion during the 2002 year. For many developed countries, the accumulated funds channeled through stock exchanges ranged between $ 6 billion in Italy and $ 26 billion in London and from both new issues and already issued shares in the year 2002. For emerging stock exchanges, the accumulated funds ranged between one billion in Jakarta and seven billions in Shanghai stock exchange (WFE, 2006). The stock markets especially in emerging countries may offer an alternative to the financing systems offered by banks, or work besides banks to supply the needed funds for establishing new projects and expansions. This may be accomplished through primary stock markets as well as the international public offerings. The accumulated investments may be generated from local and national sources and from foreign investments as well.

Third: Investment Allocation: the financial markets help the mutual funds, pension funds, insurance companies, and households to articulate the relevant portfolios, and to diversity their investments. Financial markets offer the right opportunity for reducing risk through diversifying their investment portfolios, especially in case of having foreign listed instruments in their national exchanges and vice versa.

Fourth: Creating and introducing new instruments and a variety of products that may be traded in financial markets, such as options, futures, warranties, indexed options and futures and exchange trade funds products which are based on the underlying equities and bonds.

Fifth: Serving the financial institutions: Financial markets serve the financial intermediaries and institutions such as commercial and development banks, insurance companies, mutual funds, saving and provident funds, through offering the needed liquidity when needed and providing the opportunity to invest any surplus when it is available.

Sixth: Establishing economic projects and raising the needed funds in the case of primary markets through establishing new corporations, as well as helping the existing companies to increase their own capital or generating loans through issuing bonds and other financial instruments.

Types of the World Financial Markets

The world stock markets include various markets, which can be categorized in different ways. For the purpose of this book, the financial markets may be articulated in various groups, based on different bases, which produce various types of markets as presented in Table 1-3. The presented groups of financial markets include: cash to derivative markets, stocks to fixed income rate (bonds) securities markets, regular to over the counter financial markets, national to international financial markets, money to capital markets, primary to secondary markets, emerging to developed markets. Not all financial markets presented in the table are existed in all regional or in each of the individual countries.

Table No 1-3. Summary of financial markets

Classifications	Types of markets	Examples
Location of trading	National markets	Home listed equities and bonds
	International markets	Eurocurrency, Eurobonds, Cross-listed equities, currencies, Euro- equity issues, ADR.
Time of implementing trade	Cash (spot contract)	Shares, bonds, currency, and other financial instruments
	Derivatives markets And innovative instruments	Futures, options, index futures, and index options, covered warranties, ETFs equities
Profit to fixed rate	Stocks	Common shares, preferred shares
	Bonds	Government bonds, treasury bills, corporate bonds, municipal bonds
Market place	Regular; Levels of secondary markets	Listed securities (shares and bonds)
	Over the counter (OTC)	Unlisted securities
Period of instrument	Money market (less than one year maturity)	CDs, instruments of less than a year maturity, commercial papers, Eurocurrency, repurchase agreements
	Capital markets	Shares and bonds, and treasury bills due in more than one year
Timing of issuing	Secondary markets	spot markets and derivatives markets
	Primary markets	New issues, including IPO
Level of economy	Developed markets	Financial markets located in economies with per capita income of more than $ 10,000
	Emerging markets	All financial markets located in economies with per capita income of less than $ 10,000

However, majority of developed economies have almost all the presented markets of the seven groups and sub-groups, while the emerging economies have mainly national capital financial market with trading in equities based on cash (spot contract), with no derivatives market, and with a small share of money market and bonds trading. The financial markets are working and organized based on their respected national commercial laws, which have significant differences between countries.

Some financial markets are neither existing nor permitted in some countries, while other financial markets are permitted but work based on different regulations, conditions, and environment. The following section will briefly discuss the major merits of the most significant types of financial markets based on the environment of both developed and emerging economies. However, it should be noted here that the presented features for each type are stated based on the existing practices in the majority of the financial markets, considering the fact that the world financial market is still far from being a harmonized market. The world financial markets are operated based on national related laws and regional practices which are significant different from each other rather than unified laws and regulations.

National and International Financial Markets

The national financial market refers to trading in financial securities and instruments in a national currency based on a single jurisdiction. The international financial market refers to markets where trading occur under two or more jurisdictions or using two or more currencies. This means that all transactions involved in two or more jurisdictions or currencies may be identified within international markets.

The concept of international financial markets has extended from currency trading, Eurocurrency and Eurobond markets to include bonds and equities markets that trade outside their home exchanges through either a direct cross listing in foreign stock exchanges, or through ADR (American Depositary Receipts) instruments in the case of US exchanges or through International public offering in case of trading in primary market. In addition, other transactions are considered within the context of international markets such as buying national listed shares by non- residents investors, trading in bonds and equities issued by foreign currencies, issuing instruments deposited outside the national issuers countries.

Capital and Money Markets

Capital markets refer to stock and bond markets and other instruments of long -term maturity. The money market refers to trading in short term-maturity instruments and currencies. The currencies market known as foreign exchange market is considered as an example of money market. It aims to change a currency on return of another currency based on a price known as foreign exchange rate. It is considered as a money market in which the exchange of currencies occurs between national and foreign currencies or between two foreign currencies. The purpose of currency exchange is to pay for import goods and services, for traveling or for speculation and trading purposes. The foreign exchange market transactions include both the spot transactions and the forward and futures transactions. However, the majority of trading is related to spot transactions.

The exchange price between two currencies is determined in general based on the supply and demand, as well as considering other factors, which are reflected to determine the right price. Such factors include what is known as the purchasing power parity (PPP), which is related to the price levels of the two countries. Other factors reflected in the stated price of a currency are the productivity, the economic and political situations in the related countries. Finally the variance of a national currency against other currencies is mainly based on the type of the adopted currency system, and whether it is floating or fixed exchange rate against the dollar or other main currencies. Trading of currencies may be located directly between the concerned parties, or through financial exchanges.

Stock and Bond Markets

A stock is a share of capital of a corporation, which will be discussed during the next chapters. The bond is a financial instrument represents a share of a loan with a stated face value issued by a corporation, central government, local government or a non- for profit organization. The bondholder buys a bond on return for a fixed annual interest as well as to get the face value at maturity date. At the due time, the bond may be paid once or through installments plan. The bond may be sold at a discount that produces a high yield (rate of return). The bond has various merits including the stated face value, the discount, the interest rate, and maturity period and other merits such as the ability to be converted to equities or callable before maturity or to be a secured bond. The fixed rate on bonds in international markets ranged between 3% and 15% in the last three decades. However, in some countries such as Japan the governmental bond rates are significantly less than that.

The possible buyers of bonds include many groups of investors, such as individuals, banks, insurance companies, pension funds, and mutual funds. It is less risky than equities, with reliable annual income. The bond markets may be affected by changing in interest rate, inflation, and political situations. Investment in bonds has various merits compared to shares and other instruments that it has less risk, with dependable annual income, and has tax advantages in the case of buying governmental bonds in various countries. The bonds may be listed in the home stock exchanges as well as in foreign exchanges and may be issued in the national currency or in foreign currencies known as foreign bonds such as the Yankee bonds. In addition, financial derivatives based on bonds also may be issued and traded on either organized or over the counter markets.

The types and features of bonds vary and depend on the related laws of the countries. The securities laws, which organize the issuance and trading of bonds, vary from one country to another. For example, some countries prevent or do not permit issuing bonds by corporations, while others require conditions for corporations before using the option of issuing bonds as a source of long-term financing. Considering the world bonds markets we find various types, and merits used in the majority of the world financial markets as presented in Table No 1-4.

Table 1-4. Major types and merits of bonds as existed in the majority of the world financial markets

Major Types of Bonds	Sub- types
Corporate bonds	Bearer- registered
	Secured –non secured bonds
	Fixed interest rate, floated rate, zero coupon, revenue bonds
	Converted- non –converted bonds
	Callable- Non- callable bonds
Public bonds	Government bonds (from 10 to 30 years)
	Municipality bonds (Fixed, revenue)
	Treasury bills (less than one year)
	Treasury notes (from one to ten years)
National bonds	Corporate and government
Foreign bonds	Foreign corporate and government listed in national exchange

The variety of bonds may be referred to the type of the issuer, type of attached merits, location of trading, and maturity period. There are three groups including governments, local municipalities, and public business corporations mainly issue bonds. There are various types of government bonds based on maturity, such as short treasury bills, which have a period of less than one year, intermediate maturity bonds with a period ranging from more than one to ten years, and long-term bonds, which known in some countries as developed bonds, have a maturity ranging between ten to thirty years. The majority of corporate bonds have a maturity period ranged between ten to thirty years.

Each bond has a face value, which is considered as the selling price in the primary market. The bonds may be sold for less than the face value by being sold at discount rate. The face value may be between $ 1 and $ 10 such as that issued by corporations in many emerging economies and up to $ 1000 of a face value such as that issued in USA. The majority of the world related corporate laws state the minimum and the maximum of face values of issuing bonds. This is also applicable to central governmental bonds and local government bonds which are organized by different laws, with an average face valued ranged between $ 10 and $ 10,000. Some types of bonds are attached with the right for calling, known as the call provision, which gives the right of the corporation to recall and redeem these bonds before maturity date, and offer the issuer flexibility to pay its own debt before maturity. Issuers of such bonds are likely to do that when commercial interest rate fall down. However, the yield for such types of bonds is higher than other types of bonds that do not have the call rights. In addition, there is another type of bonds which has a zero coupon, and does not pay any interest payments until maturity. Other types of securities may be known as secured bonds, which are attached with a mortgage or physical assets, while on return there are non-secured bonds. In addition, Laws in some countries permit issuing a bond to be attached with the possibility or the right to be converted to a preferred or common stock. The bond certificate may be registered holding the name of bondholders or a bearer certificate, based on the related national corporate laws. Some countries prohibited the bearer bonds recently for various reasons such as for tax purposes or for contolling the cash flow reason. In addition, there are many innovative instrument may be considered as bonds. For example, in Arab economy special types of bonds issue by Arab governments and corporations known as corporate Sukuks and Sovereign sukuks articulated based on Islamic finance principles and now are expanding mainly in Arab Gulf States.

The value of listed bonds have been increasing significantly in the majority of the world bonds markets in the last decade and increased from $ 6,618 billion in 1990 to $ 25,760 billion in 2005, while the traded value of listed bonds increased about five times in the last 15 years and reached about $14,021 billion as presented in Table 1-5. The major bond markets as expressed by annual trade value or capitalization value have been moving from one stock exchange to another in the last decade. However, the top four major bond markets as expressed by trade value are located in Luxemburg, Osaka, Tokyo and London as expressed by market capitalization, while BME Spanish, London and OMX were the top bond markets as expressed by total of trade value in bonds in 2006 (WFE, 2006).

In some countries, the value of traded government bonds is much higher than the corporate bonds while the corporate bonds value is higher than government bonds in others. For example, the government bonds market represents 56% of the GDP in Korea, while it forms only 31% in case of corporate bonds. This is also applicable to many developed and emerging countries, such as India, Hungary, France, Italy and USA. While in other countries, the share of corporate bonds value is much higher than the share of government bonds such as in the Germany and Czech Republic economies. In Italy, Japan and USA the government and corporate bonds traded value may form more than 100% of the GDP (World Bank and IMF, 2001). The market value as well as the number of listed foreign bonds has been also increasing significantly in the last decade for many world bond markets. For example, the foreign listed bonds in Luxembourg increased four times in one decade and reached about 28, 625 listed bonds (WFE, 2006).

Table 1-5. Summary of the world bond markets in $ million between 1990 and 2006

	Value of bond trading (domestic & foreign)			Market Capitalization	Listed Bonds
	1990	2005	2006	2005	2006
First: Total bond markets	3,180,306.6	13,003,334.0	14,020,702.90	25,759,704.3	111,670
Second: Top markets in traded value					
BME Spanish		4,092,370.6	4,985,000.0		4129
London SE	1,019,053.0	3,008,685.9	3,309,000.0	2,574,315.9	12171
OMX		3,100,530.8	2,894,000.0	686,293.9	4,727
Colombia		721,000.0	463,000.0	56,200.4	463
Istanbul		407,000.0	532,000.0	187,536.8	185
Euronext		367,000.0	178,000.0		3,366
Korea Exchange	4,537.0	355,088.0	304,000,0	714,294.7	8195
Deutsche Börse	603,929.3	381,052.6	288,000.0		18,292

Source: WFE, 2006 and WFE Focus, 2007.

Primary and Secondary Markets

The main financial market is the secondary market that deals with already issued stocks, bonds and other financial instruments between various investors. On the other side the primary market is related to newly under-establishing firms that to be traded for the first time based on their face value announced by the founders. It includes only new issued shares and bonds, and does not include derivatives. The mechanism of primary market depends on the related laws of the various countries. Another form of primary market is known as the Initial public offerings, which involves the transfer of private corporation to public corporation through selling the shares in the stock exchange at a stated price, which is supposed to reflect the financial position of the firm besides the future expectation of the firm. A private company goes public to raise funds and increases its own capital instead of borrowing. The regulations, conditions and procedures of going public and initial public offering vary from one country to another.

The role of the primary stock exchanges for a newly established public corporation is to manage the process of subscriptions of the new stockholders who join the establishing group of the corporation, and to trade the equities for the first time according to the par values of the related equities. Some countries permit selling the equities with discount or premium based on stated conditions. The primary markets sell corporate bonds at their face value, while the government bonds may be sold using auction trading. However, the shares and bonds may be sold in the primary market, for a price less or more than the face value such as in the case of selling at a discount rate or at a premium. The local primary market plays a critical role in accumulating the needed capital either for share or bond markets. For example, the primary market raised funds was about $ 15 trillion between 1991 and 1995 in 32 emerging and developed countries (Aylward and Glen, 2000). The primary market may serve issuing corporate shares, corporate bonds, government bonds, and may be located in regular market or in the over the counter markets.

Regular and Over-the-Counter (OTC) Markets

The regular financial market is the official regulated market in which the main securities are listed and traded based on specific criteria. The regular market may be classified into different levels (A, B and C levels) based on the capital value of the corporations. Other securities which do not meet the stated requirements of any level of regular markets may be traded in the over the counter. Over the Counter market (OTC) is a less regulated financial market, which is attached to the regular financial markets in almost the majority of the world stock exchanges. The unlisted securities and firms, which may not meet the requirements of any level of the regular market, may be traded in the OTC.

The OTC is not an auction place, but it is a network, where brokers and dealers negotiate directly, through the phone, or through special networks to implement and execute the selling and buying transactions. The majority of the de-listed firms move to OTC Market, because it has fewer regulations compared to the regular market. Firms listed in regular stock exchange may not trade their issues on the OTC market. However, some countries permitted listed firms' equities to be traded inside and outside the stock exchanges. The largest OTC market in the world now is in the NASDAQ in USA, which includes American as well as foreign securities. Some companies in some countries may prefer to go to less regulated markets when they emerge from private to public corporation, as it is the case, when a small European or Asian firm prefers to be listed in NASDAQ market rather than that in their home exchange which may have strict list of requirements.

Derivatives and Cash Markets

The normal financial market is known as the cash or spot market, while options and futures markets are known as derivative markets. The financial derivative is a new instrument which has been introduced to the world financial markets just in the last three decades. It is a financial instrument stated in a contractual form and attached to a specific underlying real instrument. The real or the basic instrument may be a share, a bond, an interest rate, and a currency. The concept of introducing this kind of financial derivatives has been derived from the forward contracts, which obligate the buyer to pay a specific price at a specific date and to receive the commodity on return. The buyer may experience profit or loss based on the price at the time of settlement. This concept is used with various applications to produce various types of derivatives. The derivatives markets offer the opportunity for investors, to reduce their risk through hedging from potential future financial markets in cases of payables and receivables, for speculators, and for arbitraging by taking offsetting positions in various instruments. These are the futures contract, the options, and the swap contracts. The three derivatives are produced based on shares, bonds, interest rates, and currencies.

The future contract is an agreement to buy or to sell an underling share, bond or currency at a stated future time for a pre-determined price in a regular exchange. The trading of future instruments or currency may occur in OTC Market and is considered as a forward contract. The option markets also provide contract agreements, which give the holder the right –not the obligation- to buy (call option) or to sell (a put option) a defined underling stock or bonds at a stated price called a strike price, and during a specific period of time. The striking price is the price at which the holder of the call option can buy, or holder of the put option can sell the derivative instrument prior to the expired date. The buyer of the call option has to pay a premium to the writer of the option as well as the holder of put option has to pay a premium to the writer of the option. However, the option and future markets may be attached to equity markets and traded in four forms, including options, index options, futures, and index futures. In recent years, the index options and index futures has become more important than options and future trading. The financial derivative instrument is a contract between two parties that agree to buy or sell stated quantity underling instruments at a specific price known as the strike price. The financial derivative has no attached annual profit or fixed interest rate such as the underlying issue.

Individual investors as well as various financial intermediates and mutual funds are the major traders. The trading of derivatives is not connected to the trading of underling instruments. The trade is implemented and settled separately from the underling instrument transactions. Buyers and sellers trading in derivatives may not necessarily own or sell the underling instruments. However, prices of the derivatives are stated based on the present and expected future prices of the underling instruments. The relationship between derivative prices and underling instruments prices works on both sides and affects each other.

The derivative markets are attached to the secondary markets not to the primary markets and may be traded on regular secondary markets as well as on over the counter markets. However, some believe that the OTC derivative activities may increase the instability in institutions, markets, and international financial system as found by Schinasi, et al. (2000, p. 49). The derivatives may be connected to money markets or to capital markets. Financial derivative payment should be settled in cash or within few working days. However, the majority of option and future markets may require paying a margin in advance as a collateral obligation and to reduce risk. The trading markets of financial derivatives occur in the world stock exchanges. However, there are specialized options and future markets that trade exclusively in the derivative instruments only. Various stock exchanges may use the margin ratio in derivatives trading as a control tool. They may decrease or increase the ratio to control the liquidity and stability of stock markets in times of unstable trading. All stock option contracts have the option to purchase a specified number of shares on or before stated future date at stated price.

The world trading of derivatives are located in USA, eight European states, Japan, Singapore, Hong Kong, and South Korea. There are few emerging markets that deal with the financial derivatives. The most important exchanges in the world are the specialized exchanges such as the Chicago Board of Trade, the Chicago Mercantile Exchange in USA, the London International Financial Future and option exchange in London, and the Option market in Netherlands. Based on the traded contracts in 2006 the Korea exchange, the Chicago Board of Options, Sao Paulo, Eurex, and Chicago Mercantile exchanges, Philadelphia, and American stock exchanges are considered as the top stock exchanges in trading derivatives respectively. The number of all derivatives equity contracts was about

6,462,796,669 in 2006 (WFE, Focus 2007). All stock option contracts are for 100 shares, accordingly, the notional value of derivatives is the number of contracts traded, multiplied by 100, multiplied by the contracts' underlying market value of the shares. Table 1-6 summarizes the world derivatives markets as existed in 2006. As shown in the table there are four major types of equity derivatives, the most important are the stock index options and the single options, which forms about 78%, while futures contracts for both single and index stocks forms only 22% of the world equity derivatives markets.

Table 1-6. Summary of the World Derivates Equity Markets in 2006

Type of Derivates	Number of Traded Contracts	Share in Markets
Stock *Options*	1,770,424,576	27%
Stock Single *Futures*	276,145,142	4%
Stock Index *Options*	3,268,505,940	51%
Stock Index *Futures*	1,147,721,011	18%
Total traded contracts in 2006	6,462,796,669	100%

Source: FEW, focus, 2007.

Developed and Emerging Markets

The classification of financial markets to developed and emerging markets is not based on the features of each group, instead, it is based on the level of economy for that country, which is measured by the income per capita and the stated level by the International Financial Corporation of the World Bank. The country with a gross domestic product per capita that exceeds 4 10,000 is considered as a developed country. Other countries with less than this value are classified as emerging countries. Based on this classification there are about eighty emerging markets and thirty-one developed markets in 2003 (S&P, 2003). The majority of the developed financial markets are mainly large markets as expressed by the number of traded products and instruments, capitalization and traded values. The largest stock markets in the developed countries are located in US, followed by Japan, UK, France, Germany, Canada, Switzerland, and Italy respectively. The largest stock markets in the emerging economies are located in China, Korea, Taiwan, Russia, Malaysia, and Brazil. In spite of the fact that China and Russia stock markets were just been initiated in the last decade, and have developed so fast. China stock market increased about eight times in the last ten years. The traded value of China stock market increased from $ 43,395 million in 1993 to $ 333,369 million in 2002 (S &P 2003).

It should be noted here that neither the developed market nor the emerging markets form harmonized segment markets. There are significant differences that exist within each group regarding the types and features of traded securities as well as the related corporate, security and exchanges laws and regulations (Sabri, 2003, Sabri, 2005, and Sabri, 2007a). The varieties are extended even to a single listed firm or issue. For example, a firm may issue dual classes of shares with vote non-vote shares, par –non par value shares, bearer- registered shares.

However, if we would like to point out the market differences in general between the developed and the emerging groups, the following features may come up: The majority of emerging markets are merely trading in common shares, with limited trading in bonds, future, and options derivatives. There are limited foreign securities listed in the majority of emerging markets. The capitalization and the traded values are still limited and form about 10% of the world total market. However, the number of listed shares is almost equal to the developed market (S &P 2003). The average capital of the listed firm is much smaller than that in developed market, and finally, the majority of the value of emerging stock markets forms less than 100% of their respected GDP.

The pervious conclusion is a general observation, because there are some emerging markets that are more important than some developed markets. Such as the size of equity market in China, the size of bond, option, and future markets in South Africa and Korea. On the other side, some developed financial markets are classified as developed markets, simply because they are located in oil producing countries. In addition, in the last decade, various new features have materialized in the majority of the emerging stock markets, such as eliminating restrictions imposed on foreign trading and ownership whether fully or partially, increasing the share of non- residents' transactions as well as in the foreign ownership of listed firms, introducing cross listed shares to emerging markets, and trading in derivatives such as that of Korea, Brazil, South Africa, Taiwan, and Malaysia stock exchanges.

INTERACTIONS BETWEEN FINANCIAL MARKETS

Financial markets are so connected to each other with a positive or negative impact, due to the fact the each financial market represents an alternative investment to the others. In addition, the interactions between the prices of products in the financial markets and the volatility spillovers from one market to another have been increasing during the last decade. For examples, the existed interactions between the stock and the bond markets, the interaction between derivatives, and the underling instruments, that occurs when new derivatives are introduced or traded. The effect may be on prices, volatility of return, and volume of the underling equities or bonds. This issue is one of the most critical aspects when dealing with stability of the world stock market.

In addition, the break down between the pricing of the future contracts and stock index is considered by some official reports as one of the main causes of 1987 crashes (Kamphuis el at. 1989). Accordingly, the IOSCO adopted a resolution on coordination between cash and derivative markets in 1993 which stated that it is important to designed the derivative products in a way that does not impair both cash and derivatives market and to reduce the risk of disruption (IOSCO, 1993). The interactions between cash markets and derivatives markets are also applied to currency markets, which is one of critical variables affecting the stock volatility (Sabri, 2004 and Sabri, 2007b). The interactions between stock market and other markets is extending to bonds markets, interest rate, and other financial instruments.

Several studies reported that there are strong interaction and linkages between bond, currencies, interest rates and stock markets, and stock market overreacts to bond yield and rating. For example, Lim et al. (1998) found that bi-directional causality exists between both stock and bond return markets. In addition, the effect of one market on another is not confined to one country or region but it extends to other regions. For example, the changing in the interest rate in USA affects the share and the bond markets not only in the USA, but also in other regions and countries, such as South Asian financial markets (BIS, 2003). In addition, the importance of the world financial markets is moving from one market to another and from one place to another.

However, the top financial markets are distributed all over the world, and moving towards concentrating to selected financial instruments besides trading in equities as existed in 2006. For example, the top stock market as expressed by share trade value and market capitalization are NYSE, Nasdaq, London, Tokyo and Euronext, as shown in Table 1-7. While the world top markets in derivatives are distributed between CBOE, Korea, CME, India, Deutsche and NYSE. The main locations of foreign trade are located in London, NYSE, and Swiss. The top markets in bonds are located in Luxembourg SE, Osaka, and Tokyo as expressed by market capitalization, while the BME Spanish, London and OMX represent the top in traded value of bonds (WFE, 2006 and 2007).

Table 1- 7. Summary of the World Financial Markets (Equities and Bonds) as in 2006

	Major Merits	Top Markets
Equity market	Traded value and market capitalization	NYSE, Nasdaq, London, Tokyo and Euronext
	Number of foreign listed shares	NYSE, Nasdaq, and London
	Number of local listed shares	TSX (Canada), NYSE, Nasdaq, London, and Tokyo
	Value of foreign trading	London, NYSE, and Swiss exchange
Derivatives	Stock option	Chicago Board Option Exchange
	Stock index option	Korea Exchange
	Stock index future	Chicago Mercantile exchange
	Single stock future	National Exchange of India
	Warrants	Deutsche Borse and Hong Kong
	ETFs	NYSE
Bonds	Traded value	BME Spanish, London and OMX
	Market capitalization	Luxembourg SE, Osaka, and Tokyo
	No. of domestic *private* bonds	Deutsche Borse
	No. of domestic *public* bond	Korea exchange
	No. of listed *foreign* bonds	Luxembourg SE
	Bond options and futures	Chicago Board of Trade, and Euronext.liffe

Source: Complied by the author based on: (WFE, 2006; and WFE, focus, 20007).

CONCLUSION

This chapter indicates the role of financial markets in the world economy, and states the most important types of financial markets, classified in seven groups. The chapter aimed to introduce the various types of financial markets in order to emerge to the next chapter which is devoted to the stock market. The theme of this research book is devoted to discuss the regular rather the OTC market, the secondary rather than the primary market, the cash (spot) stock market rather than derivatives markets. Covering both emerging and developing markets as well as national and international environments. Other forms of financial markets and instruments are to be discussed only in case of interactions with the main theme of this book, or when it is needed.

However, types and categories of the financial markets are not independent or separated, but they are overlapped. Examples of overlapping of financial instruments and markets are: corporate and government bonds issued in local and /or foreign currencies. Issuing corporate shares in both foreign and national currencies by the same corporation. Cross-listed national equities traded in different currencies, times and locations. Issuing a single national security using international public offering as well as local public offering. A national company issuing a security using international public offering in foreign jurisdiction without issuing it in the home country. Emerging based firms list their shares in developed stock exchanges and visa versa in few cases. Government bonds may be a long-term security, or a short-term treasury bill traded nationally or internationally. Some firms issue stocks in different classes, traded in primary markets, while at the same time other issues by the same issuer are traded in the secondary market. In addition, the above stated financial markets are so connected and have interactions with each other, which will be discussed extensively in the following chapters, in this book.

REFERENCES

Aylward, Anthony and Jack Glen (2000) "*Primary Securities Markets: Cross-Country Findings*" (IFC, The World Bank, Discussion Paper Number 39).

BIS, (2003) "International banking, and financial market developments *BIS Quarterly Review* (Bank for International Settlements, December).

Demirguc- Kunt, Asli and Ross Levine (1996) "Stock Market Corporate Finance and Economic Growth: An Overview" *The World Bank Economic Review* 10 (2); 223-240.

IFC (1998) *Lessons of Experience, Financial Institutions* (International Finance Corporation, World Bank, Washington D. C.).

IMF (2001) *International Financial Statistics Yearbook 2001* (International Monetary Fund, Washington D. C.).

IOSCO (1993) A Resolution on coordination between cash and derivative markets (the International Organization of Securities Commissions, October)

Kamphuis, Robert W., Roger C. Kormendi, and J W. Henry Waston, eds., (1989). *Black Monday and the Future of the Financial Markets* (Dow Jones- Irwin, Inc., Homewood).

Levine, Ross (1991). "Stock Markets, Growth and Tax Policy" *Journal of Finance* 46; 1445-1465.

Levine, Ross and Sara Zervos (1996) "Stock Market Development and Long-Run Growth" *The World Bank Economic Review* 10 (2); 323-339.

Lim, Edward S., John G. Gallo and Peggy E. Swanson (1998) "The Relationship between international bond markets and international stock markets" *International Review of Financial Analysis*, 7; 181-190.

S&P (2003) *Global Stock markets Factbook, 2003* (Standard &Poor's, McGraw- Hill Company, New York, USA).

Sabri, Nidal Rashid (2003). "Using Treasury "Repurchase" Stocks to Stabilize Stock Markets" *International Journal of Business* 8 (4); 426-450.

Sabri, Nidal Rashid (2004) Stock Volatility and Market Crisis in Emerging Economies *Review of Accounting and Finance* 3 (3); 59-83.

Sabri, Nidal Rashid (2005). "Legal Features of Traded Securities and High Price Volatility" *Advances in Financial Economics* 11; 237- 249.

Sabri, Nidal Rashid (2007a) Recent Developments and Stock Market Stability" (Manuscript under publication).

Sabri, Nidal Rashid (2007b) High volatility and stock market crises in developed economies" (Manuscript under publication).

Schinasi, Garry J., R. Sean Craig, Burkhard Drees and Charles Kramer (2000) *Modern Banking and OTC Derivatives Markets; the Transformation of Global Finance and its Implications for Systemic Risk* (International Monetary Fund, Washington DC).

WFE (2001). *Annual report of 2001* (World Federation of Exchanges, Paris).

WFE (2003) Maureen O'Hara, *World Federation of Exchanges Trading Survey 2003* (World Federation of Exchanges, Paris).

WFE (2006) World Federation of Exchanges Data Base, (World Federation of Exchanges, Paris) available on line http://www.world-exchanges.org.

WFE (2007) *Focus* Issue No. 167 (World Federation of Exchanges, Paris, January, 2007).

World Bank and IMF (2001) *Developing Government Bonds Markets: A Hand Book* (The World Bank and International Monetary Fund, Washington D. C.).

Chapter 2

INTRODUCTION TO INTERNATIONAL STOCK MARKETS

INTRODUCTION

This chapter is devoted to explore the basic fundamentals of stock market in general, while the next chapters will discuss the various issues attached to such market in more details. Accordingly, we will present first the major participants in the stock market, thereafter, the types and features of traded stocks as they exist in the majority of the world financial systems, including developing and emerging economies. Finally, the chapter will explore the various values of the stock as well as to examine features of the traded securities and their impact on stock market stability.

The stock market is a capital market where a share of corporate ownership is traded. The trading of stocks occur for various reasons, including speculations, arbitrage between markets, short term and long term investments, hedging, reducing risk and diversifying investments. In addition, there are other purposes such as changing the ownership structure through hostile or voluntary takeover of a corporation. The stock market aims to offer the relevant environment to determine the right price of a share as well as for ordering, implementing, and settling the related trading transactions.

The stock market is the most significant market in the world economy for both developed and emerging countries. It moved from being a national market to become an international market, due to trading in national as well as foreign securities, through international public offerings, cross-listing or ADR instruments' systems. The number of cross-listed firms increased significantly during the last decade and extended to include many firms located in the emerging economies. In addition, there is an increase in trading foreign shares in both developed and emerging stock exchanges. Moreover, there is an increase in linkages among national stock price indices, and integration among national and regional markets. It moved from being an independent market to be relatively a part of the world or regional integrated market. And from being a restricted market built on national laws and regulations to be a liberal market, integrated to other markets and cross-borders market.

In addition, the stock market is the most growing financial sector in the world economy as expressed by market capitalization, trading value and number of traded securities. The number of the listed firms was doubled in the last decade, and increased from 27,706 in 1992 to 48,375 securities in 2002 (S& P 2003; and IFC, 1999). The trading value of the world stock markets increased more than two times during the last seven years, it increased from $ 33,074 billion in 1999 to 71,169 billion in 2006. The size of the world capital stock market increased from $ 35,005 billion in 1999, to $ 52,145 billion in 2006 (WFE, 2006) as shown in Table 2-1. The rapid development of financial markets has been extending to emerging economies, and to both members and non members of the World Federalization of exchanges as expressed by market capitalization, and trading value.

Table 2-1. Size of the World Stock markets (1999 and 2006) in Billion US dollars

Stock Markets	Capitalization		Trading volume	
	1999	2006	1999	2006
Members of WFE	35,005	49,924	33,074	69,521
Non- members		2,221		1,675
Total of the world stock markets		52,145		71,169

WFE, Focus, 2007.

Accordingly, this market is witnessing the most prospected period during a century of trading, and it is the most vital sector among all financial markets. However, in spite of these facts, this market is also witnessing unstable periods of trading as expressed in the frequent high price volatility and market crises, which will be explored in next chapters. In addition, there are various sudden setbacks, such as the increasing numbers of de-listed firms from many stock exchanges due to various reasons. For example, the total number of de-listed firms was about 1571 firms during 2005 which forms about 3% of the total listed firms. Out of the total, one- fourth of the de-listed firms were listed in London stock exchange (WFE, 2006).

Participants in the Stock Market

There are five groups of participants in the stock markets, the buyer and seller group, the listed firms and issuers of financial instruments group, the stock exchanges, and the commissions who regulate the stock exchanges, and the intermediaries group including brokers, dealers, banks, and market markers.

Buyers and Sellers

There are so many individual investors who are always looking for selling or buying in the financial markets, and they represent investors or borrowers. Other specialized institutions buy and sell in the financial markets including householders and individual investors, state and public sector, mutual funds, pension funds, insurance companies, development and commercial banks and other financial firms. Taking into consideration the world stock markets, individuals, mutual and pension funds represent the majority of owning the traded securities.

In addition, significant changes have occurred in the nature of investors and sellers groups in the last decade. This is duc to several reasons: First, the wide use of web-internet trading, which plays a significant role in increasing the number of the interested individuals in the stock market trading. This group may not deal directly to implement the trading transactions. Nevertheless, they follow and monitor the market and give their instructions to implement their requests. Second: the majority of the world countries have removed restrictions on foreign ownership of national corporations fully or partially in the last two decades, and that is applicable to emerging countries. For example, the European and Latin American markets removed restrictions with few exceptions concerning ownership of banks and air transportation (S&P, 2000). This means an increase of the share of non- resident investors in national stock exchanges as reported by the last survey of FESE. It is clear that the non- resident investors have become the driving force of European markets. Third: the decrease in the share of the public sector in the majority of the world stock markets, especially after privatizations of the public sector in Eastern European countries and many emerging economies (FESE, 2002).

The investors (the shareholders) in the world stock markets may represent from 5% to 40% of the world population for various individual countries. For example, the number of shareholders of securities, in USA is about 84 million, in Australia 5.4 million (37% of population) in Taiwan; 24 million, in Korea; 4 million (8% of population), in Japan is 35 million (30% of population) including individuals and institutions, (WFE, 2003, and ASX, 2002). The investors in the world stock markets include all groups of investors such as government, financial institutions business firms and residents and non- residents individuals. For example, the share of individuals in Japan stock markets was about 20.6% compared to 21.5% to business firms as presented in Table 2-2, which shows groups and ratios of investors in Japan as in 2003 based on the market value.

Listed Firms and Securities

The second group of players is the listed firms and securities. The total listed securities in the world stock exchanges is about fifty thousands shares traded in the world secondary stock markets. The listed securities represent shares of owners' equities of qualified public corporations. The face value of such securities varies from one jurisdiction to another as well as within a single jurisdiction from one firm to another. The listed securities should meet stated general, capital, legal and financial requirements, before applying to the stock exchange. The application offered to the stock exchange should include various data concerning the security, the firm, and the officials of the firm.

For example, the application for listing should include the stated par value, classes to be listed, jurisdiction of the security, future issuances, total securities issued, the outstanding shares, number of freely tradable issues, number of holders, size of holding. In addition, the financial statements for the last fiscal periods for the firm as well as other business and personnel information for the applicants should be submitted. Based upon the offered information and according to examining the application, the security may be accepted in the regular secondary market, or traded on the over the counter market. Many securities may be de-listed the moment they violate the stated requirements.

Table 2-2. Groups and ratios of investors (shareholders) in Japan stock markets in 2003 based on market value

Groups of Investors	Shareholding at market value
Government	0.2%
Regional Banks	7.7%
Trust Banks, Investment trust funds	21.4%
Life insurance companies	6.7%
Other Insurance companies	2.6%
Other Financial Institutions	0.7%
Business corporations	21.5%
Securities companies	0.9%
Individuals	20.6%
Foreigners	17.7%

Source: WFE, 2003.

Brokers, Specialists, and Dealers

This group is directly related to the process of trading in stock markets, in order to facilitate, implement, and execute market orders from all parties. They are authorized to receive, process, state prices, and execute orders in the stock exchanges. This group includes dealers, brokers, specialists, and market makers. The brokers are supposed to work for the account of other inventors, as most of the seats organized exchanges are owned by brokerage firms, while dealers may trade for their own. The functions, qualifications, rules, definitions, and names of specialties also vary from one stock exchange to another based on the related laws and procedures. For example, the Swiss exchange (SWX, 1999) classifies dealers into five groups, including: professional dealers who trade in securities for their own account on a short-term basis, dealers who underwrite securities issued by their parties and offer them to the public in the primary market, dealers who create derivatives and offer them to the public, market makers who trade in securities for their own account in short basis and offer prices in securities permanently and on request, and these who trade in securities for the account of clients.

However, in some stock exchanges brokers should be specialized companies, certified individuals, or registered members of the stock exchanges, or banks. Other exchanges prevent banks or their direct representatives from dealing as brokers in the trading of stock exchanges, while other exchanges such as Frankfurt stock exchange considers banks as the certified brokers who may deal in the stock trading. In general, and no matter of the their names as brokers, specialists and dealers, they are considered as significant members in the stock exchanges, and they are participating in the ownership of the majority stock exchanges partially or fully in various world stock exchanges. In some stock exchanges, the related laws distinguish between the brokers, specialists and dealers and assigned different duties in the trading process of equity and fixed income securities. The role of this group is still significant in the stock trading, even after computerizing of stock exchanges and moving from floor trading to screen trading.

The Stock Exchanges

The third group is the exchange where the trading is conducted. A stock exchange is a legal entity, which is authorized by related laws to organize the trading facilities and the process of securities' transactions. The stock exchange is supposed to grant the exclusive or non-exclusive right for trading of securities. Many countries permit trading to be exclusively inside the stock exchange for the listed firms either through the regular or over the counter markets, while other countries permit trading in both inside and out side stock exchanges. The largest world stock exchanges as expressed by the annual traded value are NYSE, NASDAQ, London, Tokyo, Euronext, Deutsche, BME Spanish, Borsa Italiana, Swiss and Korean, stock exchanges respectively (WFE, 2007).

The legal entity of the stock exchange varies from one country to another. In general, there are about five legal forms of stock exchanges; a public sector owned and run by a government agency, a cooperative owned by members of the exchange, a non- profit organization, a monopoly company (profit seeking) owned by insiders including brokers, dealers, listed firms and other related parties, and a profit seeking company owned by outsiders and insiders. The stock exchange charges fixed fees for admission, commissions, and fees for memberships, as well as for trading transactions. The fees and commissions vary from one jurisdiction to another. The stock exchanges collect a commission of less than 0.1% of the market value of stock trading from each of the contracting parties. In addition, they collect annual fees for listed securities based on the par value or nominal capital. Other annual fees may be collected from brokers and dealers for their subscriptions and working in the stock exchange. The total revenues of the Federation of stock exchanges which includes the world major stock exchanges reached to $ 10.5 billion in 2004(WFE, 2005).

The structure of stock exchange may differ from one jurisdiction to another. The majority of stock exchanges may include subunits to conduct other related functions such as bonds markets, derivative markets, and the depositary agency for the securities certificates, the settlements agencies, and clearing houses. While in other jurisdictions, we find that those subunits may work separately and independently outside the stock exchanges. The world stock exchanges are usually organized in regional and world associations and commissions. The majority of the world stock exchanges are organized in the World Federation of Exchanges (WFE) formerly known as (FIBV) located in Paris. The WFE is the trade organization which aims to enhance the regular stock exchanges, and to encourage using harmonized practices in the stock exchange industry. It adopted stated trading principles and guidance, which should be considered as a minimum level of regulatary by exchanges wishing to become a member of the World Federation of Exchanges (WFE, 2002).

The Regulator Commissions

The majority of the world stock exchanges operate under the supervision of government securities commissions or authorities, which regulate and supervise the functions of stock exchanges. The main function of such agencies is to control the operation of stock exchanges, to monitor prices and activities and to protect all parties involved. The stock commissions issue policies, standards and regulations to control the inside trading, the margin requirements, and imposing market interruptions measures, such as trading halts, stated price limits, and circuit breaker measure. Examples of the government securities commissions are: the SEC of USA, The Financial Services Authority of United Kingdom, Indonesian Capital Market Supervisory Agency, Financial Services Agency of Japan, and Capital Market Commission of Greece.

The individual world securities commissions are assembled in a body known as the International organization of securities commission (IOSCO). It was established in 1983 and based in Montreal of Canada till 1999 when it was moved to Madrid. Currently, it includes about 181 members, of the total, 104 members are ordinary members, and 67 are affiliated and associated members. The major concern of this international commission is to promote high standards of regulations in order to maintain efficient and sound markets. For this end, the IOSCO adopted thirty principles to protect investors, ensuring efficient market and reducing the systematic risk of trading (IOSCO, 1998).

TYPES OF EQUITY MARKETS

The types, features, and classes of shares traded in the world stock markets are stated based on the related laws including the national corporate and securities laws. Based on a study conducted by the author found that there are about thirty different types of shares traded in the world stock exchanges as presented in Table 2-3. The number of shares traded in a stock market differs from one jurisdiction to another and from one corporation to another. For example, in some countries, there is only one type of registered common stock with par value. On the other side there are many countries, especially in developed markets, have up to ten varying types of shares, such as in Swiss stock markets, Germany, British Virgin Islands, and South Africa. Their stock markets include restricted and unrestricted common, preferred, bearer, registered, various voting powers classes, multi par values, and other combinations of such types.

However, the majority of the world stock markets deal with types ranging from five to ten types of shares. It should be noted here that there are some stock exchanges that prohibit listing of specific types of shares, such as the superior voting share in the NYSE, or in the case of dual shares such as in the case of the Brazil stock market, or in case of the bearer shares in some countries. Finally, the most traded share in almost all the world stock markets is the common, registered, fully paid, with one vote and par value. Other types with various merits may be traded besides the above share based on the national corporate laws and the corporation by-laws. The following section is devoted to explore the general features of the main types of shares as traded in the world stock markets.

Common Share

The common share represents the main owner equity of the corporations in all over the world jurisdictions, without exception. The common share is the share of capital issue, when the corporation establishes, and traded firstly in the primary market. The common shareholder has the voting rights, dividend's right, preemptive rights, the right to sell the share whenever needed, and the right of remaining assets in case of liquidation. Common shares have various merits based on the related laws, such merits may be in the form of registered and bearer share, par value and no par value, one class and dual class, one for residents and non-residents, fully or partially paid. However, in regards to the voting right, all common shares are characterized by this merit, while they differ in the power of voting based on the class of the common shares. The other rights as related to dividend distribution, liquidation value, and the freedom of selling rights are the same regardless of the type of the common share.

Table 2-3. Groups and classes of shares traded in the world stock markets

Based on	Types
Right of dividends	Common share
	Preferred share
	Saving share
	Participation share
Treasury (repurchase) shares	For specific reasons
	For limited period; non- limited period
Certificate share	Bearer share
	Registered share
Class share	Single common share class
	Dual class for voting rights
	Dual class for residents- non –residents
	Dual class for special owners
Voting rights	One- share - one vote
	No- vote share
	Superior vote share (two times)
	Inferior vote (up to one-tenth)
	Special voting rights
Face value	Par value with no limits
	No- par value (stated value)
	Stated minimum and maximum for par value
	Minimum limit only for par value
	Par value with premium
	Par value with discount
Paid value	Fully paid
	Partially paid
	Installment paid
Status of shares	Authorized shares
	Issued shares
	Outstanding shares
	Net-outstanding shares (minus repurchases)

Source: Sabri, 2005.

Preferred Share

The second type of shares that based on dividends and voting merits is the preferred share. The preferred share is a different class of shares which has characteristics of the common share and the bond at the same time. It may be issued with a maturity date or may be perpetual with no maturity date. Preferred shareholders get stated percentage of dividends before the common shareholder. The trading size of the preferred share is very limited as compared to the common share. Various Jurisdictions do not permit the trading of preferred shares and only a limited number of the world corporations issue preferred shares. There are various types of preferred shares as may be attached with various merits, based on the related corporate laws, including the convertible share, which may be converted into common shares at the corporation option, the participating share (to participate in extra revenues), the cumulative profit share, which transfer the profit from year to another. In addition, there are other features that may be connected to the preferred shares such as the callable at the corporation options. The majority of the traded preferred shares have no voting rights, with few exceptions in some of the jurisdictions such as in Germany, Britain, Poland, Canada, Denmark, South of Korea, and Italy.

Registered Share

The majority of the world stock markets deal with registered shares, the registered share includes the name of the shareholder, the face value of the share, the number of shares owned by the shareholder, and the serial number of the shares. Many stock markets deal only with registered shares such as USA (except Nevada which permit the bearer share), Colombia, Pakistan, Jordan, Palestine, Italy, State of Jersey, Australia, and Brazil. The registered share may be a common share or a preferred share, and may be with par value or no par value. The transfer of the registered shares from one holder to another needs stated procedures to reissue a new certificate to the new holder with the number of purchased shares and another certificate to the old holder with the number of the remaining balance.

Bearer Shares

The bearer share is a share with a certificate that does not show the name of the shareholder and carry groups of number of shares such as 100 shares, and 1000 shares. The transfer of ownership in the case of the bearer share occurs by handling the certificate and without changing the names in the corporation records. This means a corporation does not know the holder unless a specific procedure is followed. Accordingly, a company should find a way to identify the bearer shareholders, by asking the holder to deposit their shares in the company or in banks when they vote. The distribution of dividends to bearer shareholders is based on the attached coupons to the bearer share or through the banks in which the bearer shares are deposited.

Different conditions have been found in the world stock markets regarding the bearer share as presented in Table 2-4. Such conditions may be represented by markets which deal with both bearer and registered shares. Other markets imposed restrictions regarding the voting right on bearer shares. In addition, some markets assigned bearer shares only to either common or preferred shares. Finally, there are some markets that deal only with bearer shares for all classes such as Sweden. However, issuing both registered and bearer shares for the same corporation may produce differences in the share prices. For example Gardiol, et al.

(1997) found that the bearer share and ownership transfer regime are significant variables in explaining the differences between prices of dual shares.

Having bearer shares is one of the most contradicting issues in the world stock markets. Various legislations support the concept and consider it as a sign for liberalization of stock markets, while others consider it as a way for tax evasion and money laundering. Accordingly, some countries have prevented the use of bearer shares during the last decade such as Brazil and Australia, Bahamas, and Mauritius, while other countries have an intensive debate for this issue. On the other side we find some countries are introducing it recently like Egypt. In addition, various countries have varying conditions for bearer shares, especially in identifying the bearer shareholders and to the requirement of depositing the bearer share certificate in a financial institution or custodian. Other legislations increased the fees on issuing bearer shares compared to registered shares, and imposed obligation to disclose the changes in ownership of capital and voting rights such as in Sweden, France and Switzerland.

Table No 2- 4. The Bearer to Registered Shares in the World Stock Markets

	Examples of Jurisdictions
Bearer share only	Sweden
Registered share only	USA (except Nevada), Colombia, Pakistan, Jordan, Palestine, Italy (only saving may be bearer), State of Jersey
Both bearer share and registered	Denmark, Franc, Germany, Greece, State of Czech, Switzerland, Taiwan,
Both are permitted, but bearer prohibited recently	Australia, Brazil (previous bearer should converted)
Registered share may be exchanged to bearer and visa- verse, there are some restrictions on bearer shares voting	British Virgin Islands
Registered shares issue to promoters, state, and investments institutions, bearer shares issue to other groups	China
Registered, bearer permitted but not common	UK
Preferred share should be registered not bearer, bearer share only for common shares and should be fully paid	Poland
Registered, and bearer, but the bearer shares should not exceed certain limit of the outstanding shares	Egypt, South Korean

Source: based on corporate laws of respected countries.

Voting Share

Almost all worlds' jurisdictions grant the voting right for the common shares but with different merits. In general, the one- share one vote is the main alternative that prevails in the majority of the world stock markets. Along of that, there are no voting shares or the inferior voting shares that are associated mainly with either preferred shares, bearer shares or dual common class shares. The voting shares are mainly connected to the registered shares as well as to the common shares, with few exceptions. There are three types of voting shares that exist in the world stock markets, the one vote to one share that represents the majority of the world trading shares, the inferior voting share up to one-tenth of the voting right, and the superior voting share which has double voting rights.

Table 2-5 presents the voting rights of traded shares in the majority of the world stock markets. However, many studies examined the voting rights and indicated that the aim of issuing dual class shares with different voting rights is to keep the control right of the corporation. For example, Ehrhardt and Nowak (2000) reported that separation of cash rights and voting rights by using dual-class share aims to create a controlling shareholder structure. Lemmon and Lins (2003) reported that there is a large separation between cash flow ownership and control rights, which indicates that insiders have the motivation and the ability to get engage in expropriation. Finally, Becht and Roell (1999) concluded that there is a high degree of concentration of shareholder voting power in Continental Europe relative to the USA and the U. K.

Table 2-5. Vote and Non-Vote Shares in the World Stock Markets

Situations	Examples of Jurisdictions
One vote to one share	exist in all stock exchanges for common shares
One share one vote, no vote share mainly for preferred, dual class voting for multi voting rights	Australia, Denmark, Germany, France (Preferred shares either have no vote or have double voting rights,) Poland, Taiwan, South Africa
One share one vote, dual class for voting rights, superior vote, inferior vote (one- tenth)	Canada, British Virgin Islands
One share to one vote for common share, most of Preferred shares have no voting rights	USA, Greece
One share one vote Dual class shares for voting rights A share has ten times voting rights than B share.	Sweden
No voting for saving and preferred shares, multi voting rights for dual class share	Italy
One share one vote only, no class share, no preferred	Jordan, Palestine, Pakistan
No vote or different voting rights for bearer share, No vote for foreign common share	Switzerland
One vote to one share, dual class is limited, superior voting is multiple voting power	UK
One vote to one share, no dual class voting, no voting for bearer shares	Egypt

Source: based on corporate laws of respected countries and Sabri, 2005.

No- Voting Share

The No -vote shares are mainly related to preferred, bearer or class B shares that exist in some of the world stock markets. The preferred shareholder is supposed to abandon his voting right in return for specific privileges. The no vote share is limited to few countries, which issue class B shares to keep management under the control of the holders' minority. Such situation should be permitted by national company laws as well as by the company by- laws. On the other side, there is the superior (A common class) share that is issued in some countries to serve the same purpose.

Dual Class Share

Dual class shares may be issued for various reasons; for resident non-resident, for one group of investors, for promoter- non-promoter investors and for voting rights as it has been indicated in the previous paragraphs. The dual class shares exist in Sweden, Switzerland, South Korea, France, Germany, Denmark, Mexico, Canada, Australia, and People's Republic of China. Dual classes may produce significant differences in the stock price of the same security.

For example, the Chinese listed companies issue Class A, B and H shares to Chinese, foreign, and Hong Kong investors, respectively. Entitled to exactly the same rights and obligations, the three classes of shares are, however, traded at significantly different prices (Zhang and Zhao, 2003 and 2004).

Par and no -par Value Shares

The majority of the world shares are issued with a stated value known as the face value or the par value, which is the price at which the first issue of stocks is sold. This process is known as the subscription process, and it allows the investor to pay only the partial price of the par value as a first installment. After completing the subscription process the share becomes a secondary market security based on stated conditions. The value of the share may have nominal or face value known as par value, or can be without a stated par value. The minimum or maximum par value may be stated by the corporate national law, or the corporation's by-laws. When the corporation issues a new issue of stocks, its national laws should state whether to use the same stated par value as the first issue, or to add a premium or deduct a discount. These possibilities are presented in Table 2- 6.

As indicated in the table, all the world stock markets use the par value shares or permit both choices except Australia, which recently has abandoned the par value share. In addition, some developed markets are discussing the issue of eliminating the par value share such as the British company law (DTI, 2000) However, the stated regulations for the par value vary from one legislation to another. Table 2-7. Shows various jurisdictions determine the minimum and or the maximum of the par value, while others leave the value limits for the by-laws of the corporations.

Table 2- 6. The share par value and no par value situations in the World Stock Markets

Par Value Situations	Examples of Jurisdictions
No par value only	Australia
Par Value only	British Virgin Islands, Danish, Greece, China, Egypt, Italia, Jordan, Pakistan, Palestine, Poland, South Korea, Sweden, Taiwan, Switzerland, State of Czech
Both are permitted	Brazil, Canada, France, Germany, South Africa, UK, USA, State of Jersey

Source: based on corporate laws of respected countries.

Table 2-7. The share par value conditions in the selected corporate laws countries

	Conditions and explanations
Australia	Recently eliminated par value, a company have no par value
Brazil	partially paid share is permitted,
China	Par value with premium is permitted but not with discount
Egypt	Minimum par value of LE 5 and maximum LE 1000, per value with premium is permitted
France	No- pare value introduced in 1998
Germany	Recently no par value added to the par value shares
Jordan	Minimum and maximum limits of par value, premium yes no par value with discount
Palestine	Minimum and maximum limits of par value, premium yes
Poland	Minimum par value of 500 zlotys, par value with premium is permitted but not with discount
Sweden	Nominal value should be determined
Switzerland	The minimum pare value reduced to 1 centime and the zero par value eliminated
Taiwan	Par value with premium is permitted but not with discount
UK	It is recommended to eliminate par value for private company,
USA	Par value may be with premium or discount

Source: based on corporate laws of respected countries and Sabri, 2005.

Treasury (Repurchases) Share

In the majority of the world stock markets, a firm may repurchase its own shares traded in the stock markets, entering the market as independent legal entity, and acting as one of the investors. Repurchasing a part of its own shares by a firm is known as share repurchases or shares buyback. The purchased shares ratio should not exceed 10% of the total of the outstanding shares in many countries, while this percentage may be different in other markets. The repurchased shares can be held for a limited or unlimited time for future usage, which may be considered as treasury shares, thus as an investment rather than as a temporary or permanent reduction of its own capital, based on the related regulations of the various jurisdictions. However, the International Accounting Standards Committee (IASC, 2001) stated that treasury shares should be presented in the balance sheet as a deduction from equity and should not be considered as financial assets, and no gain or loss should be recognized in the income statement on sale, or cancellation activities, but to be presented as a change in equity.

The general known methods of shares' repurchasing are to repurchase from the open market, Dutch auction, fixed –price tender offer repurchases or to repurchase from off market and equal access repurchases. In various countries, a corporation might repurchase part of their own common stocks, which are fully paid, legally issued, in order to be cancelled or to be held for reselling. While it is considered as illegal trading by many other countries because this may be considered as a reduction in their own stated capital. The mechanism, rational, conditions and methods of share repurchases are different from one country to another, based on different corporate laws, stock exchange stock laws, tax laws, and accounting practices applying to repurchases activities.

However, the number of firms that have repurchased their own shares is still limited in the entire world compared to the regular trading in the stock markets, with exception of USA, Canada, and UK. The share repurchases activity has existed merely outside the US stock market before 1980. It has increased significantly in the last decade in most of the world stock markets in both developed and emerging economies. For example, the number of firms that repurchased their own shares form the stock markets was about 4,743 firms between 1985 to 1996 (Jagannathan, et al. 2000), the number in Canada was about 1060 firms between 1989 and 1997 (Ikenberry, et al. 2000), while the number of firms repurchased their own shares from stock markets was about 293 firms between 1985 and 1995 in UK (Rau & Vermaelen 2000).

A firm may repurchase a part of its own shares for various reasons. First: to buy investments as a part of the pension and compensation plans for the firms' employees. Second, to use it as a substitute for dividends, this may have a positive impact on the stock market prices of the company. Third: to establish a market and to create additional demand for the company's shares. However, this purpose is prohibited in the majority of the world stock markets and may be considered as illegal interference in the market to raise the price of its own share. Fourth: to adjust its owners' equity and capital structure for some reasons. Fifth: is to take over defensive steps by reducing the public floating shares in the stock market. Sixth: is to gain tax advantages, but it depends on the tax regulations of that country. However, some countries consider repurchasing programs as distribution of profits to the extent that the price paid for the shares exceeds the par value of the share and thus is applied for tax. Seventh: to increase earning per share by reducing the outstanding shares of the firm. Eighth: to meet merger needs and procedures (Sabri, 2003).

Recently, various changes have been taking place regarding the share repurchases in the world stock market. First: the size of repurchases trading volume as an alternative to dividends has increased significantly. Second: many countries introduced the concept of share repurchases by corporate firms during the last five years. Third: many countries that already have legitimized the share repurchasing activities are deregulating, and relaxing the conditions and rules to encourage corporations using repurchases as an alternative to dividends, and serving other purposes including improving stock prices. Fourth: other countries are moving from share repurchases activities towards holding the repurchased shares in treasury. Fifth: some countries are introducing more liberal rules to be applicable as treasury shares, in order to enhance the stability of stock markets. Finally, the corporate share repurchases practices in the world stock markets may be classified into five groups as presented in Table 2- 8.

Table 2-8. Repurchasing practices based on related laws as existed in selected countries

Repurchasing practices based on related corporate laws	Example of countries
A corporate may not repurchase its' own share under no conditions.	Jordan, Oman, Lebanon, Morocco, Poland, Saudi Arabia, Republic of China
A corporate may repurchase its own share under specific conditions for purpose of capital reductions limited to 10% of outstanding shares as a maximum.	South Africa, Australia, Taiwan, Sweden, Singapore, Japan, Germany, Netherlands, Denmark, Taiwan, Belgium, New Zealand, Canada, France, Finland, Korea, Norway, Italy, Spain, Ireland
A corporate may repurchase its own share under specific conditions for capital reductions, but it is permitted to exceed 10% of outstanding share	UK, Australia, Hong Kong, India Bermuda, Cayman Islands
A corporate may repurchase its own shares for the purpose of capital reduction and to be held for a limited period.	Switzerland, (6years) Greece (3years) EC directives (one to three year)
A corporate may repurchase its own share for various purposes, and for employee option plans, and reissue or redeem without limited time.	USA Malaysia UK (In process) Hong Kong (In process)

Source: (Sabri, 2003) and based on the related laws of the above countries.

The first group: A corporate can not repurchase its own shares under no conditions. Reduction of capital should be conducted for all shareholders equally. There are some countries in which corporate laws do not permit the firm to buy its own shares under any circumstance, including the reduction of its own capital. They stated in their corporate laws that a firm may not buy its own share under any condition, while specifying the way and the conditions under which the firm may reduce its own capital, such as reducing the par value of each outstanding share on equal basis, after getting the consent of several parties including the creditors and official corporate controllers. Moreover, in case of merging two firms, if one firm used to own shares of the other firm before merging, such shares should be dispatched, as it is the case for the Jordanian corporate law (HKJ, 1988) as an example. Other countries adopting such laws are Lebanon, Morocco, Poland, Saudi Arabia, and Republic of China.

The second group: A corporate may repurchase its own shares under specific conditions for the purpose of capital reductions up to a limit of 10% of the outstanding shares as a maximum. The majority of this group permitted share repurchases only during the last five years. They still have limited experience in share repurchasing activities as expressed by the trading volume. Countries of this group are: South Africa, Australia, Taiwan, Sweden, Singapore, Japan, Germany, Netherlands, Denmark, Taiwan, Belgium, France, New Zealand, France, Finland, Korea, Norway, Belgium, Italy, Spain, and Ireland. Some countries such as

Canada limited the size of repurchased shares to 5% of outstanding shares or 10% of public offering shares (Ikenbury et al. 2000).

The third group: A corporate may repurchase its own shares under specific conditions for capital reductions, but it is permitted to exceed the 10% outstanding shares. An example of this group is the UK which requires specific regulations when the percentage of purchased shares is more than 15%, Hong Kong requires meeting specific regulations, in case the volume is more than 10% of outstanding shares and the company has to get an independent financial advisor (SFCHG, 1998 and 2000).

The fourth group: A corporate may repurchase its own shares for the purpose of capital reductions with the intention of holding the shares for a limited period. EEC directive stated that "where the laws of member states permitting a company to acquire its own share, it must dispose them within three years of their acquisition" (EEC, 1999). European countries, which laws permit corporations to repurchase their own share, have to comply with the European second directive.

The fifth group: A corporate may repurchase its own shares for various purposes and hold them as treasury stocks, and may reissue or redeem them without a limited time. USA and Malaysia have no limits on the volume of holding treasury shares other than the minimum requirements of float shares in stock exchange, while UK and Hong Kong suggesting 10% of outstanding shares as maximum.

TYPES OF STOCK VALUES

Trading of stocks inside or outside stock exchanges is based on the market price, which is supposed to be determined according to supply and demand for that specific share. In addition, the market price for a share reflects other values for that share. This section explores the various values of a share and the relationship between such values and their usages. Generally, and regardless of the related laws and jurisdictions, there are about eight different values of the share used for different purposes as presented in Table 2-9.

However, all of the presented values may have direct or indirect impact on the market value, in spite of the fact that there is no significant correlation between such values. Various studies examined the response of stock prices to other fundamentals, such as book to market value, fair value accounting and size of the firm, and other economic factors as reported by: Cornett et al. (1996) and Chui and Wei, (1998).

Book Value

The book value is the value of a common share calculated based on the financial statements of that firm as prepared based on the generally accounting principles including the continuously principle. The formula to calculate the book value which is know as accounting stock value, is to divide the common capital owner equity over the number of the outstanding shares for a fiscal period. The accuracy of the book value of a stock is based on the generally accepted accounting principles, methods of depreciation and accounting practices related to the intangible assets. The general accounting principles, standards and interpretations have various differences from one country to another, and from stated national accounting principles to others, such as the FASB standards of USA, the ASB standards of UK and the international Accounting standards published by the IASC which is known now as IASB which has been adopted by European Union countries and many emerging countries. In addition, there are no stated written standards in some countries, in which they use what is known as generally accepted accounting principles.

Table 2-9. Types of stock values and their uses

Stock values	Time of Calculation	Uses
Book value	One time a year	To measure profit ratios, and financial analysis
Market value	Continuous basic	Selling and buying in secondary market
Adjusted book value	Occasionally and when it is needed	For emerging and takeover buying, or determine premium attached to new issues
Par value	First time of issuing and establishing corporation	The price of first stock issue in primary market, To determine the distributed dividends
Stated value	First time of issue for no-par value stocks	The price of first stock issue in primary market, To determine the distributed dividends
Premium attached to par value	Times of second issue of capital	The price of next issue stock in primary market, and in case of selling authorized shares.
Discount attached to par value	Times of second issue of capital	The price of next issue stock in primary market, and in case of selling authorized shares.
Liquidated value	One time a life	In case of buying or liquidation of the whole firm

The book value may be above or below the market value and par value based on the financial position of the related firm as well as the market status. The calculation of thee book value should consider the preferred shares in case the corporation has issued preferred shares. The value of the preferred shares should be deducted from the total equity to determine the owner equity of common capital. However, the book value for preferred share may, also be calculated considering the par value of preferred share, number of outstanding preferred shares, and the cumulated dividends assigned for preferred shares.

Market Value

The price for unlisted securities is determined outside the regular exchange, either over the counter market, or just between buyers and sellers in case of trading outside official markets. Some countries' laws permit trading of listed securities outside exchanges, while others confine that to the official exchange. The control on trading and thus on stated market price is very difficult in case of trading in bearer stocks. On the other side the market value of a listed share is stated inside the regular stock exchange based on supply and demand of that particular security, and considering the book value, the expected future value, and other fundamentals data. The stock prices should respond to fundamentals and real economic data, including dividends distribution, repurchasing of shares announcements, earning per share, earning announcements and forecasting, inflation, employment data, monetary policy and other economic fundamentals. Other performance and profitability measures are reflected on the market price. The stock market assumes to state a relevant market price for a stock assuming the efficient market hypothesis.

However, to predict the future market value of a stock, more financial analysis should be conducted. The analysis of financial statements may include the last fiscal periods. The analysis of the financial statements for one year considers ratio analysis and cross sectional analysis. It compares ratios of the firm with the standards of the respected industry and the performance of other similar firms. The ratio analysis includes five groups: liquidity ratios, activity ratios, credit to owner-equity ratios, leverage ratios, and profitability ratios. In addition, it may use more than two financial statements, which becomes time- serial analysis, in order to determine the trends overtime concerning the major financial ratios.

Many studies examined the factors that affect stock prices and found positive relations between the fundamental values and movements of stock prices and that reported positive signals to stock prices, such as: price earning per share, earning announcements, accounting earnings, financial ratios, and forecasting. Many studies reported positive impact on stock prices in various stock markets such as Bandyopadhyay, et.al.(1995); Han and Wild, (2000); Terpstra and Fan, (1993) and Chung and Lee, (1998). The majority of the above studies reported that there was a positive impact of earning information on stock market prices.

Accordingly, various performance measures may have significant impact on the market price of a security. Such as the earning per share, the price-earning ratio, return on equity and market price- book value ratios. Earning per share is calculated by dividing the amount of reported income available for common shareholders over the outstanding shares. The earning per share is the available amount for distribution as dividends to the shareholders after deducting various reserves for reinvestments as stated by the related laws. Recently, the earning per share is considered as a requirement to the financial statements as stated by the International Accounting Standards, IAS, 33 of 1997, and became effective in 1998. It applies to firms whose ordinary shares are publicly traded or in the process of issuing ordinary shares (IASC, 2000). Return on equity ratio is calculated by dividing net income after taxes over owner's equity. The price-earning ratio is determined by dividing the stock market price by earnings per share. The market price is the stated price in the stock market in the last day of the fiscal year. The financial analyst uses the above ratios and measures amongst other fundamentals to direct customers to trade in a specific security. Other measures may be considered to forecast the expected future market price for a share such as the beta factor, and the ratio of ownership by institutions ratio as a loyal holders to the total shareholders of the firm, which have positive or negative impacts on the volatility of stocks prices. The beta is a factor that compares the volatility of a share to the volatility of the stock market as expressed by the price index of that market. A beta one for a specific share means that the earnings of the share move according to the market return index.

However, the price-earning ratio is considered as the most important performance measure, which is calculated based on the market value. The price-earning ratio is calculated for a stock, a sector of industry including all listed stock for that sector and for the national stock exchange including all local listed stocks, as presented in Table 2-10. This table shows the price earning ratios in 1990, 2000, and 2005 for selected stock exchanges. It indicates that the price earning ratio, which reflects both the market price as well the annual earning, ranged between less than 9.9% such as in case of Hong Kong to 126.9% in case of Nasdaq stock exchange. In addition, the price-earning ratio may be significantly different from one year to another and mainly due to changing in the market value of traded shares.

Par Value

The par or the face value of the share is the stated value of a share, which is written on the certificate. It is the price of selling the share in the primary market or the subscribed price at which first buyers buy the stocks. The par value of a share should not be changed during the life of the firm, including the next issues, in case of increasing capital, or issuing authorized shares to sell in the market. As it was mentioned earlier, the majority of the world trading stocks have par value, which is determined based on the related laws and according to the founders or promoters' decisions. Many jurisdictions stated the range between minimum and maximum in which the par value should be stated. For example, a corporate law may state that all shares of the corporation should have a par value between $10 to $ 100.

Table 2-10. The Price Earning Ratios between 1990 and 2005 for Selected Stock Exchanges

Exchange	1990	2000	2005
Mexican Exchange	11.2	12.2	17.3
Nasdaq	11.1	126.9	NA
NYSE	14.8	25.2	NA
Australian SE	11.0	21.3	17.0
Bursa Malaysia	25.5	22.1	15.2
Hong Kong Exchanges	9.9	12.8	15.6
Korea Exchange	12.2	15.4	11.0
Singapore Exchange	15.8	20.9	15.4
Taiwan SE Corp.	31.1	14.8	17.6
Tokyo SE	39.8	85.5	50.4
Athens Exchange	20.4	27.5	29.4
Borsa Italiana	16.5	22.4	16.0
Euronext Amsterdam	10.2	21.3	13.3
Euronext Paris	10.2	18.1	15.1
Istanbul SE	23.3	16.1	19.4
London SE	10.6	23.3	14.0
OMX Stockholm	11.0	26.0	17.5

Source: WFE, 2006.

Par Value with a Premium or Discount

The total par value amount of all outstanding shares is considered as the paid capital of the shareholders. The difference between the book value and the total par value of outstanding shares represents what is known as the earned capital. The earned capital includes retained earning, premiums and various reserves. As long as the related laws in the majority of the world jurisdictions, do not permit for different par values for next issuances of shares, many legislations permit to issue the share with the same par value but may be attached with a premium. This premium which increases the par value of the share aims to be compensating to the old shareholders compared to the new ones, who will have equal right in the total equities of the firm.

In addition, it is supposed to reflect the earned capital and accumulated reserves from the first issue up to the date of the next new issues, or to meet the margin between the book and the market values. However, issuing new shares with a par value attached with a premium is done under strict control of the related legislations in most of the countries. The same concept is applicable when a share is issued with a par value attached to a discount in case the firm is facing losses. However, various jurisdictions permitting the premium to be attached to par value based on stated conditions, but preventing issuing the par value with discounts, while other jurisdiction permit issuing share attached to either a premium or a discount.

Stated Value

As presented in the previous sections many countries permit issuing shares with no par value in the share certificate. Accordingly, there is a need to determine a price to sell that share. The determined price is known as the stated value, which is the amount designated to the no-par value stocks. The total stated value of outstanding shares is considered as part of the capital for each issued share.

Adjusted Book Value

When a corporation merges with another corporation, it can prepare adjusted financial statements in order to reflect the market values of the major assets of both corporations. Reevaluating some of the fixed assets aims to consider the real market price instead of the historical cost which appears in the financial statements. This is done especially for asset items which may have appreciation value such as land and building, and long term securities.

Liquidated Stock Value

The liquidation value is the value of a share, which is calculated based on the liquidated balance sheet. The liquidated balance sheet is prepared based on a voluntarily or mandatory decision of liquidating a corporation. The assets of the firm should be liquidated and registered at the actual market price. A profit or loss may be produced as a result of the liquidation process, thus the liquidation value may be higher or lower than the book value. In general a liquidated firm has a book share value less than the par value, unless the liquidation process is connected for purposes other than losses.

Types of Shares and Market Stability

The relationship between types of stocks and market stability comes from the fact that the reaction of shareholder is significantly different from one individual or group of investors to another, based on the holding type of shares and their attached benefits. The purpose of holding a share as well as the mechanism of pricing and the possibility of trading it outsides the stock exchange will reflect on the stock return volatility. Various studies examined the stock market crisis and found that they are related to the overreaction of shareholders and investors (Rozeff and Zaman, 1998; Fung, 1999; Kiymaz, 2001, Veronesi, 1999).

Some type of shares or shareholders have negative or positive impact on stock market stability compared to other type of shares and shareholders. Table 2-11 summarizes types and features of traded shares in the world stock markets and their possible impacts towards stock market stability.

Table 2-11. The main types of traded shares and their possible adverse impact on stock market stability

Types of shares	Possible impacts on market stability
Bearer shares	Trading outside stock exchanges Trading outside price limits stated in the stock exchanges No possibility of preventing insider trading No possibility of imposing other controlling measures
Non- vote and inferior shares	Main concern is return rather than corporate control, which means less loyalty of stockholders Minority control a company No change in corporate management
No- par value share	Possibility of various prices of the same issue of shares
Dual class shares (residence- foreigner)	Various prices of the same issue based on different classes Less loyalty of foreign and inferior holders

As presented in the above table, the non- vote share and inferior share rights, and B class holders may be ready to sell as fast as possible in case of the stock market crisis and during unstable periods of stock trading, compared to minority holders who control the corporation as well as the holder of superior shares. In addition, the loyalty of shareholders of specific types of shares compared to the less loyal groups of shareholders. Some studies (Sabri 1995a and Sabri 1995b) indicated that increasing share of banks and pension funds is considered the most stabilizing factor in stock exchange as perceived by the experts of the stock market. In addition, the mechanism of trading and price determination may be vary during the unstable periods of stock trading in case of dual class of shares, or in case of no- par value shares or in case of multi par values of a class share.

There is a possibility of trading outside the stock exchanges in case of bearer shares as long as the trading is based on the delivery of the share certificates, with no changes in corporate or depositary institute records. Thus, there is no impact of measures taken by stock exchanges to control bearer shares trading. Finally, in spite of the significant changes occurred in the related laws, regulation concerning the stock trading towards harmonization and integration, but there is still a significant diversity of the related laws, which have a direct impact on the issue of stock trading stability. Such recent changes may not be enough to deal with rapid increasing of linkages, and integration occurring in the world stock exchanges

Conclusion

This chapter presented the fundamentals of the stock trading, including the major players of the stock markets, types, and merits of traded stocks, and types of stock values. There are five players in the world stock markets, including: investors and borrowers which may be estimated to be about 200 million shareholders, 200 stock exchanges, 190 securities commissions, thousands of listed brokers and dealers, and 50,000 listed securities in the world stock exchanges.

There are various types, classes, features of shares traded in the world stock markets. Which are varying not only based on the related different jurisdictions, but also between one corporation and another, and even between an issue to another for the same corporation. The types of shares which may have a negative aspect during irrational trading periods still exist and may be introduced in new legalizations such as bearer shares, dual class share, inferior voting shares and no- par value shares. Corporate laws as well as individual corporate by-laws have different regulations and practices to organize classes, types, and features of stock shares, which are traded in the world stock market today. In addition, there is an increasing movement in the world stock market towards adopting or deregulating the share repurchases programs, and there is a toleration to use the treasury shares in enhancing the stock market stability during stock crises and extraordinary market price volatility.

The corporate ownership and the controlling structure is a significant issue concerning the stability of prices in stock markets. For example, family controlled, control chains, public holding, residents ownership, cross holding firms, have positive impact in case of noise and irrational trading compared to widely held firms, individual investors and foreign ownership. This is because decisions of selling shares is based on the degree of loyalty or objectives of holding that shares, and whether shareholders are long-term oriented or they are waiting to sell. Another aspect is related to the imposed measures by the majority of the world stock exchanges, which have different impacts on the various types of shares. Imposing such measures may not be possible in the case of the bearer shares, which may be traded outside the stock exchanges.

REFERENCES

ASX (2003). *Australian Share Ownership Study, 2002* (Australian Stock Exchange, Sydney, Australia).

Bandyopadhyay, Sati P., Lawrence D. Brown and Gordon D. Richardson (1995) "Analysts' use of earnings forecast in predicting stock returns: Forecast horizon impacts" *International Journal of Forecasting*, 11, 429-445.

Becht, Marco and Ailsa Roell (1999) "Corporate governance in Europe Block holdings in European: An international comparison" *European Economic Review* 43; 1049-1056.

Chui, Andy C. W. and John K. C. Wei (1998). "Book-to- market, firm size and turn-of-the year impact: Evidence from Pacific- Basin Emerging markets" *Pacific- Basin Finance Journal*. 6; 275-294.

Cornett, Marcia Millon, Zabihollah Rezaee and Hassan Tehranian (1996) "An investigation of capital market reactions to pronouncements related to fair value accounting" *Journal of Accounting and Economics*. 22; 119-154.

Chung, Heetaik and Bong-Soo Lee (1998). "Fundamentals and non-fundamentals components in stock prices of Pacific-Rim countries" *Pacific- Basin Finance Journal*. 6; 421-446.

DTI (2000) *Modern Company Law for a competitive economy: Capital maintenance and other issues* (Trade and Industry Department, U. K).

EEC (1999) *Fourth Council Directive* 78/660/EEC of 1978 and its amendments to 1999 (EUR Lex).

Ehrhardt, Olaf and Eric Nowak (2000) "Corporate governance changes, dual- class share structure and long-run stock performance of IPOs of German family- owned firms" (working paper, Humboldt- University, Germany).

FESE (2002) Share Ownership Structure in Europe (Federation of European Securities Exchanges, Economics & Statistics Subcommittee).

Fung, Alexander K.-W. (1999) "Overreaction in the Honk Kong stock market" *Global Finance Journal* 10; 224-240.

Gardiol, Lucien, Rajna Gibson-Asner, and Nils S. Tuchshmid (1997) "Are Liquidity and Corporate Control Priced by Shareholders? Empirical Evidence from Swiss Dual Class Shares" *Journal of Corporate Finance* 3; 299-323.

Han, Jerry C. Y. and John J. Wild (2000) "Pre-disclosure Information, Firm Capitalization, and Earnings Information Transfers" *Journal of Business Research*. 49; 274-288.

HKJ (1988) Corporate Law of 1989, Article No. 124 (Amman, Jordan).

IASC (2001) *Interpretation SIC-16 Share Capital- Reacquired Own Equity Instruments: Treasury Shares* (International Accounting Standards Committee, United Kingdom).

IASC (2000) *International Accounting Standards IAS 33* (International Accounting Standards Committee, United Kingdom).

IFC, (1999) *Emerging Stock Markets Fact Book 1999* (International Finance Corporation, Washington D. C.).

Ikenberry, David, Josef Lakonishok, and Theo Vermaelen, (2000) Stock Repurchases in Canada: Performance and Strategic Trading *Journal of Finance*, 55; 2373-2397.

IOSCO (1998). "*Objectives and Principles of Securities Regulation*" (International Organization of Securities Commissions, September).

Jagannathan, Murali, Clifford P. Stephens and Michael S. Weisbach (2000) "Financial Flexibility and the Choice between Dividends and Stock Repurchases" *Journal of Financial Economics* 57; 355-384.

Kiymaz, Halil (2001) "The impacts of stock market rumors on stock prices: evidence from an emerging market" *Journal of Multinational Financial Management* 11; 105-115.

Lemmon, Michael L. and Karl V. Lins (2003) "Ownership structure, corporate governance and firm value; evidence from the East Asian Financial Crisis" *Journal of Finance* 58; 1445-1468.

Rau, Raghavendra P. and Theo Vermaelen (2000) Regulation, Taxes and Share Repurchases in the UK (November, working Paper).

Rozeff, Michael and Mir A. Zaman (1998) "Overreaction and insider trading: Evidence from growth and value portfolios" *Journal of Finance* 53; 701-1-716.

S&P (2003) *Global Stock markets Factbook, 2003* (Standard &Poor's, McGraw- Hill Company, New York, USA).

S&P (2000) *Emerging Stock Markets Fact Book 2000* (Standard & Poor's, McGraw- Hill Company, New York, USA).

Sabri, Nidal Rashid (1995a) "Stabilization of Stock Markets; the Case of the Frankfurt Exchange" *Journal of Multinational Financial Management* 5; 23- 32.

Sabri, Nidal Rashid (1995b) "Experts' Opinions Toward Price Stability During the Stock Market Crisis" *International Journal of Commerce & Management* 5; 130-146

Sabri, Nidal Rashid (2003). "Using Treasury "Repurchase" Stocks to Stabilize Stock Markets" *International Journal of Business* 8 (4); 426-450.

Sabri, Nidal Rashid (2004) "Stock Volatility and Market Crisis in Emerging Economies" *Review of Accounting and Finance* 3, (3); 59-83.

Sabri, Nidal Rashid (2005) "Legal Features of Traded Securities and High Price Volatility" *Advances in Financial Economics* 11; 237- 249.

SFCHG (1998) *Consultation Paper on Treasury Shares* (Securities and Futures Commission of Hong Kong, November).

SFCHG (2000) *Code in share repurchases* (Securities and Futures Commission of Hong Kong).

SWX (1999).*Stock Exchange Ordinance, SESTO Ordinance on Stock Exchanges and Securities Trading* (Stock Exchange, Geneva).

Terpstra, Robert H. and Dennis K.K Fan. (1993). "Dispersion of financial analysts forecasts of earnings per share and trading volume: the Hong Kong experience" *Pacific-basin Finance Journal* 1; 277-285.

Veronesi, Pietro (1999). "Stock market overreaction to bad news in good times: A rational expectations equilibrium model" *Review of financial Studies* 12; 975-1007.

WFE (2002) *Market Principles* (The World Federation of Exchanges, Paris)

WFE (2003) *Share Ownership Surveys* (World Federation of Exchanges, Paris) available on internet www.world-exchange.org.

WFE (2005) *Annual Report and Statistics, 2005* (World Federation of Exchanges, Paris).

WFE (2006) World Federation of Exchanges Data Base: available on line http://www.world-exchanges.org)

WFE (2007) *Focus* Issue No. 167 (World Federation of Exchanges, Paris, January, 2007).

Zhang, Yimin and Ronald Zhao (2003) "Risk under "One Country and Two Systems": Evidence from Class A, B and H Shares of Chinese Listed Companies" *Review of Pacific Basin Financial Markets and Policies* 6: 179-197.

Zhang, Yimin and Ronald Zhao (2004) "The Valuation Differential between Class A and B Shares: Country Risk in the Chinese Stock Market" *Journal of International Financial Management & Accounting* 15; 44 -60.

Chapter 3

Recent Legal Developments and Stock Market Stability

Introduction

In formulating laws, regulations and practices of financial systems for a country various aspects should be considered, including the public interest, social and political aspects and believes, liquidity of trading, cost of trading, efficiency, and stability of prices and volatility reduction. Various studies examined the existed laws towards the cost, efficiency, and liquidity of the laws related to stock trading practices, but studies that scrutinized laws and aspects of stability and reduction stock price' volatility is still limited. The issue of stock market stability has been considered as one of the most critical issues to improve the world economy in the last two decades, due to the fact that various stock market crises hit the world stock markets. One of the major reported causes of the stock market crises is the inefficiency of the laws and regulations related to stock trading.

For example, Carstens and Schwartz, (1998) suggested the need for upgrading financial regulatory framework in emerging countries to handle highly volatile capital flow. Chui, et al. (2001) found that distinguishing between common law and civil law provides an indicator to whether a market includes a momentum effect prior to financial crises or not. Alba et al. (1999) reported evidences that the weakness of legal institutions and the poor corporate governance had an important effect on the stock market declines in the Asian crisis in 1997. Finally, the World Bank report (2000) argues that further economic progress in emerging markets is related to adopting the appropriate measures to reduce capital flows volatility, which needs to set the relevant instruments, policies, and institutions.

Accordingly, this chapter will be devoted to discuss this issue, which includes two parts: The first part of this chapter will explore situation as existed in the world stock markets at present, including objectives of the laws as well as the framework of the related laws which organize the trading process in the world stock markets as it is applied to both developed and emerging jurisdictions. The next part of this chapter is devoted to discuss changes in laws of stock trading which have been introduced recently to cover the new incorporated practices to the world stock markets that were introduced in the last decade.

OBJECTIVES OF STOCK MARKET LAWS

Considering the new changes including the advanced technology, the internet trading, using electronic network trading, globalization, integration, liberalizations and introducing new derivative products and indexed funds, there is a need to reconsider the stated purposes of the laws related to assure stability, liquidity and low cost of trading. The present related world laws of stock markets are varied based on various backgrounds and different objectives. Accordingly, the following section is devoted to synthesize the expected objectives for the world stock markets, which may be summarized as follows:

- To protect the public and government interest: the first objective of the related laws of stock markets should protect and serve public and government interest including collecting the stated taxes and fees imposed on stock trading and other transactions. The related laws should also be stated according to the government economic and policies of the respected country as well as the accepted related regional and international standards.
- To protect the concerned participating parties: The second major objective of the related laws should protect the concerned parties participating in the world stock markets, including present and expected investors, creditors, shareholders and other concerned individuals and agencies.
- To fit with the high competition from other markets: There is a need to reform and modify the related laws to compete with the new international business environment. Mainly, to attract other foreign stocks for dual listing and to increase equity portfolio investments in the national stock exchanges as well as for cross- border trading. In the USA, there are arguments stating that there will be more non- US companies, listed on the NYSE if the IASC standards are applied instead of the American accounting standards of the FASB, because they are too extensive and complex to use in cross-border securities (Mueller, 1999).
- To follow up new changes in technology and assets management industry: To cope with the rapid changes in the assets management industry and technology, there is a need to continuously update the related laws and regulations, and to regulate the new innovated instruments traded in stock markets such as index products, index funds, and warranties which have been introduced recently.
- To balance between interests of the related parties: To maintain the relevant balance between corporate governance, investor protection, and liquidity of the stock market. This objective is one of the most difficult targets to be maintained in the world stock markets, and it has been treated in different ways by the world jurisdictions. Because imposing restricted laws to enhance protection for investors may lead to reduce liquidity and thus impair the market stability.
- To avoid market failure: The efficiency of related laws for stock trading means more developed, more competitive market and more relevant to cope with and to absorb the stock market crises and the extraordinary high price volatility. Various studies that were conducted in the majority of the developed and emerging stock markets concerning the relevancy of the existing laws have found inefficiency of various

aspects of the related laws and procedures that may affect or increase the possibility of initiating the stock market crises.

- To assure efficiency and countinous flow of information: To assure a minimum level of efficiency of financial markets, there is a need to adopt relevant laws and regulations, to permit the flow of information concerning the stock trading (information asymmetry).

FRAMEWORK OF THE RELATED LAWS

Generally, the legal framework of a jurisdiction as well as the attached legislative powers should accord with political, economic, and marketing features of a country. Accordingly, the framework of the related laws varies from one jurisdiction to another, and it is based on original laws. In general, the related laws that organize the world stock trading and have direct or indirect effect may be stated in various groups as presented in Table 3-1. It shows that the framework of the related laws of stock markets may be arranged in six levels as follows:

First Level: The Social, Economic, and Political Philosophy

The aspects of social, economic and political policies in a country should be considered as the base for stating objectives and the framework of the related laws and enforcement bodies for any jurisdiction. The general directions issue to the regulators when establishing any related laws should reflect the economic and political views of the respective country. For example, if a country is directed towards the liberalization of its own economy, this leads to reorganize the related laws and regulations to protect the concerned parties including national economy and local investors.

Second Level: The Original of the National Law

The world related laws are grouped into two major laws including the civil law group and the common law group. The majority of the world jurisdictions are built on civil laws, while some countries such as USA, UK and previous British colonies are based on the common law. In addition, the original of laws produce significant differences among jurisdictions. For example, there are significant differences between, French, German, and Scandinavian original laws. The majority of the world jurisdictions including developed and emerging countries are based on English, French, Germane, and Scandinavian original laws. For example, Jordan and Egypt have a civil law with French original, while Malaysia has English original, and Taiwan has civil German original law.

Concerning the stock markets, some economists believe that common laws can be more relevant to stock markets than civil laws. For example, La Porta et.al. (1997) questioned why some countries have bigger capital than others and concluded that countries with poor relevant laws have smaller and narrower capital markets. In addition, reported that French civil law countries have the least developed capital markets. Levine and Zervos (1998) stated that countries with relevant accounting standards and investor protection laws lead to better developed stock markets.

Table 3-1. The framework of the major laws, and regulations of the world stock markets

Levels	Laws, regulations, codes and practices
Social, Economic and Political aspects	Economic policies Monetary and financial policies Financial policies and objectives
Original Laws	Civil law, common law,
Corporate laws	Corporate share laws, types and features of shares, issuing of shares regulations
	Corporate governance laws and codes of ethics
Securities laws	Securities laws, trading regulations,
	Disclosure of stockholders requirements
	Derivatives products (Future and options), warrants laws
	Index products and instruments indexed funds, traded exchange funds, index options, index futures regulations
	Disclosures requirements, reporting requirements, Accounting principles, price -earning ratio, other requirements
Stock Exchange regulations	Stock exchange by-laws
	Market organization
	Market supervision and authorization, and arbitration rules
	Brokers and membership requirements
	Equity indices composition and weighting regulations
	Calculation of index, methodology, and dissemination process
	Trading mechanism, floor trading, electronic trading, call auction, continuous methods, type of orders regulations
Trading and price Control	Block trading and special deals regulations
	Insider trading laws
	Price limits regulations
	Margin requirements
	Circuit breakers Trading halts, Reducing trading hours regulations

Third Level: Corporate Laws

Corporate laws organize the types, features, and conditions for issuing the traded securities in the world stock markets which are reflected on the efficiency and liquidity of the stock markets. The main aim of a corporate law for the stock trading is to maintain the balance between corporate governance, investor protection, and the liquidity of stock market. In addition, there are many aspects of corporate laws which may have positive or negative impact on stock market liquidity and stability, such as monitoring rules, minority shareholder protection issue, block holding shares rules, repurchases shares rules, type of shares (bearer to registered; vote -non vote).

Many studies were carried out in the last decade to discuss the issue of corporate governance and stock market activity and liquidity. These studies concluded that classes and features of shares might affect the liquidity and volatility of stock market prices. Different corporate laws have different classes of stock shares, including: bearer share compared to registered share, vote share compared to non- vote share. The bearer shares which may be found in the majority of European countries may be traded outside stock exchanges accordingly may increase the volatility of stock prices and may moderately destabilized market during stock crises periods based on the opinion of stock market experts (Sabri, 1995a 1995b, and 2002).

Fourth Level: The Securities Laws

The IOSCO stated 30 principles for the securities regulations, which are based upon three objectives including the protection of investors, ensuring that markets are fair, efficient and transparent; and the reduction of systematic risk (IOSCO, 2003a). The securities laws organize the price and trading processes of the world stock markets including clearing and cash settlements procedures, listing requirements, delisting requirements, disclosure of stockholders requirements, disclosures requirements of securities, generally accepted accounting principles, and other requirements. The details and regulations of the above-organized issues are related to securities laws that vary from one jurisdiction to another. Since 1987 stock market crash, many empirical studies were conducted in various stock markets to investigate the role of institutional features of stock exchanges in stock market crises. This includes trading mechanism, cash settlements, clearing period, type of orders, trading hours, transactions cost, and computerizing of trading activities. The world stock exchanges using different trading and pricing systems, different settlements cycles that range from one to seven days, few of the world stock exchange still use floor-trading systems, while the majority use various models of computerized systems. The point here is to find out the most appropriate mechanism to cope with stock market crises.

Fifth Level Stock Exchange Laws

The stock exchanges' laws regulate the stock trading activities including: stock exchange by-laws, market organization, pricing regulations, settlements regulations, market supervision and authorization, arbitration rules, brokers and membership requirements, equity indices, index composition and weighting, calculation of index and methodology, and dissemination process. However, it should be noted here that there is an overlap between regulations and rules stated by securities laws and exchanges laws in some of the world jurisdictions.

Financial experts started to examine whether some of the present institutional features and the structure of the stock market are associated with stock market crisis in certain events.

Some believe that the 1987 crash might not have been as large as it was the case if more orderly trade mechanisms had been maintained (Harris, 1989). However, the empirical examinations of institutional features reported contradicting observations regarding the relevancy of the existing mechanism to cope with stock market crises. This applies for example to the various methods of stock trading:

Sixth Level: The Controlling Rules

The majority of stock markets impose various regulations to prevent manipulations, protect investors and to reduce volatility. Price limits, safe harbor rules, insider trading rules, investment protection rules and margin requirements are examples of such controlling measures. This part will be discussed later in this chapter as one of the introduced regulations to the world stock markets.

Recent Development of the Related Laws

The recent developments occurred in the world stock markets that had occurred in the last decade were intensive in responding to the new changes that were introduced to the world stock trading. The legal changes cover almost all aspects and levels of related laws and regulations. However, this section considers the most recent changes that may have direct or indirect effect on the stability of stock markets, and have the merits of globalization in such a way that it forms a general trend in both developed and merging markets. This includes changes in the legal entity of the world stock exchanges, altering the corporate laws and corporate governance codes and regulations, new trends in legalizing and regulating some features and types of shares, and other regulations were introduced to the world stock markets to authorize and organize some new practices such as; introducing the alternative trading systems as supplementary to the traditional stock exchanges, and the regulations related to the cross border financial services.

Changing the Legal Entity of Stock Exchanges

The majority of the world stock exchanges witnessed extensive changes in almost every aspect of stock exchange features. The majority of these changes have just occurred in the last few years. The legal entity of the stock exchange in the majority of the world stock markets has been changed after one century of using the same legal entity. The changes were introduced in the last ten years including the economic statue, the profit target, types of owners, legal entity, work conditions, sources of revenues, place of trading, capital shares, and other aspects as presented in Table 3-2. In the last decade, the world stock exchanges went through demutualization and privatization process of many developed stock exchanges. The movement of privatization of the world stock exchanges started in Europe and is extending now to some Asian stock exchanges.

Table 3-2. New trends in the legal entity of the world stock exchanges

Legal and Economic Aspects	Past and present	New Trends
Economy Status	Monopoly	Competition
Profit target	Non- Profit oriented	Profit seeking company
Owners	Government and insiders	Outsiders and insiders
Legal entity	Government, semi public, and cooperatives	Private and public Corporations
Work under	one jurisdiction	Cross border jurisdictions
Revenues	Fess and commissions	Mainly information services, Fees, commissions,
Listed	Not listed	Listed in the exchange
Capital	No capital	Common shares of equity base up to one billion (e. g.; London)
place of trading	Exclusive house for trading	Competition with alternative trading systems (ATS)
Perception	Local	Regional and global

Sabri, 2007.

For example, Stockholm Stock Exchange was the first to get into demutualization in 1993, followed by the majority of European stock exchanges, Hong Kong, Singapore, and Toronto. In addition the majority of these stock exchanges are now publicly traded and listed in their own stock exchanges such as Australian;1998, Hong Kong; 2000, Helisniki; 2000, Singapore; 2000, Deutsche; 2001, Oslo; 2002, London (2001), the market capitalization of London exchange is one billion pounds (Aggarwal, 2002).

In addition, some of these stock exchanges may be dual listed in more than stock exchanges. However, the changes of legal entity of stock exchanges are extending to the rest of the world. The annual report of World Federation of Exchanges annual (WFE, 2001), indicated that there was a significant changes in the legal entities of the world stock exchanges, and based on a survey of 48 members of the World Federation of stock exchanges 46% of the world exchanges were profit firms or non- profit organizations with insider ownership, while 37% are profit organizations with outsider ownership, and 17% are public and other entities. In addition this situation has been moved more and more towards demutualization, in 2004, 69% of members of FEW exchanges become for profit enterprises (WFE, 2005).

Accordingly, it can be concluded that the legal entity trend is shifting; from public to non- for profit organizations, and to private company with insider owners, from private company with outsider owners, to public companies with outsider owners. Eventually, the majority of the world stock exchanges will end as public corporations owned by both insiders and outsiders that are listed in the stock exchange and may have dual listed in foreign exchanges. Changing legal entity of stock exchanges reflects on various aspects including profit target, working conditions and ownership.

In addition, there was a change in the size and structure of revenues in almost all the world stock exchanges. For example, the total revenue of the federation of stock exchanges organized in the WFE increased from $2.1 billion in 1991 to $ 8.4 billion in 2002, which means an increase of 300% in last decade (WFE, 2003). The revenues of stock exchanges used to be generated mainly from two resources, trading fees and listing fees. However, this situation is now changing by adding new sources of revenue, such as selling of information and other financial services. This new source formed about half of the European stock exchanges revenues, while trading fees offered 44% and 7% was from listing fees in 2002. The contribution of information services and others amounted to 67% in Stockholm stock exchange as compared to 5% from listing fees. However, the trading fees represent the main sources of revenue in the case of in Deutschue Borse that generates about 57% of total revenues, Helsinki 52%, and Swiss exchange 57% (Anderson, 2003).

The effect of changing the legal entity of the world stock exchanges on the market stability is not clear yet. In addition, it is supposed to increase the efficiency, reduce the cost of trading, and to increase the liquidity of trading. However, there is no empirical investigation being conducted yet to compare between the performances of stock exchanges under different legal entities, nor there is enough experience to find out if the profit oriented companies will have more relevant place of trading in case of high price volatility and in stock market crises.

Changes in Corporate Governance Regulations

The corporate governance laws articulate the way a business corporation being operated, directed, and controlled. The corporate governance efficiency has a direct impact on the performance of stock markets. Accordingly, the issue of corporate governance in all over the world is expected to increase in the coming years for various reasons:

First: The 1997 stock market crisis in South Asia: The last stock crisis took place in South Asia, raised the issue of efficiency of the related regulations of corporate governance and their behaviors that lead to the crisis.

Second: The recent corporate accounting fraud scandals: During the last few years major auditing scandals occurred in the USA and other developed countries. Such issue impaired the creditability of the external auditors significantly, and led international, regional, and national jurisdictions and commissions to reconsider the accounting and disclosures requirements, and standards.

Third: The issues of corporate governance received a lot of debates and was reorganized in the last decades to cover various aspects, and can be different from one jurisdiction to another as presented in Table 3-3. It includes the major issues of concern in corporate governances for selected jurisdictions. Some jurisdictions emphasize the internal and external control, disclosures, and transparency issues. Others emphasize majority and minority of stockholders meetings and rights, the protection of creditors' rights, employees as shareholders, and the rule of labor union in appointing the board of directors.

In general, the major issues of the corporate governance in the world corporate laws are related mainly to better disclosures and transparency, the equity treatment of shareholders, the board composition, the monitory committees, and non-executive directors, separation of the post of the CEO and chairman posts alternatives, the participation of employees in the management and in the board of directors. However, in spite of the new changes in corporate governance, there is still much to be done in this field to assure protection for all concerned parties in the world stock markets. In a survey conducted by Investment Company Institute (ICI, 2000) to examine the legal practices of corporate governance in 11 jurisdictions including concluded that they were certain countries with no assurance to the minimum level of protections for shareholders, and there are restrictions on the ability of the holders, who may face cumbersome requirements to exercises their voting rights. Shleifer and Vishny (1997) reported that the corporate governance mechanism around the world still varied. While USA and England rely on protection for inventors, Europe and Japan rely on large investors and banks, and the rest of the world relies on families' ownership.

Fourth: Recently, various international and regional organizations issued general principles, guidelines and best practices concerning corporate governance.

Table 3-3. Examples of the major issues incorporated to corporate governances in selected jurisdictions

Jurisdictions	Issued	Major Issues
Italy	2002	Role of chairman of board of directors, confidential information, appointment, and remuneration of director, internal control, shareholders meetings, and relationship with institutional investors.
Taiwan	2002	Composition, duties, responsibilities of the board of directors, supervisory board, proxy solicitation, monitoring of minority shareholders, disclosure and transparency, disgorgement again insider's short- swing profit.
Netherlands	1997	Supervisory board, conflict of interest, functions of general meeting, priority shares, preference shares, proxy solicitation, rating agencies, monitory, buyback of shares
German	202	Shareholders and general meeting, cooperative between management board and supervisory board, management board, supervisory board, transparency, reporting and audit of annual financial statements.
Other Jurisdictions	1995-2000	Participation of employee in the board of directors, protection of creditors rights, employees as shareholders, the rule of labor union in appointing the board of directors

Source: The Corporate Government Cods and Regulations in the respective jurisdictions.

This includes:

- The Organization for Economic Co-operation and Development, which issued principles of corporate governance (OECD, 1999) and was adopted by 29 OECD countries. Moreover, thereafter in 2002, these general practices were recommended by the International Organization of Securities Commission to be followed by emerging countries. In 2004, a revised and updated edition was issued to restate the principles. They intended to provide guidance for stock exchanges, investors, corporations that have a role in developing good corporate governance. It includes five major principles and detailed recommendations (OECD, 2004a). The major groups of principles are the rights of shareholders, the equitable treatment of shareholders and their role in corporate governance, disclosure and transparency requirements, and the responsibility of the board of directors as presented in Table 3-4.

- The OECD business sector advisory group on corporate governance adopted twenty standards for public policy improvement of corporate laws. This includes flexibility in responding to the changing competitive environment, the regulatory intervention to be fair, transparency and accountability, policy makers and regulators should be protecting shareholder rights, to have sound audit practices, to consider investor competition, to ensure that corporations abide by laws, to support and encourage education and training efforts, and promoting the welfare of individuals (WGM, 2002).
- The OECD also issued guidelines for multinational enterprises that included general policies and disclosure requirements, employment and industrial relations, environment issues, bribery combating, consumer interests, science and technology, competition, and taxation issues (OECD, 2000).
- International Corporate Governance Network issued statements on global corporate governance principles stating that where codes of the best corporate governance practices, they have to be applied pragmatically, and should adhere to all applicable laws of the jurisdictions in which they operate. Each member of the board director should stand for election on periodical basis, to disclose accurate and timely information to allow investors to make decisions in case of acquisition, ownership and sale of shares (ICGN, 1998).

Table 3-4. OECD Principles of Corporate Governance

Main groups	Examples of Code Principles
The rights of shareholders	Secured methods of ownership registration, obtaining, the shareholder should have the right and opportunity to participate in general meetings, to disclose any capital arrangements that enable certain shareholders to obtain a degree of disproportionate control on their equity ownership
The equitable treatment of shareholders	All shareholders of the same class should be treated equally; insider trading should be prohibited, to disclose any material interests in transactions belong to managers and board of directors; unrestricted cross border voting should be facilitated.
The role of shareholders in corporate governance	Assuring that the rights of stockholders that are protected by the law are respected, permitting performance -enhancing of stockholders participations and they should have access to relevant information
Disclosure and Transparency	Disclosure should include material information, to be prepared, audited and disclose based on high quality accounting standards, an annual audit should be conducted by an independent auditor, and the dissemination of information to relevant users, analysts brokers, rating agencies and others who provide analysis should disclose any material conflicts of interest.
Responsibilities of the board	The board should act on the best interest of the company and shareholders and treat them fairly, ensure compliance with applicable laws, and should have access to accurate and timely information

Source: OECD, 1999 and OECD, 2004a.

Modernization of Corporate Law

Modernizing of companies laws are found in almost all European countries in the last decade including Austria, Germany, Spain, Italy, Finland, France, and Denmark. In addition, in UK the final report of modernizing the corporate law has just been offered to the UK Parliament, after four years of debates (DTI, 2002). The most recent changes in the corporate laws are related to defining the audit functions, in which about 13 jurisdictions witnessed changes in this area, including US, Belgium, Spain, Austria, Ireland, Netherlands, Greece, Czech, Turkey, Poland, Switzerland, Canada and Japan. Other issues such as improving transparency were reconsidered in 17 countries. Laws related to control of interest groups issue was reconsidered by 10 countries, the role of independent directors was reconsidered by 8 countries, and the issue of improving voting rights was reconsidered by 11 countries (OECD, 2003 and OECD, 2004b).

Trends towards Dual Class Shares

There are various announced international and regional standards and recommendations which adopted the concept of one vote one share, and the equity of shareholders. For example, the global share voting principles stated that the same voting rights should attach to shares and stated how to implement voting principles (ICGN, 1998 and 2000). Nevertheless, there are still various countries that accepted dual class shares for different voting rights, and it is expected to increase in the world stock markets. The dual class shares are issued either for voting purposes, or to distinguish between foreign -resident owners, and to distinguish between special owners or promoters and other shareholders.

Accordingly, major issues are needed to be treated including: the issue of controlling a corporation by a minority using the dual class mechanism, the issue of imposing measurements to control or eliminate the bearer's share, the issue of keeping inferior or superior voting rights, the issue of keeping special classes for foreigners and other groups of stockholders. For example, in some countries, the holders of class B with inferior voting rights have the right to elect a minority board of directors, while in other countries, such as Australia, the holders of class A shares have the right to elect the majority of the board of directors. A similar situation concerns the saving shareholders in Italy, who have their own assembly (Sabri, 2005, Sabri, 2007). Table 3-5 presents a summary of types and uses of dual class shares traded in the world stock exchanges.

The shareholders of dual stock classes either for less voting rights, for foreigners or for non –promoters, or for other purposes, are considered as inferior stockholders; thus their reactions may impair the efficiency of stock markets and may have an adverse effect on stock markets during unstable periods of stock trading in the world exchanges. It is expected that the inferior shareholders will be first to sell their shares as long as other purposes of holding shares are not considered such as the purpose of management control of the firm or the long term commitments. In addition, the variety between the prices of the different classes of a security will increase significantly, which may increase the price volatility for the securities traded in the stock markets.

Table 3-5. Examples of the dual class shares traded in the world stock exchanges

	Types and Purposes of dual Class
Australia	For special type of shareholders, special stockholders meeting
Brazil	Dual classes of shares are admitted, but companies listed companies should have one common class
Canada	For voting and special owners
China	To distinguish between foreigners -residences For voting purposes Special stockholders groups such as public owners
France	Preferred Shares either have no vote or have double voting rights,
Germany	Different classes of shares based on different voting rights, non- voting preferred should not exceed 50%
Italy	For voting purposes
South Africa	Dual class for multi voting rights
South Korean	Preferred share, no voting of shares should be more than 25% of outstanding shares
Sweden	Dual class chares for voting rights A share has ten times of voting rights of B share.
Switzerland	For voting purposes For bearer to register For foreigners to resident
Taiwan	Dual class share for different voting rights

Source: The related laws of the respected countries, Sabri, 2007.

Trends towards no- par Value Share

There is a new trend that more jurisdictions are permitting using the no- par value shares as supplementary to the par value shares or as a conclusive alternative. Various countries have accepted the concept of issuing no- pare value shares in the last decade as presented in Table 3-6, while the par value share was the only alternative for the majority of the world corporate jurisdictions for a long time.

Examples of such jurisdictions which introduce the no- par value concept besides the par value shares are France, Germany, Guernsey, and Sate of Jersey. Other states considering this issue such as Hong Kong and Taiwan, while Australia selected the no- par value share as a conclusive alternative for the new issues. In addition, in some jurisdictions firms may have both par and no- par value in an issue at once.

The issue of no- par value received an intensive attention in the last decade due to the process of converting the capital amounts of the European companies stated by the European national currencies to the Euro currency, which created various accounting problems during the redenomination process of the shares into Euro. This situation may encourage the concept of using the no- par value shares. However, using no- par value concept may create various technical, legal, and accounting problems, which will have to be organized, reconsidered and solved.

Table 3-6. Example of Jurisdictions which have recent changes related to no- par value shares

	Year	Explanations
Australia	1998	Exclusively using no par value shares since 1998
France	1998	Introducing the no- par value share besides par value
Germany	1998	Introducing the no- par value share besides par value
Guernsey	2002	Introducing the no- par value share besides par value
Martinis	2001	shares issued after 2001 will be no par value share
State of Jersey	2002	Introduced in 2002
UK	1999	It is recommended to eliminate par value for private company,
Hong Kong	2003	In process of adopting a law to allow issuing shares with no par value
Taiwan	2004	In process of adopting a law to allow issuing shares with no par value

Source: The related laws of the respected countries.

Examples of such problems are:

- Partial payments for no -par value shares,
- Repurchases programs of no- par value shares
- Tax treatments for related activities of no- pare shares
- Redemption and cancellation of no- par value shares
- Issuing both the no- par value and the par value shares at once or by the same firm in jurisdictions, which permit such issuing.
- The issue of protection of creditors: the par value capital represents the minimum paid capital of a firm which represents the first guarantee for the creditors.
- The discount and premiums accounts that are attached to next issues may not be possible, which is supposed to reflect the difference between book and market values of the firms' shares. This situation may jeopardize the interest of other shareholders and may impair the concept of equity for all shareholders.
- Issuing no- par value with different stated or market values in different times or with par and no par value at once may increase the high price volatility of the respective security. In addition,
- When a company increases its own capital while the market price falls below the stated price, it has to price it below the last stated price, which decreases the stock price sharply in the stock exchange.

Repurchasing Shares Programs Regulations

Repurchasing shares, means that a firm buys its own shares for specific purposes using one of the generally accepted ways and programs. This process may help in stabilizing stock markets although it may impair the efficiency of stock market, especially when the holding period of such shares is not restricted nor dumped from the capital. Repurchasing programs that are implemented by listed firms have been increasing significantly as a way of managing their capital efficiency. Accordingly, there is a need to organize such activities in the majority of the world stock markets, thus various new legal developments have been incorporated in different jurisdictions, which may be summarized as follows:

First: The International Organization of Securities Commissions issued a report concerning the stock repurchasing programs in 2004. The IOSCO considered the repurchased programs as material regarding existing and potential investors; thus, it stated four principles to organize such process including: First: the stock repurchasing program should treat shareholders in a fair manner. Second: The regulatory authorities should ensure that their insider dealing regulations apply to the issuers trading during the program. Third: It should be consistent with market integrity. Fourth: the additional risk should be considered in case of derivative transactions attached to the repurchased underlying shares (IOSCO, 2004a).

Second: The majority of the world jurisdictions witnessed new developments in the legal aspects of repurchasing activities programs. For example, in a study conducted by the author (Sabri, 2003) it was reported that about eighteen stock markets witnessed a change in the related laws of share repurchases during the period 1995 to 2000. Moreover, there is a toleration to use the treasury shares in enhancing the stock market during stock market crises and during the existing of extraordinary market price volatility. Based on investigations of the related corporate laws, it may be concluded that various countries witnessed a change in one or more of the related laws of share repurchases during the period 1995 to 2000 in the world economy as presented in Table 3-7.

Some of these changes are related to introducing the concept of share repurchase for the first time, after being illegal, by amending corporate and other related laws. These countries are Finland in 1997, Germany in 1998, India in 1999, Japan in 1995, Norway in 1999, Malaysia in 1997, Singapore in 1998, Denmark in 2000, Sweden in 2000, South Africa in 1999, Taiwan in 2000, and France in 1998. Other countries witnessed changes in share repurchase laws and regulations. For example New Zealand in 1999, Singapore in 1999, Netherlands in 2001, who changed tax laws to encourage share purchase activities. UK issued two consultation papers suggesting the amendment of share repurchases laws; the first one is related to allowing investment companies to repurchase their own shares using capital profits (DTI, 1999a). The other document is related to financial assistance offered by a company for the acquisition of its own share (DTI, 1996).

Other significant changes in share repurchases were related to moving from corporate share repurchase to the concept of holding those shares in treasury for limited or unlimited periods as presented. Malaysia and USA permitted holding of the repurchased shares in Treasury. UK issued a consultative document in 1998 aimed at changing the current law that imposes cancellation of repurchased shares, in order to adopt the concept of holding them as treasury shares (DTI, 1998). In 1999, the department of UK Trade and Industry accepted recommendation of consultation document and decided to deregulate company law in respect to holding shares in Treasury (DTI, 1999b). In Hong Kong a consultation paper was issued to consider permitting treasury shares. It stated five arguments in favor of legalizing treasury shares, including: better management of the balance between debt and equity, providing flexibility in fund raising, better management of employee share schemes, disposing shares in the relevant time, and permitting investment in a company's own shares (SFCHG, 1998). US adopted in 1999 (SEC, 1999) an amendment to Rule 10b-18 (Rule) under the Securities Exchange Act of 1934 in order to improve liquidity during severe market downturns, by modifying timing conditions during the trading session immediately following a market-wide trading suspension.

Table 3-7. Changes in laws occurred in selected countries regarding share repurchase between 1995 and 2000

Country	Effective Year	Major changes
Australia	1995 1999	Deregulate the share buybacks including removing the limit of the 10% To organize the repurchase program in case of no- par value shares
Denmark	2000	New Law related to share repurchases applied since March, 2000
Finland	1997 1998	Permitting listed firms to repurchase their own shares Change in tax regulation in favor of repurchasing shares
Germany	1998 1998	Permitting companies to buyback their own shares Modify the Security Act related to disclosures of firms buy own share
Hong Kong	1998	Consultation paper to introduce treasury shares
IOSCO	2004	Stating international principles for implementing repurchase programs
India	1999	Permitting companies to repurchase their own shares
Japan	1995	Permitting listed companies to repurchase their own shares
Malaysia	1997 1998	Permitting a listed firm to buy its own shares A firm has the choice to hold its own share in treasury
Netherlands	2001	Changes in Tax laws to encourage repurchase of shares
Norway	1999	Permitting listed companies to repurchases their own share
New Zealand	1999	The buybacks of own shares law was amended
Singapore	1998 2000	Permitting companies to repurchase their own share Issue tax treatment of repurchases
South Africa	1999	To allow listed companies to repurchase their own share
Sweden	2000	To allow listed companies to repurchase their own share
Taiwan	2000	To allow listed companies to repurchase their own share
United Kingdom	1999	A consultation paper to allow Investment firms to repurchase their own shares using capital profits

Sources: Compiled by the author (Sabri, 2003) based on the related companies Laws, Regulations of stock exchanges and other related laws and consultation papers for the above states.

In addition, other recent legal issues which have been introduced to the world stock markets concerning the repurchases programs are related to the ways of implementing such programs. Some jurisdictions stated conditions on the mechanisms that may be used such as Italy, Malaysia, Singapore, and Switzerland, while others do not state any specified mechanisms to be used. There are four possible ways which are used in the world stock markets including open market repurchase program, self-tender offers program, over the counter repurchases program and derivative- based share repurchases (IOSCO, 2004a). Other issues are related to repurchasing activities such as in case of no- par value shares or when a share buy-back premium or discount arises (AARF, 1998a and 1998b).

Inside Trading Regulations

Recently, the majority of the world stock markets work under regulations to prohibit insider trading. Such regulations were incorporated to the world stock markets in the last fifteen years. For examples, the European Community issued the Insider Trading Directives in 1989 (EEC, 89, 592). In USA, recently, the Congress passed the Act of Insider Trading and Securities Fraud Enforcement (Garfinklel, 1997). The number of stock markets adopting insider trading regulations increased from 34 markets before 1990 to 87 stock markets in 2000, which formed about 85% of the world stock markets (Bhattacharya and Daouk, 2002). The insider trading means trading based on information which is not publicly available, and if it is available, the stock price may change significantly. The insider trading covers trading directly in the stock markets or sharing insider information to other parties, or to recommend others to invest in the related equities based on insider information.

The insider traders include members of the board of directors, corporate managers, supervisors and deputy managers, stockholders who own a certain percent of total equities, appointed CPAs and their staff, and any other staff who own insider information which materially affect stock prices. Accordingly, the related laws preventing the insider traders to trade during those periods before the annual meetings that announce earning decisions. However, it should be noted that the definition of insider information, insiders, insider trading, legal liability, prohibited activities, sanctions, and the powers of related regulators as well as the self-regulatory organizations might be different from one market to another (IOSCO, 2003b).

The concept of imposing insider trading has legal, social, economic and ethical aspects. Recent empirical and theoretical studies showed contradicting pros and cons aspects. The effect of this new phenomenon on the efficiency, stability, liquidity and cost of trading is not explored yet. For liquidity, imposing insider trading restrictions decreases liquidity of stock markets which may lead to instability of stock prices. For example, if the stock prices fall sharply in the period before the annual meetings, the major traders may not trade based on insider trading regulations, while such traders may stop falling prices if they are not prohibited from trading. In addition, imposing restrictions on insider trading may impair the efficient hypothesis in its strong form and may not be possible, as long as insider traders may not use insider information to gain extra profit compared to other investors trading in equities. For the stock value, imposing insider-trading restrictions might have a negative effect on target firms' stock value (Persons, 1997).

The effect of imposing regulations on insider trading were examined empirically in many stock exchanges and the majority concluded that such rules are not effective, and may have disadvantages related to reducing liquidity and are not justified. The concept of imposing control on insiders' traders is to prevent them from getting abnormal profit as compared to outsider traders who are trading under conditions of no insider information. However, such regulations may prevent insiders from trading in the stock markets when they are mostly in need during the period of falling stock prices. For example, Kabir and Vermaelen (1996) indicated that stock market in Netherlands became less liquid, when insiders were not allowed to trade due to imposing new regulations. Garfinkel (1997) reported that the threats of legal sanctions affect the trading behavior of insiders in the stock market. Accordingly, many experts question the wisdom of imposing such regulations, entrepreneurs and society may disagree on the conditions of imposing the insider trading restrictions and prefer to allow insider trading even when it is not socially optimal (Khanna and Slezak, 1994).

Trading Interruption; (Control Price) Regulations

Recently, the majority of the world stock markets works under different regulations of market interruptions, to reduce stock volatility and cease trading in case of extraordinary fluctuations of prices. The used measures range from discretionary instruments such as trading halts, and market disclosures to automatic measures such as stated price limits, circuit breaker for the entire market, trading suspension, and margin requirements to control liquidity of the stock markets.

The interruption regulations may be imposed on a security, group of securities and the whole market. For the circuit breakers for example, the SEC of US established new circuit breaker rule sets of 10%, 20%, 40% of one-day decline in the Dow Jones and modifying the market- wide trading halt (SEC, 1999). For price limits, the majority of stock markets in both developed and emerging markets imposed price limits ranged between 5% and 30% in a daily trading. For example, the price limits is 10% in Italian Exchange, 10%, in Istanbul, 15% in Korean stock exchange, 5% in Egypt, 7% in Taiwan, 20% in Czech, and 30% in Thailand stock exchange. Various markets use both price limits and trading halts as presented in Table 3-8. Another control measure is the margin requirement, which it is the amount to be paid as a down payment in stock trading, which limits the maximum amount of credit the buyer can obtain from the broker. Changing the margin requirements used to reduce the liquidity and to control the trading activity.

Table 3-8. Control measures imposed on selected sample of the world stock exchanges

Stock Exchanges	Price limits	Circuit breaker rules	Margin requirements
Danish	No	No	No
USA, NYSE	No	Yes	Yes 50%
Czech	20%		Yes
Italian	10%		
Istanbul	10%		
Korean	15%		
Egypt	5%		Yes
Australian	No	No	No
Taiwan	7%		Yes
Thailand	30%		
Canada		Yes	
France	Yes	Yes	
Irish		Yes	No
Bahrain	10%		Yes
Australia	No	No	No

Sources: a- Sabri, 2007 b- The related laws for the respected jurisdictions c- Survey conducted by the Author.

The effects of the above measures on efficiency, liquidity, and stability of stock markets are not clear. The majority of published research found contradictory conclusions about the desired need effect on stock trading. However, in spite of the non- conclusive results of empirical studies, imposing such measures in order to control the high stock volatility may impair the efficiency of stock markets, especially, when such interruptions occur frequently. For example the frequency of trading halt reached to 1145 halts in Canada and more than 500 times in Brazil, Malaysia and NASDAQ stock exchanges in the year 2001 as presented in Table 3-9.

Regulations of Cross-boarded Stock Trading

The issue of regulating cross boarded transactions concerning stock trading is one of the new challenges facing the legislations all over the world. In practice there are various cross-bordered activities taking place in the world stock markets including cross-borders licensing of financial services which is related to offering services to parties located in other jurisdictions (IOSCO, 1995). Various new practices and conditions were introduced to the world stock markets which required regulations responding to the issue of cross border legislations. Financial services products, activities and transactions of stock market trading occurred, conducted and originated in a home base as may impact stock markets activities based on foreign jurisdictions and vice versa.

Table 3-9. Number of trading halt occurred in selected stock exchanges during 2001.

Stock Exchanges	Number of halts	Halts per year a company
Brazil	594	0.7
Canada	1145	0.7
Hong Kong	489	0.6
Istanbul	209	0.4
Mexico	51	0.3
Italy	73	0.2
Australia	169	0.2
Poland	72	0.2
Switzerland	159	0.2
Malaysia	505	0.2
NYSE	376	0.1
NASDAQ	714	0.1
England	72	0.04
Spain	54	0.03
Taiwan	27	0.02

Source: IOSCO, Report on Trading Halts, 2002, p.38.

Accordingly, the world regulators countered many questions and situations which needs to be verified, related to whether to accept regulations of the counter partners jurisdictions in case of providing financial services related to stock trading and cash settlements, when, where and to what extent in case of contradictory regulations which may exist between the supplier of services and the receivers' jurisdictions. In addition, the cross boarders' regulations issue is expanding due to the cent practices; environment and conditions which may be summarized as follows:

- Electronic transfer of cash and securities cross boarders: Recently various countries regulated the reporting process of cross border currency and securities transferring including stocks and bonds requirements. In matters related to when, where, who and how to report, The EC regulations defined the cross- boarder payments as transfer of credit transfers' electronic payment transactions, cash withdrawals by means of electronic payment instrument and cross- borders checks from one state to another (EC, 2001). Other issues attached to electronic transfer of cash and securities also regulated recently such as money laundering. The IOSCO adopted a resolution on money laundering in 1992, which should consider customer identify costumers' information and keep adequate record requirements (IOSCO, 1992).
- The integrations among regional stock exchanges which emerged more than stock exchanges in one company or one legal entity, such as the merging between Paris, Brussels, Lisbon, and Amsterdam stock exchange in one legal entity known as Euronext.
- Cross borders financial services including consultation, ordering, and implementing, over the internet websites. In addition an investor may open an account with brokers attached to different jurisdictions. This means that the Internet financial services for the providers and recipients are based on different jurisdictions. This situation creates the problem of organizing such multi jurisdictions trading transactions. The IOSCO indicated that the regulators in response to the internet cross trading stock markets should balance between the benefit of internet services and the possible disadvantages such as the misconduct, and should consider consumer protection, transparency and clarity, and regulators should facilitate cross- border transactions.
- Alternative trading systems: This issue has also been more significant to regulators after introducing what is known as the alternative trading systems by which trading occurs through electronic networking systems cross boarders. This practice will be explored in the next section of this chapter.
- Cross- boarder clearing and settlements: The cross –border clearing and settlement means that clearing or settlements occur in a jurisdiction other than jurisdictions of one or more of involved counterparties. In other world it involves two or more national clearing houses and settlement agencies or currencies. Various regulators organized this practice in order to avoid as much as possible the attached risks of such operations such as credit and systematic risk. Other regulators modified the related laws in order that a national stock exchange may deal with more than national or foreign clearing houses and settlements agencies under conditions that be accredited in advance. Cross –border settlements are produced mainly from trading in cross listed firms, internet trading, alternative trading systems and other cross-border transactions. More details concerning the clearing and settlement issue will be presented in the next chapter.
- Cross- boarder public offerings of securities: this issue received intensive debates, proposal and active plans in the EC, in order to facilitate the raising of capital within the EC states. There are various proposals issued to facilitate cross-border securities

offerings such as the European passport for issuers, but this report has been under debate and criticism (St. John, 2001).

- The cross-listed securities in two different jurisdictions: A new challenge facing the world stock markets due to the increasing number of dual listed securities in two or more different jurisdictions. It creates many questions that the regulators have to respond about how to deal with different regulations in which one single security has been priced and traded. The regulators have to regulate the requirements and conditions of foreign securities to be listed in their own stock exchanges. The conditions and requirements of their home securities listed in foreign stock exchanges. The regulations, which organize the relationship between the trading in two stock exchanges affiliated to two jurisdictions. For example if a trading interruptions imposed on the security in one market, the question here is to whether the other stock exchanges where the same security is listed should be accord with such measure in a parallel manner.
- The IOSCO reported on traded halt indicated that the stock exchange implementing a trading halt should notify other stock exchanges and share with them the information underlying the trading halt. However, a few jurisdictions have formal agreements to organize their actions to trading halt notifications, and two jurisdictions have jointed a pilot program to impose an automatic trading suspension every time a market imposes a trading suspension on the dual listed security (IOSCO, 2002).
- Other issues such as settling cross- border financial disputes, multi jurisdiction mergers of two listed firm, cross border tax issues and issues related to option and futures products traded in specialized international stock exchanges.

The choices that are confronting the world regulators are so various in dealing with the cross- borders stock transactions, including harmonization of the world stock market regulations, which is unrealistic, bilateral and multilateral agreement between various jurisdictions and cooperative agreements, other jurisdictions may choose the mutual recognitions between twin or regional stock exchanges in which each jurisdictions accept the regulatory of the partners jurisdictions in trading and settlements transactions as well as licensing requirements. Others have unilateral cooperatives in case of regional experience such as the EC region. While other countries accepted that to recognize foreign transactions based on stated conditions. Finally some countries insist that their respected laws and regulation to be fulfilled.

For example, the USA applies all local requirements in all cross- border transaction under all circumstances; Mexico and Japan require foreign intermediaries to have presence in their countries. The EU selected the mutual recognition of authorization known as EU Passport in which a financial institution located in one EU state may work in another EU state. Other countries such as Australia developed principles to regulate the cross- boarder services (IOSCO, 2004b).

Australia is an example of countries, which have developed regulations to organize the cross- boarder financial services. It stated ten principles by the ASIC, Australian Securities & Investments Commission, and issued in 2002 (ASIC, 2002). It includes also, the purposes of the stated regulations, and the uses and conditions of applying such regulations. Table 3-10 presents summary of cross border financial service regulations in Australia.

Table 3-10. Framework for cross border financial services' regulations in Australia

Framework	Details
Purposes	To ensure that foreign facilities services and products do not affect the integrity of Australian markets or create systemic risk for it. To protect Australian investors who access foreign facilities, services, and products
Uses	To recognize a foreign regulatory regime or regulators To enter into bi- or multi- lateral recognition agreement with foreign regulators.
Principles	To recognize foreign regulatory regimes that are sufficiently equivalent to the Australian regulatory regime,
	To give the possible recognition to sufficiently equivalent foreign regulatory regimes.
	To have effective co-operation arrangements (bi-lateral or multilateral) with the home regulators of foreign facilities, services and products available in Australia.
	To enforce the Australian laws that applies to foreign facilities, services and products.
	Adequate rights and remedies must be practically available to Australian investors who access foreign facilities, services or products in Australia.
	Adequate disclosure must be made of information that Australian investors may reasonably require.
	An equivalent regulatory regime is clear, transparent and certain.
	An equivalent regulatory regime is consistent with the IOSCO Objectives and Principles of Securities Regulation.
	An equivalent regulatory regime is adequately enforced in the home jurisdiction Principle
	An equivalent regulatory regime achieves equivalent outcomes to the Australian regulatory

Source: ASIC Australian Securities & Investments Commission, 2002.

Regulating of Alternative Trading Systems (ATSs)

One of the recent developments in the legal aspects of the world stock markets is the adoption of a newly regulations of stock trading which is known as the alternative trading system or the non- exchange trading system. It is an alternative trading method to the traditional stock exchange, or it may be working as a supplementary vehicle to the stock exchanges and may handle the business trading in case of an increase in trading volume. The traditional stock exchanges no longer work as a conclusive pace of stock trading, in which the stock prices are determined. The new practice which uses electronic communication networks known as ECNs offers the opportunity to investors to send their orders directly to the electronic system, which will do the match electronically, as non- discretionary action set by the system operation. This trading method which increases access to cross boarder markets now exists in various developed markets and trade in equities as well as in corporate and government bonds.

Trading outside the traditional stock exchange has various advantages. Such as, First: it may play a distinct role in the market and solve the conflict of interest problems that exist between brokers and dealers as reported by Macey and O'Hara (1999). Second: There is the benefit of offering a trading system round the clock, Third: it fits more with retail investors and trades unanimously which is not permitted in the traditional stock exchanges, Forth: it offers the opportunity to trade with less cost under less regulatory environment and it may be considered as a complementary method to handle a part of the stock market trading in case of booming seasons of trade.

On the other side there are various critical problems that are attached to this way, which are mainly related to:

1. Market fragmentation: dealing with the ATSs system along with trading in traditional stock exchanges lead to market fragmentations where the orders in both markets are not matched or interacted. Accordingly, this situation may impair the efficiency of stock markets, and thus creates instability for both stock exchange and non- stock exchange trading. However, the argument against this phenomenon has not been settled yet, and some economists believe it is acceptable to have such a variety and both markets should not be consolidated, rather should deal independently, and the AST system should not be treated in the framework of the market concept.
2. There is no assurance concerning the information asymmetry, and may not be fully disclosed. Therefore new national rules may be required to use an electronic board to announce quote prices on a continuous basis.
3. There is no minimum degree of investor protection, and may include manipulation and fraud and there is no assurance for a minimum degree of public transparency.

Accordingly, there was an urgent need to regulate such activities, in which the related jurisdictions respond for this new challenge so fast on national, regional, and international levels. On the regional level, the European Securities regulators amended or in process of adopting regulation concerning this type of stock trading. The new regulations stated and defined the system, the rule of conduct and standards for alternatives trading system as presented in Table 3- 11. The standards of European Securities Regulations cover the following topics (CESR, 2002):

1. The notification of establishing a qualifying system including the trading process, type of orders and quote information, the system design.
2. The types and number of users and the access arrangement for users and contracted liquidity providers.
3. The trading arrangement is fair and in order.
4. The publication of trading information on a reasonable commercial basis including quotes and orders.
5. Monitor user compliance with contractual rules of the system.
6. Facilitating market integrity and investor protection.
7. System is capable of delivering the proposed service.
8. Clarity of obligations for the clearing and settlement of transactions.

Table 3- 11. Regulation and standards of alternative trading systems as stated by the Committee of European Securities Regulations in 2002

Fundamentals	Standards & Regulations
Definitions	Multilateral systems excluding bilateral system Multiple third party buying and selling interests Brings non-discretionary rules set by the system operator
Standards	Notification Fair and orderly trading Publication of trading information Monitoring Market integrity and investor protection
Conduct rules	To clear the nature relationship between operator and user Supplying sufficient information about the system Providing sufficient publicly available information
Type of system	A qualified system
Multilateral system Merits	Limit order matching book Electronics periodic auction system Price-taking system and crossing network Multiple market maker Bulletin board if execution takes place inside the system

Source: CESR, 2002.

For national level, the majority of developed jurisdictions adopted new regulations in the last few years concerning the use of the ATSs. For example in the USA, the SEC adopted a rule to allow an alternative trading system to register as national securities exchange, or as broker- dealers and to comply with other requirements based on their trading volume. The recording requirements include daily summary of trading, transaction volume, time-sequenced records of order information and a record of subscribers to alternative trading systems. The size of ATS trading was about 20% of orders in securities listed on the NASDAQ, and 4% of orders related to stock exchanges (SEC, 1998). The Finnish securities market act (SMA) was amended in 2002 to include regulations on ATSs, which allows only limited securities to be traded on ATSs (Wist and Mikkola, 2002). In UK which already has about 20 based ATSs actives in markets for equities, bonds, financial derivatives and commodities, the Financial Services Authority of U. K. issued a consultation paper in 2002, and thereafter, issued the final policy and handbook text related to the regulation of ATSs in June 2003. The major concern of trading thought ATSs is to assure public transparency of prices and transactions occurring in the system, monitoring and detecting market abuse by means of the system, and ensuring users have access to information about instruments traded (FSA, 2003).

However, in spite of the newly introduced regulations of the ATSs, there are various issues that have not been settled yet, and need to be answered. Such as: whether the traded securities have to be registered in the ATS system, and to what extend this system should be different and less regulatory from the stock exchange system. Should the new system be as alternative or supplementary system to the traditional stock exchange. Should this new system be regulated based on market place concept or based on a new concept of remoate trading.

Other issues are related to the necessity for registering the traded securities, and the licensing requirements, for the firms working in this field. Because some of the concerned parties and market participants believe that more regulations will increase the cost of trading and lead to the loss of the expected benefits of having an alternative system to stock exchanges which is already heavily regulated.

CONCLUSION

This chapter presented purposes and frameworks of the related laws of the world stock markets. Thereafter, the chapter explored ten new legal changes, which have been incorporated, to the world stock markets. These changes including the new legal entity of the stock exchanges, changes in corporate governance and laws, trends towards dual class and no- par value shares, adopting regulations to repurchases programs, adopting regulations concerning insider trading and control price procedures, cross- boarder regulations for stock trading processing, and regulating of the ATSs as a supplementary way for the stock exchange markets.

REFERENCES

AARF (1998a) *Accounting for share Buy- Backs, Abstract 16* (Australian Accounting Research Foundation, Australia, January).

AARF (1998b) *Accounting for share Buy- Backs of no- par value shares, Abstract 22* (Australian Accounting Research Foundation, Australia, November).

Aggarwal, Reena (2002) "Demutualization and corporate governance of stock exchanges" *Journal of Applied Corporate Finance* 15; No. 1, 105-113.

Alba, Pedro, Amar Bhattacharys, Stijin Claessens, Swati Ghosh and Leonardo Hernandez (1999) "The Role of Macro-economic and Financial Sector Linkages in East Asia's Financial Crisis" (Working Paper, Working Bank and Central Bank of Chile).

Andersen Atso K. (2003) "Competition between European Stock Exchanges" (Helsinki School of Economics Working Paper No. W-342).

ASIC (2002) *Principles for cross border financial services regulation: Making the regulatory regime work in cross border environment* (Australian Securities & Investments Commission, November).

Bhattacharya, Utpal and Hazem Daouk (2002) "The world price of insider trading" *The Journal of Finance* 57; 75-109.

Carstens, Agustin and Moises J. Schwartz, (1998) "Capital flows and financial crisis in Mexico" *Journal of Asian Economics* 9 (2); 207-226.

CESR, (2002) *Standards for Alternative Trading Systems* (The Committee of European Securities Regulations, CESR/02-86b, France).

Chui, C. W., Sheridan Titman and K. C. John Wei (2001) "Momentum, Legal Systems and Ownership Structure: An analysis of Asian stock markets" (SSRN, Working paper series, Social Science Electronic Publishing).

DTI (1996) *Financial assistance by a company for the acquisition of its own shares: a consultative document* (May, Department of Trade and Industry, UK).

DTI (1998) *Share Buybacks*: A consultative Document (May, Department of Trade and Industry, UK).

DTI (1999a) *Using Capital Profit*: A consultative Document (May, Department of Trade and Industry, UK).

DTI (1999b) *Purchase by Companies of Their Own Shares for Holding in Treasury* (December, Department of Trade and Industry, UK).

DTI (2002) *Modernizing Company Law* (Presented to the Parliament, Trade and Industry Department, U. K).

EC (2001) Regulation on cross- broader payment in Euro *Official Journal of the European communities* (28.12.2001).

EEC (1989). *Coordinating regulations on insider dealing*" (Council Directive 89/ 592/ EEC, of 13 November 1989).

FSA (2003) *Alternative Trading Systems*: Feedback on CP153 and made Text (Financial Services Authority, U. K).

Garfinkel, John A. (1997) "New Evidence on the Effects of Federal Regulations on Insider Trading The Insider Trading and Securities Fraud Enforcement Act (ITSFEA)" *Journal of Corporate Finance* 3 (2); 89-111.

Harris, Lawrence (1989) "The October 1987 S & P 500 stock futures basis" *Journal of Finance* 44; 77 - 99.

ICGN (1998) *Global Share Voting Principles* (International Corporate governance Network, San Francisco)

ICGN (2000) *Statement on Global of ICGN Voting principles* (International Corporate governance Network, London)

ICI (2000) Global *Corporate Governance Issues for Mutual funds* (Investment Company Institute, Washington, DC available on line www. ici. Org

IOSCO (1992) *Report on Money Laundering,* (Report of the Technical Committee International Organization of Securities Commissions, October).

IOSCO (1995) *Resolution Concerning Cross- border transactions* (Presidents' Committee, International Organization of Securities Commissions, February).

IOSCO (2002). "*Report on Trading Halts and Market Closures*" (Technical committee, International Organization of Securities Commissions, October).

IOSCO (2003a) *Objectives and Principles of Securities Regulation* (International Organization of Securities Commissions, May).

IOSCO (2003b). "*Insider Trading: How Jurisdictions regulate it*" (Technical committee, International Organization of Securities Commissions, March).

IOSCO (2004a) *Report on Stock Purchase Programs* (the International Organization of Securities Commissions, February).

IOSCO (2004b) *Regulation of Remote Cross- Border Financial Intermediaries* (Technical Committee of the International Organization of Securities Commissions, February).

Kabir, Rezaul and Theo Vermaelen (1996) "Insider Trading Restrictions and the Stock Market: Evidence from the Amsterdam Stock Exchange" *European Economic Review* 40; 1591-1603.

Khanna, Naveen and Steve L. Slezak (1994) "Insider trading, outside search, and resource allocation: Why firms and society may disagree on insider trading restrictions" *The Review of Financial Studies*, 7, (4); 575-608.

LaPorta, Rafael, florencio Lopez-de-Silanes, Andrei Shleifer and Ropert W. Vishny 1997. "Legal determinants of external finance" *Journal of Finance* 52; 1141-1150.

Levine, Ross and Sara Zervos (1998). "Capital control liberalization and stock market development, *World Development* 26; 1169-1183.

Macey, Jonathan and Maureen O'Hara (1999) "Regulating Exchanges and Alternative Trading Systems: A law and Economics Perspective" *Journal of Legal Studies* 28; 17-54.

Mueller, Gerhard. (1999) "Global Financial Accounting Standards Setting at Crossroads" *Emerging Issues in International Accounting* (Niagara University, USA) 7-11.

OECD (1999) *Principles of corporate governance* (Organization For Economic Co-operation and Development, France)

OECD (2000) *The OECD guidelines for multinational enterprises* (Organization For Economic Co-operation and Development, France).

OECD (2003) *Survey of corporate governance developments in OECD countries* (December, Organization For Economic Co-operation and Development, France).

OECD (2004a) *OECD Principles of corporate governance; Draft Revised Text* (Organization For Economic Co-operation and Development, France)

OECD (2004b) *Experience from the regional corporate governance roundtables* (January, Organization For Economic Co-operation and Development, France)

Persons, Obeua S. 1997. "SEC's insider trading Enforcements and Target Firms' stock values" *Journal of Business Research* 39; 187- 194.

Sabri, Nidal Rashid (1995a) "Experts' Opinions Toward Price Stability During the Stock Market Crisis" *International Journal of Commerce & Management* 5; 130-146

Sabri, Nidal Rashid (1995b) "Stabilization of Stock Markets; the Case of the Frankfurt Exchange" *Journal of Multinational Financial Management* Vol. 5; 23- 32.

Sabri, Nidal Rashid (2002) "Roots of stock market volatility and crises: a synthesis and suggested remedies" *International Review of Comparative Public Policy* 13; 1-53.

Sabri, Nidal Rashid (2003). "Using treasury "repurchase" stocks to stabilize stock markets" *International Journal of Business* 8, (4); 426-450.

Sabri, Nidal Rashid (2005). "Legal Features of Traded Securities and High Price Volatility" *Advances in Financial Economics* 11; 237- 249.

Sabri, Nidal Rashid (2007) Recent Developments and Stock Market Stability" (Manuscript under publication).

SEC (1999) *Final Rule: Purchases of Certain Equity Securities by the Issuer and others* (Release No.34-41905, SEC, New York).

SEC (1998) *Regulation of Exchange and Alternative Trading Systems* (Release No. 34-40760, File No. S7-12-98, SEC, New York).

SFCHG (1998) *Consultation Paper on Treasury Shares* (Securities and Futures Commission of Hong Kong, November).

Shleifer A. and R. Vishny, (1997) "A Survey of Corporate Governance" *Journal of Finance* (Vol. 52) 737-783.

St John, Alexander, B. (2001) "The Regulation of Cross- borders public offerings of securities in the European Union: Present and Future" *Denver Journal of International Law and Policy* 29 (3); 237-258.

WFE (2003) *the Significant of the Exchange Industry* (August, World Federation of Exchanges, Paris).

WFE (2001) *World Federation of Exchanges Annual Report* (World Federation of Exchanges, Paris).

WFE (2005) *World Federation of Exchanges Annual Report* (World Federation of Exchanges, Paris).

WGM (2002). *Discussion Of Individual Corporate Governance Codes Relevant To The European Union And Its Member States, ANNEX IV* (Weil, Gotshal & Mangos in consultation with EASD and ECGN)

Wist, Tarja and Irine Mikkola (2002) "New regulation of alternative trading systems in Finland" *International Business Lawyer* 30, (4); 166-169.

World Bank (2000) *Global Development Finance 2000* (The World Bank, Washington, DC).

Chapter 4

RECENT TRADING DEVELOPMENTS AND STOCK MARKET STABILITY

INTRODUCTION

Various new practices are taking place and becoming essential in the world stock markets. Such practices have been introduced so rapidly to the stock market as a result of the advanced technology, communications, and internet evolution, the advancement of assets management industry, adopting the concept of liberalization, globalization and the world's economy integration. These practices became acceptable in both the emerging and the developed countries. This new situation creates challenges to the management of stock exchanges and subsidiaries, investors, listed firms, brokers, financial intermediates and other related parties, as well as to the related legislation bodies in all countries.

Accordingly, there is a need to identify the major recent practices that have been introduced to the world stock market. In the previous chapter, the recent developments in the related laws and regulations were presented and discussed. This chapter is devoted to other recent developments, which may be connected to the trading process and practices of stock trading, while the next chapter will discuss recent developments related to globalization, including liberalization, integration and increasing linkages among financial systems and among stock markets.

Recently, and mainly in the last decade, various practices have been incorporated to the world stock market, justifying examination in the light of the stock market stability. Therefore, this chapter aims to synthesize the major changes occurred in trading of stock markets, to indicate which changes have impact on the stock market stability based on theoretical analysis and published empirical studies. However, other changes, which have little impact on stock market stability, will be excluded. The following new practices and issues that have direct or indirect impact on the stock market stability will be explored in this chapter. They include: using internet trading and investment advice in stock trading, increasing stock price volatility, changes in stock trading practices and settlement systems, increasing the role of international credit rating agencies on the equity markets, the use of stock price indexation on stock trading, including its use as a performance measurement, as a basis for indexed products and index funds including the ETFs and mutual funds, increasing the volatility of equities portfolio flows and increasing the impact of derivatives and other financial markets on stock markets.

Internet Trading and Investment Advice

Besides what was presented about the ATSs stock trading, there is a new practice related to using the internet in stock trading. This service is one of the most significant new practices introduced to the world stock market. The internet services cover both internet investment advising through interactive websites and trading online through certified brokers, using computer software based models, but unlike the ATSs, it should be concluded in the traditional stock exchanges. This new practice is increasing and has reached billions of dollars as expressed in traded value channeled directly or indirectly through internet stock trading. In addition, it is gradually changing the direction and the mechanism of trading decisions of the world stock markets.

The trading decisions are becoming spreading all over the world websites, rather than being concentrated in and around the stock exchange. In the last five years, the number of investors including sellers and buyers using the internet services has been increasing rapidly. For example, a NASDAQ report (2001) found that there are about over 28 million on line brokerage accounts in 2001. In addition, a survey conducted in 2002 indicated that 31% of the European online consumers own shares, one third of them researched and used online, which they represent 10% of the European shareholders (IOSCO, 2003a).

The internet services include variety of activities that are offered to the investors such as:

- Offers investment advice services, through specialized and non- specialized corporate and individual firms using interactive websites.
- Monitoring and observing the movements of the stock prices and the trade volume.
- Following the financial news in general and the activities of stock markets in particular.
- Selling or buying directly online through accounts connected to the online-certified brokers. However, this activity is still limited compared to the regular way of requesting buy and sell orders.
- Getting instant stock quotes of the traded stocks in continuous basis in more than stock exchanges on the same time.
- Monitoring the price movements and trade volume for more than stock markets in case of cross-listed securities.
- Introducing the possibility of using internet as a stock exchange facility and as an alternative to stock trading exchange system.
- Introducing the possibility of conducting clearance and settlement procedures using online financial services.
- Having a permanent electronic bulletin board to publish the prices in a continuous basis.

However, to reduce the risk accompanied to internet stock trading and investment advisory services, the majority of the developed countries' jurisdictions issued and adopted regulations and policy statements to organize such practices including license' conditions, and features of firms which may offer advising services without a license. The majority of these regulations adopted or revised in the last five years to organize both online trading and online investments advising. The major problem of internet trading and advising is the connection between the world websites and the complicated links between the investors, advisors and brokers who may affiliate to various jurisdictions. A substantial part of internet trading and advising is considered as cross boarder transactions, which involve more than one jurisdiction. For example, the Australian Securities' Commission stated that the policy statements for an internet investment advice will apply to investment advice sent by overseas internet advisors using email addresses of Australian investors, as well as for advisors who place advice on the internet in Australia for outside users (ASIC, 2000, PS, 118, 56- 57).

Using internet advising of stock trading is supposed to increase the dissemination of information and thus improving the stock market efficiency. However, the investment websites advising activities may create adverse effect on certain securities upon issuing recommendations for selling such securities. Such recommendations being announced in the internet websites may intentionally or unintentionally impair the efficiency of stock markets. The quality and effect of such recommendations issued by internet websites about stock prices movements has little impact on stock prices so far. It has been found by a study that the internet stock recommendations are mostly positive with a ratio to buy compared to seven to one, and the recommendations have no informative value (Dewally, 2003). However, this conclusion may be different in case of stock market crisis or during the instable trading periods.

The use of the internet services has a direct advantage on increasing the trading activities significantly. However, the effect of internet trading on the stock market stability is not clear yet. The last regional stock market crises occurred in 1997, while the internet use was still limited. Especially, the online stock trading is considered as more actively, more speculative and less profitable as reported by Barber and Odean (2002). The reaction of internet advisors, specialists, and investors may be unpredicted during instability of stock markets. Other issues related to internet trading such as the possibility of trade abuse, dissolving of boarders, less loyalty of stock holders and difficulty of enforcing related rules may have negative aspects concerning the stock market stability. The irrational trading is considered one of the most causes of initiated a stock market crisis.

Recently, the International Organization of Securities Commissions (IOSCO) discussed this issue, which is related to the challenges created by the internet technology to regulators, listed firms and investors, and stated 24 recommendations in this regard. The recommendations are related to application of domestic regulatory requirements to securities activities on the internet, including communications to customers and recordkeeping, exercising of regulatory over cross –border activities on the internet, using the internet to foster investor education and transparency and to enhance cooperation in enforcement matters (IOSCO, 1998). The second report discussed the issues related to system capacity, security, day trading, mitigate risk, advertising requirements, internet discussion site (IDS) and enforcement. The last report was published in 2003 which concentrated on the issue of barriers to cross-border transactions and the attached risk, security control measures to prevent unauthorized trading, online fraud and breaches of privacy as well as other issues such as record retention requirements and enforcement issue (IOSCO, 2003a).

INCREASING THE STOCK PRICE VOLATILITY

The volatility is a statistical measure of the movements of a share price in terms of rising or falling within a short period of time, while the implied volatility is related to the options of price changes rather than the fluctuations of underlying shares. The volatility of stock prices has become the most critical issue in the world stock market, simply, because increasing the volatility of stock prices when prices fall to a low level, may lead to stock market crisis at certain conditions. This new phenomenon in the world stock markets created and contributed to the instability of stock markets. The instability of stock prices lead to major stock crises, such as crashes in October, 1987, regional crises in 1995 and in 1997-1998. The high stock price movements raise the question of the efficiency of the stock market.

The stock prices are supposed to respond to accounting data, dividends, and economic facts under the hypothesis of market efficiency. The monthly changes ratio (up and down) in stock prices indices reached in many of the international stock exchanges two digit numbers during the nineties, which is not justified by the market or economic rules. For example, the average rate of price indices for the major twelve international stock markets fell down about 22% during 1990 (ASE, 1991). It shows that the stock market price index lost more than 25% in various European stock markets during the 1987 stock crisis. During 1990 stock market transactions, the majority of the world stock market indices declined from 20% to 50%. In addition, during the month of March 2000, the Asia IFC index declined about 44%, other individual stock markets witnessed a decline of more than 60% such as NASDAQ, 24% in Germany,19% in Canada and 14% in London during one-month transactions. During August transactions, the stock markets price indices declined from 10% to 45% in most of the World stock markets. The very high price fluctuations -up and down- continued in 1991, 1992, 1998 and 2000.

To indicate the increasing phenomena of the stock market high price volatility, Table 4-1 presents examples for the price movements of both developed and emerging stock markets using local indices during the 2006. The high changes of the stock market prices are not confined to one direction, but also move up and down in an irrational manner during specific periods. For example, the percentage between high -low price of stock indices in the majority of the world stock markets was between 36% and 97% during the 2002. The average percentage of high-low change (lagged) was about 60%, for the year 2002, while it was about 91% for selected stock exchanges indices during the 1998 stock trading (WFE, 2006).

The moderate level of the stock price volatility may be good for speculators and investors. The problem arises when the stock price volatility increases to high levels during the period of falling prices, which, may lead to a stock market crisis. In addition, the transmission of stock volatility concept is considered as one of the major factors that transfer the stock market crisis and high volatility to other markets. The spell out of stock volatility exists between the world stock exchanges, within regions stock markets, and among various pairs and twins markets. The transmission of volatility increases (decreases) during high (low) fluctuation of prices, and the mechanism of volatility transmission varies overtime. The degree of transmission of volatility varies from period to another and from one marker or region to others. Aspects of this model may be found in the following interpretations:

First, during the stock market crises periods, the world stock indices become so integrated and stock price movements move so closely, and retain independently during normal situations.

Second: There are some leading stock markets, which have significant effect on the majority of the world stock markets.

Third: spell out of volatility may occur during overlapping hours of trading as well as from closing to opening trading information.

Fourth: The majority of the empirical studies found that stock market volatility interactions exist, reciprocal and transmitted from one market to other markets.

Table 4-1. Changes in % of local price index for the selected developed and emerging stock markets during 2006

Exchange	2006				% Change
	January	April	September	December	2005-2006
Buenos Aires SE	81,085.71	90,025.91	80,581.41	103,164.27	49.9%
Nasdaq	2,305.82	2,322.57	2,258.43	2,415.29	9.5%
NYSE	8,106.55	8,471.43	8,469.65	9,139.00	17.9%
Korea Exchange	1,399.83	1,419.73	1,371.41	1,434.46	4.0%
Stock Exchange of India	2,585.95	3,064.70	2,988.25	3,295.05	34.0%
Shanghai SE	1,258.05	1,440.22	1,752.42	2,675.47	130.4%
Singapore Exchange	621.41	674.72	667.26	783.28	30.3%
Taiwan SE Corp.	6,532.18	7,171.77	6,883.05	7,823.72	19.5%
Tokyo SE	1,710.77	1,716.43	1,610.73	1,681.07	1.9%
Athens Exchange	3,977.84	4,139.96	3,931.05	4,394.13	19.9%
Cairo & Alexandria SEs	7,930.19	6,633.71	6,444.93	6,973.41	10.3%
Euronext Amsterdam	672.68	705.22	712.97	748.77	16.4%
Euronext Brussels	11,594.37	12,070.05	12,516.43	13,489.35	23.5%
Euronext Lisbon	2,653.04	3,077.30	3,208.42	3,485.63	33.3%
Istanbul SE	44,590.00	43,880.00	36,924.86	39,117.46	-1.7%
Malta SE	5,420.92	6,038.38	5,141.01	4,873.46	-2.8%
Oslo Børs	267.28	303.62	271.48	321.22	28.4%
Wiener Börse	1,433.01	1,510.64	1,471.21	1,676.70	26.6%

Source: WFE, 2007.

Changes in Stock Trading Practices

The stock trading operations include receiving and executing selling and buying orders, formation of stock pricing, and the settlement process. The trading practices witnessed various changes and trends, including changes from floor trading to computerized screen system, the trend of using the continuous auction method in formatting the security price compared to other ways. Using multi currencies in trading local and foreign listed securities and using the screen-based order driven compared to other orders. The following paragraphs will elaborate more about these issues.

Trading Orders

There are so many types of orders being used in the world stock markets. For example, there are about 12 different orders used in the world stock markets, including Limit orders which are used by all stock exchanges, market orders (the best available price order) used by 88%, all or non orders used by 69%, odd lot orders by 55%, hidden orders used by 50%, stop loss orders used by 36%, market at close orders 26%, basket orders used by 24%, orders for forward deal used by 10%, orders for a premium deal used by 7%, scale orders used by 5% and other orders used by 31% (WFE Trading Survey, 2003). However, most of the world stock exchanges use more than one type of orders. The selected type of orders and its merits may be stated based on stock exchange rules, whether the stock exchange uses floor or electronic trading, whether it uses auction, call or continuous trading in determining the stock prices. For example, some stock exchanges determine the auction stock price based on the limit and market orders at a particular time such as in Frankfurt Stock Exchange (DBG, 2003a).

Price Determination Method

The second process is related to the main trading process, which is stating the stock prices. The price of security is a sophisticated manner in the world stock markets. Various stock prices to be stated such as the open price, reference price, single price, closed price. In addition, there are various differences in the merits and mechanism of stating share prices, which are mainly based on rules and regulations of that individual stock exchange, and whether the process is implemented thought floor trading or computerized trading, and the applied mechanisms. Generally, the world stock exchanges use auction- call or continuous trading methods to determining the stock prices of the computerized system. Generally speaking, there is a trend to move towards the continuous trading method for price setting. Today, the majority of the world stock markets use the continuous price system compared to the other systems such as the call system as presented in Table 4-2.

Using Multi- currency

Another new practice incorporated to the world stock markets is related to using multicurrency in the world stock exchanges' trading, mainly using the national currency in addition to one or two foreign currencies. In all the world stock markets, it was only the national currency being used in trading including price determination and cash settlement. Due to globalization, liberation of stock markets and increasing the number and volume of cross-listed firms, multi currencies may be used in the same stock exchange. Today about 37% of the world stock exchanges allow for multicurrency trading (WFE Survey, 2003).

Table 4-2. Summary of equity trading systems in the world stock markets

Stock Markets	Ratio of using the system
Trading mechanism	
Floor	5%
Electronic	79%
Both	17%
Trading Process	
Continues	36%
Call	2%
Both	62%
Orders Systems	
Pure order system	76%
Hybrid system	19%
Both	5%

Source: WFE Survey, 2003.

Table 4-3. Trading systems for selected stock exchanges in 2006

Exchanges	Trading Systems
Athens	Screen Based
Australian SE	Electronic Trading – SEATS
Buenos Aires	Open out-cry (floor trading)
Canadian	Trade Screen based order driven
Copenhagen	electronic continuous trading with open call
Deutsche	Floor trading and screen based
Hong Kong	Automatic Order Matching
Korea	Fully Computerized - (KATS)
Madrid	SIBE (Screen based)
Osaka	Screen-based trading
NASDAQ	Small Order Execution System and SelectNet
New York	Floor Trading, Auction market with specialists
Santiago	Floor trading & electronic system
Swiss	Fully integrated electronic trading
Shanghai	Screen Based

Source: WFE, 2006.

Changing from Floor to Computerized Trading

By the end of the twentieth century, related business transactions and activities in the stock exchanges have been fully computerized. In 1998 there were 18 stock exchanges conducting the floor system, while in 2003 there were few stock exchanges such as NYSE and the Tokyo stock exchanges, still using floor trading (WFE Survey, 2003). Another study (Jain, 2003) reported that out of 118 stock exchanges, there are 100 exchanges have adopted automated screen trading systems. The main objective of computerizing the operation of the stock exchanges is to reduce the cost of trading and facilitating the work, to be faster and more efficient. However, automation of stock markets including the process of receiving order, determining the prices, executive trades, conformation of the deals, clearance, and cash settlement, may impair the efficiency of stock markets especially during emergency periods. The atomization of the world stock exchange does not mean that they have now a homogenous trading system. Various systems still exist in the world stock exchanges as presented in Table 4-3. In spite of the fact that the majority of the world stock exchanges are using screen system and order driven systems, significant differences between the trading systems of the world stock exchanges still existed as being indicated according to last surveys of the World Federation of Exchanges (Wells, 2000 and WFE Survey, 2003).

New Trends in Settlement Systems

The security settlement system is the second significant factor in the world stock markets after price determination. It is the implementing instrument of processing the attached cash flow between the concerned parties. Accordingly, various significant changes were incorporated to the world settlement systems in the last decade such as:

First: changing the organization and legal entity of settlments agencies.

Second: reducing the period cycle of the settlement including the time of confirmation, clearance, and cash settlement.

Third: changing the processing of settlement operations from a settlement system with batch processing to real time processing.

Forth: there is a trend towards regional integration of the clearance housing and settlements firms.

Fifth: adopting international and regional standards by the national securities settlements systems.

The following paragraphs discuss such changes in more details.

Changing in Legal Entity of Settlements' Agencies

The securities settlement entity used to be a part of the stock exchange, today the majority of settlement organizations are profit seeking companies or non- profit organization with insiders or outsiders ownership. Other settlement organizations may be an autonomy unit attached to the stock exchange. In addition, more than settlement organizations beside the national settlement agency can offer the settlement services for the stock exchange. However, the other settlement organizations should be recognized by the stock exchange. For example, the Swiss Stock exchange states that the recognized settlement organization should meet stated merits and conditions, such as to have the relevant automated link to the home central security depository, to the home settlement agency, and the link must ensure "straight through processing" (SWX, 2002).

Reducing Period Time of Settlement

Using technology in electronic trading and transferring makes it possible to reduce the settlement cycle period. There is a continuous tendency for shorter rolling settlement cycles in the majority of the world stock markets In addition; there has been a reduction in the period for holding securities within the settlement processes in the responding markets (IFSE, 1999). The settlement cycle of the majority of the world stock exchanges, use to be around T as the trading day plus seven working days. This period is gradually reduced to one, or two or three days. However, the majority of the world stock exchange uses T (Trading day) such as in NYSE, London, Tokyo, and Toronto as shown in Table 4-4. Few stock markets use T +4 such as Colombo. In addition some stock exchange reduced the period recently to 3 days such as Tehran and Jakarta and Singapore; the last one reduced the settlement period from 7 to 3 days (WFE, 2006). The period of settlement includes confirmation, which is supposed to be implemented in the trading date, the clearance process which is supposed to be ended in two working days, and cash settlement will conclude the deal in the third working day.

Table 4- 4. The settlement cycle in examples of the world stock exchanges in 2006

Settlement Cycle	Examples of Stock Exchanges
T+1	Shanghai
T+2	Taiwan,, Irish, Frankfurt, Korea, Hong Kong, Mexican,
T+3	NYSE, London, Tokyo, Toronto, Luxemburg, Australian,
T+4 (for sellers)	Colombo

Source: (WFE, 2006).

However, the settlement process of indexed contracts is a more complicated way compared to the settlement in cash stock market. The settlement of indexed product is supposed to end by cash or delivery of the asset, but the issue is to state the contract expiry price. Methods and bases of establishing futures expiry price and settlements are different from one market to another as presented in a special survey that was conducted by the IOSCO in 2003. In general, there are two methods of establishing the price, one is the index value based on an auction process, and the second is based on the averaging index readings over period. (IOSCO, 2003b).

Changing to Multi Processing Cycle

A recent survey that was conducted by the International Federation of Stock exchanges indicated that there was a trend in the world stock settlement systems to move from the traditional way of batch process in cash settlement operation to multiprocessing cycle (IFSE, 1999). This new way which is known as real time processing, is more efficient, and speedy in the settlement of cash payments compared to the batch processing. An empirical study indicated that this way of cash settlement results in a reduction in delays payment delay and risks with the growing need of increasing liquidity (Leinonen, and Soramakia, 1999).

Integration of Clearing Agencies

The clearance and cash settlement business is moving towards integration in national and cross-national bases. This consolidation target aims to deal with cross- boarder settlements as well as to increase efficiency and reduce cost of operation. Thus, there were various emerging experiences that were taken place recently in developed economies. For example the integration took place in USA of the depositary Trust company and the National Securities clearing Cooperation in a firm named as the Depository Trust & Clearing Cooperation. In addition, there was another merger in Europe included Deutsche Borse Clearing and Cedelbank Luxembourg under a name of Clearsteam International (Schmiedel, et al. 2002).

Adopting International Standards for Settlements

In order to increase the best practices and the general environment of effective settlement in stock trading, the IOSCO and Bank of International Settlements jointly identified the minimum standards to be adopted by the world stock exchanges, and settlements agencies to organize their operations, which included 19 recommendations. The recommendations covering the legal framework, trade confirmation, settlement cycle, central counterparts, securities lending, central securities depositories, delivery versus payment, timing of settlement finality, dealing with participants failures to settle, cash settlement assets, operational reliability, protection of customers securities, governance, access, efficiency, communication procedures, transparency, regulation and oversight, and risks in cross-boarders transactions (BIS and IOSCO, 2001).

In addition, other practices were recommended to the stock exchanges in transition economies by Federation of Euro- Asian Stock Exchanges (FESA), which stated the effective and efficient system for clearing, settlement, depository, custodial and transfer agent registry services. It includes the following practices: the minimum final cash settlement is T+3 (day of trading), adopting the rolling settlement system, the securities should be dematerialized in central securities depository, there is a conformation of trading should be done by T+ 0, and in case of cross border clients should be no later than T+1, the possibility of using netting (offsetting of positions or obligations) in order to reduce the process amount in the settlement system, and applying the concept of the delivery versus payment and settlement (FEAS, 2000, Best Practice, 15).

The new trends in stock trading and settlements practices may have some disadvantages concerning the stock market stability. First: The computerized system had been broken down during some severe falling price periods due to the heavily received selling and buying orders in some European stock exchanges in the last decade. In addition, Naidu, and Rozeff (1995) found that automation of stock market increases stock volatility. Trading of stock markets using full computerized and electronic screen systems may reduce the transaction costs and increase transparency, but may raise the possibility of destabilizing stock markets through increasing the high price volatility of stock markets during periods of instable trading. Second: changing stock pricing method to a continuous method may be more efficient, but it might be more risky concerning the stock market stability. Madhavan (1992) indicated that a periodic auction trading offers greater price efficiency where a continuous auction trading fails, and suggested switching to the periodic method in times of market stress. Third:

Reducing cash settlement period may decrease the liquidity as compared to a longer period for settlement. There were rumors that the performance of clearinghouses in US was one of the causes of 1987 stock market (Bernanke, 1990).

INCREASING THE ROLE OF THE INTERNATIONAL CREDIT RATING

Due to the new trend of globalization of the world financial markets, a new phenomenon has been emerging and spreading over all regional and national markets. It is the rating of a bond, which has been a practice in almost the majority of the world equity markets. The instrument rating is an evaluating process conducted by international or regional specialized rating agency for the expected future performance and the attached default risk for a bond. Examples of the specialized international rating agencies are the Standard & Poor's, Moody's Investors services Inc., Fitch- IBCA, International Investor, and DBRS. Other regional and national rating agencies have emerged in the last decade such as the Japan credit rating Agency (JCR), the IIRA in Arab and Moslem countries, and the Association of Credit Agencies in Asia.

The idea of rating a financial security or a financial institution started with rating the ability of insurance companies to pay claims, and the risk attached to government and corporate bonds. This practice has been extending, to analyses and report outlooks for the shares performances and conveys to the potential investors. The rating agencies assign different rating scales such as letters, numbers, signs and worlds (Excellent, good, and Fair, A, Aa, Baa). The rating process is conducted for individual instrument, and thus it is reflected related instruments of the issuing firm. The rating process differs from one rating agency to another, it has different components and different methodologies to calculated. In addition, some agencies use only quantitative models and statistical analysis to get a rating, while other agencies may use both quantitative and qualitative indicators to conclude a rating process.

The increasing role of the rating and forecasting earning agencies has received critical criticism for various reasons: First: the rating agencies are mainly profit seeking companies and not independent or governmental agencies. Second, the rating process needs to be updated in a continuous basis to reflect further new emerged merits that have not occurred in most cases. Third: the downgrade rating may be due to external factors rather than to conditions attached to the issuing firms, such as increasing commercial interest rate and changes in leverage terms in case of bond rating. In addition, the majority of the world business ratings are conducted by very few agencies which create barriers to market entry for other new agencies. Accordingly, the IOSCO issued a statement of principles regarding the activities of rating agencies including: the assurance of quality and integrity of the rating process, the independence status and conflicts of interest, the transparency and timeliness of rating disclosure, and conditions of using confidential information. The conflict of interest is the most critical principle, because the larger rating agencies receive most of their revenues from the issuers that they rate (IOSCO, 2003c).

Finally, there is a possibility to create an adverse effect on the stock markets, due to announcement of downgrading rating for the respective bonds. For example, Goh and Ederington (1999) found that the stock market reacts much more negatively to bond rating downgrades. Kaminsky, and Schumkler (2002), concluded that changes in sovereign rating contributed to instability of emerging stock and bond markets.

INCREASING THE ROLE OF STOCK PRICE INDEX

Recently, the stock price index became the most dominant factor in the world stock trading. Its role and uses became more important than ever. It is now the main concern of million of individual and institutional investors, brokers, dealers, investments funds managers, and credit rating firms and managements of stock exchanges. In addition, there are significant changes in the role and uses of the world stock price, which may be presented as follows:

Index as a Performance Measure

The main function of the stock price index is to be as a performance measure of stock market activity. It is based on tracing changes in prices of securities. It may include all listed securities in one market, or in one industry, or group of special merits of securities related to capital, turnover, and trade value. The concept of measuring the price changes of a group of securities is old as initiated in NYSE for more than one century. Today more than one stock market index are found in all the world stock markets, which are announced continuously in the world internets and other locations, reflecting the stock trading movements minute by minute.

The components, methodology, and purposes of stock market index vary form one index to another, and from one market to another. The stock market index may be calculated based on different methods and weights. There are national stock indices, regional stock, and global stock indices. All listed shares in a price index must have certain merits. For example, the merits of securities to be included in the Frankfurt stock index should be listed in the prime market, traded continuously, has a free- float portion, belong to a sector included in the index, frequency of price determination and turnover (DBG, 2003b).

The new recent development in the world stock index is the increasing number of indices for the same market, and the same region, with different components and purposes. For example, Athena Stock exchange has the composite index of the main market, composite index of the parallel, sector indices, index of new listed companies, the general price index of 60 shares, FTSE/ ASE 20 Index, Dow Jones Greece Index, MSCI Greece index, IFC Global index (ASE, 2001). This multiplicity of price indices is found in almost all developed stock exchanges and in many of the emerging stock markets. However, in spite of the multiplicity of stock indices, there is usually one main stock index, for each stock exchange as presented in Table 4-5, which shows examples of the main index for selected developed and emerging stock exchanges and the percentage of changes between 1990 and 2005.

One of the important world stock price indices that relates immediately to the emerging stock markets was developed by the IFC in 1981, which measures the price index annually using month end prices. Recently this price index is run and calculated by S& P known as S& P/ IFCC index The structure of the composite index is build in market weights for the different geographical regions. For example; Asia has 51% of the composite index, Latin American has 21%, Europe has 14%, Meddle East and Africa has 14%. Another stock price index, which was developed also by the IFC in 1996, is the index for 14 less emerging markets known as frontier market. The annual fact book of emerging stock market and recently the global fact book represent a reference about the world stock market indices (S & P, 2000).

In addition, there are other global and regional indices formulated and published periodically by the IFC, and later by the S&P. There are the IFC total return indices, the IFC Inevitable indices, the IFC Global industry indices, the IFC inevitable industry indices, The industry indices cover the groups of industry as classified by the SIC Codes, which includes Agriculture, mining, construction, manufacturing, transportation communications and utilities, wholesale and retail trade, finance, services, government, and non- classified firms.

Table 4-5. Stock Market Index for Selected Stock Markets at Year-End 1990- 2005

Exchange	Name of Index	End 1990	End 2005
Mexican Exchange	(IPC)	628.79	17,802.71
Nasdaq	Nasdaq Composite	373.84	2,205.32
NYSE	NYSE Composite	1,908.45	7,753.95
Bursa Malaysia	KL Composite	505.92	899.79
Korea Exchange	KOSPI	696.11	1,379.37
Shanghai SE	SSE Composite Index		1,161.06
Tokyo SE	TOPIX	1,733.83	1,649.76
Madrid	General Index (IGBM)	223.25	1,156.21
Borsa Italiana	MIB Index	8,007.00	26,056.00
Cairo & Alexandria SEs	CASE 30		6,324.70
Deutsche Börse	CDAX	1,398.23	5,408.26
Euronext Brussels	BAS	2,974.09	10,924.01
Euronext Paris	SBF 250	1,000.00	3,300.94
London SE	FTSE All Share	1,032.25	2,847.02
OMX Copenhagen SE	KAX All Share		367.50
OMX Stockholm SE	(SAX)	50.42	302.91
Swiss Exchange	(SPI)	908.30	5,742.41

Source: WFE 2006.

Index as a Basis for Derivative Products

The second recent function for stock price index is to underline stock derivatives and produce new products known as stock index products. These financial instruments are based on common stock indexes and traded in the related stock exchanges. In the last decade, there is a flood in index equity products, including stock index warrants, stock index futures, and the stock index options. The number of traded stock index products including options and futures, traded in the world stock markets is usually around the same number of stock market indices, which ranged between two products to ten products in the different world stock markets. The increasing size of indexed stock products trading including options and futures is so significant which reached more than five times of in recent years.

Today, the indexed stock options and futures are traded in about 40 stock exchanges, mainly in US, Europe, and Korea, which form the majority of the world trading. Table 4-6 presents the number of contracts for both equity index options and equity index futures in the top major stock exchanges in 2006 for each market. The total number of contracts for index options and futures trading was about 4,416,226,951 during 2006, the Korea SE stock exchange is considered as number one concerning the number of traded contracted for share indexed options followed by the Chicago Board options exchanges, while the Chicago Mercantile Exchange represents number one market concerning the share index futures followed by the Euronext exchanges (WFE, 2007).

Table 4-6. Number of contracts for both equity index options and index futures in the world stock exchanges in 2006

Exchanges	Equity Index *Options*		Equity Index *Futures*	
	No of contact	Share of market	No of contacts	Share of Market
Korea SE *	2,409,098,242	73%		
Chicago Board Options Exchange	284,056,441	9%		
Chicago Mercantile Exchange			470,180,198	41%
EURONEXT	217,232,549	7%	270,134,951	24%
Other Stock Exchanges	358,118,708	11%	407,451,109	35%
Total Contract in the world stock market in 2006	3,268,505,940	100%	1,147,721,011	100

Source: WFE, Focus, 2007.

Index as a Basis for Fund Instruments

The third function for the stock price index, which has been introduced recently to the world stock market, is to produce fund financial instruments, such as the exchange-traded funds (ETFs) and indexed based mutual funds. The index funds may use cash or derivatives as the basic for the fund. An investment trust fund includes a group of shares assigned to the price of underlying-selected shares, and traded as a single security. The indexed funds may have various characteristics and merits based on the respected stock exchanges. However, there are two major types of funds including the index mutual fund, and the exchange-traded fund (ETF). The index funds invest in all listed firms and included in the index, while it may include only selected sample of the listed firms. The ETF is a specialized financial instrument, which uses index funds listed and traded on stock exchanges based on market price daily.

The importance of the index based fund increased significantly just in the last few years. For example, the total net assets of ETFs in US increased from $1 billion in 1995 to about $ 101 billion in 2002 to $ 2510.7 billion during 2006, while in Europe reached about $ 9 billion in 2002 and increased to $ 144 billion in 2006 (IOSCO, 2004, WFE Focus, 2007). The use of ETF has just started in the last few years, for example, it has been introduced to many developed countries after 1995, and mainly in the last few years, between 1998 and 2002 as presented in Table 4-7. In addition, the exchange trade funds (ETFs) are traded in some of the world stock exchanges without related official regulations such as in Australia, Mexico, and Spain. However, in spite of the fact that such funds are traded in about 43% of the world stock exchanges, they are still immaterial in the majority of the world stock exchanges.

Table 4-7. Dates of first initiated index based funds in selected stock exchanges

Jurisdictions	Date of first index fund	Regulated Exchange Trade Fund
Australia	1999	No
Brazil	2002	Yes
Germany	1998	Yes
Hong Kong	1995	Yes
Ireland	1998	Yes
Italy	2002	Yes
Mexico	1998	No
Spain	2001	No

Source: IOSCO, 2004.

The ETFs as a financial instrument witnessed a significant growth in US and Europe, especially during the period 2001 to 2006. The number of listed ETFs reached in the world markets was 1135 in 2005. In 2006, the trade value of ETFs jumped significant p to $ 2146.9 Billion in NYSE alone. Other exchanges such as American, Deutschue, Euronext and TSX witnessed significant increase between 2005 and 2006 as shown in Table 4-8. It shows that the tope five stock exchanges as expressed by traded values were NYSE witnessed the highest value of trading in ETFs followed by American Stock Exchange, Deutsche, Euronext, (Paris, Amsterdam, and Brussels) TSX Group, respectively. The NYSE formed about 95% of the total world ETFs trading market. (WFE, 2007).

Table 4-8. Value of ETFs (exchange-traded funds) in top of the world stock exchanges in 2006 in $ billion

Stock Exchanges	No. of Listed ETFs in 2005	Value in $ *Billion* in 2006	Ratio of Increased 2005 -2006
New York Stock Exchange	64	2,146.9	7056.0%
American Stock Exchange	133	363.8	15.2%
Deutsche Borse	77	99.5	52.8%
Euronext	95	44.5	83.1%
TSX	21	38.2	77.6%
Other Markets	745	153.5	
Total World Market	1135	2,846.4	

(WFE, Focus, 2007, p. 70, and WFE, 2006).

INCREASING VOLATILITY OF EQUITY PORTFOLIO FLOWS

In the last decade the world stock markets especially in the merging economies witnessed a high volatility of the equity portfolio flow. The equity portfolio flow between developed and emerging stock markets is not working in one direction. During the last decade, some negative political and economic changes in emerging countries led to a significant cash outflow. For example, during 1998, there was a negative cash outflow of about $ 18 billion from Asian emerging markets (IMF, 2000). However, the net private portfolio across stock market witnessed high fluctuations during the period from 1997 to 2002 because of Asia financial crises in 1997-1998 as presented in Table 4-9.

Table 4-9. Net private portfolio equity flows to selected emerging markets between 1997 to 2002 in $ billion

Countries	1997	1998	1999	2000	2001	2002
Indonesia	- 5.0	- 4.4	-.08	- 1.0	0.4	0.9
Malaysia	- 8.0	-.04	0.1	- 1.8	- 0.7	- 0.3
Poland	0.6	1.7	0.0	0.3	- 0.8	0.4
Russian Federation	1.3	0.7	- 0.3	0.2	0.5	2.6
Mexico	3.2	- 0.7	3.8	0.4	0.2	- 0.1
Chile	1.7	0.6	0.5	- 0.4	-0.2	- 0.3
Argentina	1.4	- 0.2	-10.8	- 3.2	- 0.1	- 0.1
Egypt	0.5	-0.2	0.7	0.3	0.0	- 0.2
India	2.6	- 0.6	2.3	2.8	2.0	1.0
South Africa	5.5	8.6	9.0	4.2	-1.0	-0.4

Source: World Bank, 2004.

It shows that there were negative flows of equity portfolio from almost all emerging regions during the last five years (World Bank, 2004). The high volatility of equity portfolio flows between developed and emerging markets may create instability in emerging stock markets.

The capital flow of equity portfolio to emerging markets received a lot of criticism, as a short-term rather than being a long-term investment. Thus, there are many opinions against the portfolio capital flow as reported by empirical studies and official reports. For example, the World Bank (2000) reported that the capital flow of equity portfolio has unstable structure relation between stock markets and less stable aspects compared to the foreign direct investments. Grabel (1996), and Singh and Weisse (1998) considered it as not helping developing countries in enhancing long term economic growth, and may lead to various problems. Increasing the linkages of stock markets as a consequence of increasing equity portfolio flows to emerging countries may be considered as additional negative aspect and may lead to destabilizing of emerging stock markets. The existing high volatility of equity portfolio flows between stock markets in general and between developed and emerging markets in particular may create unstable linkages.

On the other side many experts believe that investments in the form of direct foreign investments (FDI) have more positive impact than equity portfolio regarding the world stock market stability as well as regarding economic development in emerging countries. It is believed that the foreign direct investors hold securities as long term investments, rather than as marketable securities, and they have long term interest in the management of the related corporations. In addition, they are probably from the founders who bough the securities from the primary market, and usually hold a substantial part of the capital, which is more than 10% of the total owner equity. In addition, it is supposed to transfer of technology to the emerging economy. However, it should be noted that the foreign direct investment has decreased in the last few years. For example, the net inward foreign direct investments for all developing countries increased from \$ 105 billion in 1995 to \$ 182 Billion in 1999, but it fall down to \$ 147 billion during 2002 (World Bank, 2004).

INCREASING THE IMPACT OF DERIVATIVES MARKET ON CASH MARKET

The adverse impact of derivatives on the volatility of underlying stocks prices may be considered as one of the major causes of increasing price volatility, and has been increased recently. The impact of option markets on the volatility of underlying stock prices may come due to the change in option share index; interaction with underlying shares, introducing new options in the related stock markets. Several reports reported that the option market was the reason for the high stock price movements in the major stock international markets. For example, an official inquiry committee in Amsterdam stock exchange discussed the extent to which buy and sell transactions in Dutch option market determine price development on Amsterdam Stock. The report stated that there was evidence that some of the options' series did have the effect of increasing volatility, but it is very difficult to conclude that the prices' peaks are determined purely by option volumes (SEA & EOE, 1990).

In addition, the effect of index future and index equity markets on the underlying stock prices has been examined by various studies: and indicated that future markets lead cash market and stock market volatility to increase after introducing index future trading or index equity trading. For example, Sourescu (2000) found that there was a negative abnormal return due to introduction of index options that may expedite the dissemination of negative information. Chang, et al. (1999) found that stocks volatility increases compared to average volatility when Nikkei futures began trading on the Osaka Securities Exchange. Accordingly, the IOSCO addressed the issue of derivatives in general and issued reports to coordinate between cash and derivatives markets and demand for cooperation between the related supervisory bodies including local and international commissions and exchanges, when both markets are subject to different market authorities (IOSCO, 1993).

Finally, The effect of introducing the index fund instruments including exchange traded funds (ETFs) on the stabiliy of stock trading is not materialized yet, due to the fact that such investments instruments were introduced to the stock markets and have become significant in the last few years, and mainly after 1997. However, this issue between derivatives' markets and cash stock market will continue to be a contradictory issue in the literature of the world stock markets.

Increasing the Impact of Bond Markets on Stock Market

There are related markets to stock trading, which may have significant effect on the stock price volatility. Due to the fact, that such markets form alternatives for stock investments, and investments in stock markets may be transferred to bonds, currencies trading or deposits and visa versa in short times. These markets include bonds market, money markets, and short-term deposits. Accordingly, changes in bond yields, currency exchange rates, and interest rates may have significant influences on the stock market stability.

The effect of bond trading on the volatility of stock prices is due to the change of bonds yield, interactions with share trading, and improving bonds yield. The market of bonds is a strong alternative to investments in stocks; accordingly, the improvement of bond yield may shift investments and liquidity from stock markets to bonds markets. This interpretation was one of the causes of 1987 stock crises. Changes of bonds yields may increase high stock price volatility. For example the bond yield (over 10 years) changed during one year (end year of 1998 to end year of 1999) from 4.65% to 6.28% in US, from 5.11% to 9.07 in Argentina, from 21.18% to 26.66% in Brazil, from 4.94% to 5.46% in Belgium, from 4.44% to 4.84% in France, from 4.89% to 5.15% in Netherlands, from 4.45% to 4.41% in UK and from 5.01% to 6.97% in Australia (IFSE, 2001).

Various empirical studies examined the relationship between the stock and bond markets. The majority of those studies found that there are strong interactions and linkages between the bond markets and stock markets, and the stock market overreacts to bond yield and rating. Fleming et al. (1998) found that the volatility linkages between stock, bond, and money markets are strong, and has become stronger since the 1987 stock crash.

Conclusion

This chapter discussed various new practices that were incorporated to the world trading stock markets in the last decade. The new practices include the internet trading, the increase of price volatility, increase in the role of credit rating, introducing the index based investments fund vehicles and products, increasing the volatility of cash flow, increasing the impact of derivative and other financial markets on the stability stock market.

The above new changes may have a positive or negative effects on, risk, return, liquidity, transaction cost, capital cost, volatility, and eventually on the stability of stock markets. The major concern is whether the new practices may affect the stock market stability. The majority of empirical studies concluded that there is possibility of impairing the efficiency of stock market trading at certain events, thus may lead to destabilizing of the stock markets. However, the findings of the empirical research as in the state of arts may not be conclusive yet, due to the fact that the majority of the new practices have not enough time to be examined.

References

ASE (1991) The Amsterdam Stock Exchange In 1990 (Amsterdam, The Netherlands, 1991).

ASE, (2001). *The Securities Market of the Athens Stock Exchange* (Athens Stock Exchange, Athens, June).

ASIC, (2000) PS, 118, Investment advisory Services: media, computer software and internet advice, Chapter 7, Securities (Australian Securities & Investments Commissions).

Barber, Brad M., and Terrance Odean (2002) "Online Investors: Do the Slow Die First?" *Review of Financial Studies* 15; 455-487.

Bernanke, Ben S. (1990) "Clearing and settlement during the crash" *Review of Financial Studies* 4, (1); 144-151.

BIS & IOSCO (2001) *Recommendations for securities settlement systems* (Committee on Payment and Settlement Systems, Bank for International Settlements and International Organization of Securities Commissions).

Chang, Eric C., Joseph W. Cheng, and J. Michaelb Pinegar, (1999) "Does futures trading increase stock market volatility? The case of the Nikkei stock index futures markets" *Journal of Banking & Finance* 23; 727-753.

DBG (2003a) *Exchange Rules for the Frankfurt Stock Exchange* (Deutsche Brose Group Version 5.1, March).

DBG (2003b) *Guideline to the Equity Indices of Deutsche Borse* (Deutsche Brose Group Version 5.1, March).

Dewally, Michael (2003) "Internet Investment Advice Investing with a Rock of Salt" *Financial Analyst Journal* 59; 95-77.

FEAS (2000) Best Practices for the Development of stock exchanges in Transition economies (Federation of Euro- Asian Stock Exchanges).

Fleming, Jeff, Chris Kirby and Barbara Ostdiek (1998) "Information and Volatility Linkages in the Stock, Bond, and Money Markets" *Journal of Financial Economics* 49; 111-147.

Goh, Jeremy C. and Louis H. Ederington (1999) Cross-sectional variation in the stock market reaction to bond rating changes" *The Quarterly Review of Economics and Finance* 39 (1); 101-112.

Grabel, Ilene (1996) "Marketing the Third World: The Contradictions of Portfolio Investment in the Global Economy" *World Development* 24 (11); 1761-1776.

IFC, (1999) *Emerging Stock Markets Factbook 1999* (International Financial Corporation, Washington, D. C.).

IFSE, (1999) *FIBV Clearing Settlement Best Practice Report* (International Federation of Stock Exchanges, September).

IFSE, (2001) *FIBV Data Based* (International Federation of Stock Exchanges, Paris September).

IMF, (2000) *International Capital Markets: Development, Prospects and Key Policy Issues,* (World Economic and Financial Surveys, IMF, Washington, D. C. September).

IOSCO (1993) A Resolution on Coordination between cash and Derivative markets (the International Organization of Securities Commissions, October).

IOSCO (1998) *Report on Securities activity on the internet* (the International Organization of Securities Commissions, September)

IOSCO (2003a) *Report on Securities activity on the internet III* (the International Organization of Securities Commissions, October).

IOSCO (2003b) *Indexation: Securities Indices and Index Derivatives* (Report of the Technical Committee of the International Organization of Securities Commissions, February).

IOSCO (2003c) *Report on the Activities of Credit rating Agencies* (the International Organization of Securities Commissions, September).

IOSCO (2004) *Index Funds and the Use of Indices by the Asset Management Industry* (the International Organization of Securities Commissions, February).

Jain, Pankaj, (2003) "Financial market design and equity premium: electronic versus floor trading" (February. AFA 2004 San Diego Meetings).

Kaminsky, Graciela and Sergio L. Schumkler (2002) "Emerging markets instability: Do sovereign rating affect country risk and stock returns?" *The World Bank Economic Review* 16 (2); 171-196.

Leinonen, H. and K. Soromaki (1999) Optimizing Liquidity Usage and Settlement Speed in Payment Systems, (Bank of Finland - Discussion Papers 16/99, Bank of Finland - Research Department).

Madhavan, Ananth (1992) "Trading Mechanisms in Securities Markets" *Journal of Finance* 47; 606-642.

Naidu, G. N. and Michael S. Rozeff (1995) "Volume, volatility, and efficiency of the Singapore stock exchange before and after automation" *Pacific- Basin Finance Journal* 3 (1); 137-138.

NASDAQ, (2001) *The Globalization of the World Stock Markets* (NASDAQ, USA November, 14).

S&P (2000) *Emerging stock markets Factbook 2000* (Standard & Poor's, USA).

Schmiedel, Heiko, Markku Malkamäki and Juha Tarkka (2002) "Economies of scale and technological development in securities depository and settlement systems" (Bank Of Finland, Discussion Papers, No. 26, Helsinki.).

Singh, Ajit and Bruce Weisse (1998) "Emerging Stock Markets, Portfolio Capital Flows and Long- term Economic Growth Micro and Macroeconomics Perspectives" *World Development* 26. (4); 607-622.

Sourescu, Sorin (2000) The effects of options on stock prices: 1974 to 1995 *Journal of Finance* 55; 487-514.

SEA & EOE (1990) "Conclusions of the Inquiry Conducted by the FASE Committee into interaction between the Stock and Options Exchange in Amsterdam" (Amsterdam 12, November).

SWX (2002) "Recognized settlement organizations and central securities depositories" in *Swiss Exchange General Conditions* (SWX, Swiss Exchange).

Wells, Stephen 2000. "Price Discovery and the Competitiveness of Trading Systems" (A Report of the FIBV Annual Meeting, International Federation of Stock Exchanges, Paris).

WFE Survey, (2003) Maureen O'Hara, *World Federation of Exchanges Trading Survey 2003* (World Federation of Exchanges, Paris).

WFE (2006) World Federation of Exchanges Data Base, (available on line http://www.world-exchanges.org).

WFE (2007) *Focus* Issue No. 167 (World Federation of Exchanges, Paris, January, 2007).

World Bank (2000). *Global Development Finance 2000* (The World Bank, Washington, DC).

World Bank (2004) *Global Development Finance: Analysis and summary tables* (The World Bank, Washington D. C.).

Chapter 5

GLOBALIZATION AND STOCK MARKET STABILITY

INTRODUCTION

The globalization of the world stock markets is the one of the new significant development occurred during the last decade. Various factors contributed to the globalization of financial organizations including: First, advancement of technology and remote access which have been utilized in the stock trading. Second: Emerging of international financial institutions, which offer financial services regardless of the geographical and jurisdictions boarders. Third: Introducing new trends of liberalization and removing restrictions on foreign ownership, trading and cross border transactions. Fourth: the movement occurred in the world stock markets towards regional integration of stock exchanges, clearing and settlements organizations, and other financial institutions.

Accordingly, the world stock markets are moving so rapidly towards globalization. The concept of globalization simply means the free movement of goods, technology, labor and capital flow. Our main concern is related to the globalization of capital flow through the world stock trading. The globalization of financial sector means the integration of the local financial system to international financial systems and institutions through cross borders financial transactions, products, and instruments. The globalization phenomenon may be a blessing which is embraced by the majority of economic experts due to the expected benefits of such economic opening. Many experts believe that globalization may bring market to more efficiency, lowering its risk due to the possibility of diversifications, more convenience, and using arbitrage in a relevant way. On the other side, many believe that globalization may harm the interests of some groups of society, such as farmers, labors, and small-scale industries.

MAJOR ASPECTS OF STOCK MARKET GLOBALIZATION

Considering the present practices and the expected trends, it may be stated that the world stock market is heading toward globalization. The world market globalization concept has three major aspects as shown in Table 5-1: The first aspect is liberalization of international stock markets. The second aspect of the stock market globalization is related to integration of the world stock markets, including regional integration of stock exchanges, clearing and settlement agencies, regional Integration of related laws and regulations, and adopting international principles and regulations. The adopted international principles includes international general accepted accounting and disclosure requirements, audit principles and standards, cross boarders financial transactions accepted principles. The third aspect is related to internationalizing the stock trading including: cross listing of corporations on other stock exchanges, global public offerings in more than one jurisdiction, cross boarders' transactions and settlements, internet stock trading and consultation, alternative stock trading systems, increasing linkages between stock markets, International mutual fund investment. Some of these aspects were discussed in previous chapters, while the remaining issues will be investigated throughout the rest of this chapter.

Table 5-1. Major Aspects of Stock Market Globalization

Major Aspects	Practices
Liberalization of stock trading	Removing restrictions imposed on foreign ownership Attracting foreign investors to invest in national stock exchanges Permitting foreign investors for direct investments
Integration of stock markets	Regional integration of stock exchanges and settlement agencies Regional integration of related laws and regulations Harmonization of international accounting standards and disclosure requirements Adopting International trading and corporate laws, regulations and practices
Internationalizing of stock trading	Cross boarders transactions and cross boarders settlements Internet stock trading and consultations Alternative stock trading systems Global public offerings in more than jurisdictions Increasing of foreign trading in national stock exchanges Cross (Dual) listed firms in national and foreign exchanges Introducing international mutual funds

LIBERALIZATION OF STOCK TRADING

The liberalizations of stock markets may take various forms as in the world stock markets, including: removing restrictions imposed on foreign ownership, attracting foreign investors to invest in the national stock exchanges and increasing the share of foreign trading in the stock trading to permit direct investments by foreign investors. As a result, the liberalization concept of world stock markets has been materialized through the following aspects:

First: The majority of the world stock exchanges adopted regulatory changes in the last decade, most of which are favorable towards the liberalization of stock market trading and operating financial institutions. The number of countries that introduced changes to release their investments laws and cash flow mechanism, and to encourage foreign investments including direct foreign investments has increased significantly; reaching to 102 countries in

2004 issuing about 234 regulatory changes in favor of foreign investments as shown in Table 5-2 (UNCTAD, 2006).

Second: Out of the fifty two emerging stock markets states, thirty five states have removed the ceiling of ownership for listed stocks up to 100% of the total equities by the end of 1998. The other seventeen states removed the restrictions on foreign ownership partially, such as Brazil: 49%, Trinidad and Tobago: 30%, India 24%, Korea: 39%, Philippines: 40%, Taiwan: 30%, Thailand: 49%, Russia: 9%- 25%, Ghana: 74, Jordan: 50%, Saudi Arabia 25%, Tunisia: 49.9%, and Zimbabwe: 40% (IFC, 1999). In addition, most of the European countries have no foreign ownership restrictions, such as Austria, Denmark, Belgium, Luxemburg, Greece, Germany, Ireland, UK, Sweden, Netherlands and Italy.

Third: The majority of the world emerging and developed countries witnessed and concluded bilateral, multilateral, and international investment agreements to encourage foreign investments and cash flows cross borders. In 2002, eighty-two bilateral investments treaties were concluded by seventy-six countries. This is also applied to double taxation treaties, in 2002; sixty-eight double taxation treaties were concluded by seventy-six countries as reported by the UN World Investment report (UNCTAD, 2003).

The liberalization of financial markets includes removing restrictions on foreign ownership of local corporations, permitting foreign investments in local companies, increasing the national investors from emerging countries holdings foreign equities in developed markets. Liberalization of stock markets was received and interpreted as a positive signal in the development of global stock markets, which may lead to various advantages, such as: reducing the cost of equity capital (Bekaert and Harvey (2000), and Miller (1999). Increasing investments opportunities (Henry, 2000). Increasing liquidity, reducing risk, increasing diversification, and increasing the investor base (Hargis, 2000; and Jayaraman, et al. 1993).

However, in spite of the previously mentioned advantages of the world stock markets' liberalization, various serious barriers, and disadvantages had existed and had been attached to the concept of liberalization of the world stock markets, which is facing the flow of funds between countries. These legal barriers and economic disadvantages are summarized as follows:

First: There are direct legal constrains imposed by governmental laws or individual listed corporations, as well as indirect barriers such as capital gains income tax.

Second: There are various related laws of controlling local exchange rates and transferring of funds outside the borders that still exist in many jurisdictions in the world economy.

Table 5-2. National Regulatory changes for Foreign Investments between 1991- 2004

	1991	1998	2002	2004
Number of countries introduced changes in their investments regimes	35	60	70	102
Number of regulatory changes favorable to Foreign investments	80	136	234	234

Source: UNCTAD, 2006.

Third: Liberalization may harm the national economy because it is expected that liberalization of stock markets in countries with weak currency might damage the economy in case of negative equity flows. Torre, et al. (2002) suggested that developing countries who are seeking financial globalization should have a strong currency or should not be fearful of floating their home currencies against other currencies and should have a strong institutional framework.

Fourth: barriers of direct foreign trading are still imposed either by the corporate laws or stock exchanges' laws in most of the Middle Eastern countries, some of the Latin American countries and South Asia countries. However, in some countries, the restrictions on foreign investments are imposed by the individual corporation's bylaw, and not by the governmental laws as in Switzerland, Finland and Thailand (Stulz and Wasserfallen, 1995). Other restrictions of ownership may be imposed only in specific sectors such as the financial sector as in Brazil, Russia, and Sir Lanka. In other countries there are special shares that are issued for local residents, and other shares issue for foreign investors. For example, a company in Switzerland may issue as a part of its own capital bearer shares, registered shares and restricted shares with different vote rights (Gardiol et al. 1997).

Fifth: liberalization may increase the stock markets' volatility and volatility spillovers amongst stock markets that may harm the economies of emerging countries as reported by Levine and Zervos (1998) who found that stock markets have become larger, more liquid, more volatile, and more integrated as a result of stock markets liberalization of sixteen emerging stock markets. Lauridsen (1998) found that financial liberalization contributed to the meltdown of financial crisis in Thailand. Kim and Rogers (1995) found that the stock volatility spillovers have increased since the liberalization of Korean stock exchange. Kawakatsu and Morey (1999) stated that liberalization does not seem to improve the efficiency of emerging stock markets

Sixth: Liberalization may lead to incomplete integration: In majority of the developing countries, the liberalization of financial regulation may lead to incomplete integration and increase volatility of capital flows (World Bank, 2001, 70-71).

Seventh: Liberalization means high competitions facing financial systems from international financial institutions including international stock exchanges. This situation may put a pressure on the local financial institutions, and thus lead to instability of local stock markets and other local financial systems. The IMF report (2000) concluded that emerging market assets remain heavily dependent upon mature markets' developments considering investors' risk tolerance.

Eight: Fewer policy instruments: Liberalizations of the related rules regarding financial systems leave governments, especially in developing countries, with less monetary and controllable measures to cope with emergencies and financial crisis. This is because liberalization of financial regulations leads to transferring a substantial part of government power to the market mechanism, which is usually uncontrollable in the case of emergencies or during unstable periods of trading.

INTEGRATION OF THE WORLD STOCK MARKETS

The integration of international stock markets may be considered as the most significant change in the global capital market. Financial markets and institutions are moving towards a globally integrated economy. This includes stock markets, banks, and other financial intermediates in both developed and emerging markets. Integration increases substantially over time, especially since 1995, when these differentials began shrinking, and by mid-1998, six months before the official date for EMU launch, stock markets in EMU member states seem to be almost fully integrated. The average saving in the cost of capital from integration in Europe over the period 1992-1998 is estimated at around 2% (Hardouvelis, et al. 1999).

However, the integration of emerging stock markets may still not be materialized according to IMF and the World Bank reports. The IMF, Global financial stability report, (2003) indicated that the local securities markets remain highly segmented in most of emerging regions, and number of measures would have to be undertaken to fully develop integrated markets. Other studies found that integrations are still incomplete regarding to the world stock markets even within economic integrated regions such as the EC region. For example, St John (2001) reported that while the EUs' success in monetary integration has been impressive due to the introduction of Euro as a single currency and establishing the European central bank, there is one area that remains incomplete which is the integration of EU equity markets. In addition, Agenor (2003) argues that the benefits of financial integration for small open developing countries are mostly long term, while risks can be significant in the short-run. Thus, there is a need for careful preparation to ensure that short-run costs do not lead to policy reversals. This situation can be noticed in case of developed economies because increased integration of financial markets may be considered as a risk factor and may reduce expected gains from international diversification (Shawky, et al. 1997).

In addition, there are no generally accepted measurements of stock market integrations. Nevertheless, there are various aspects which indicate to what extent the world stock market is moving towards global and regional integrations. These aspects include: adopting international principles and regulations, adopting harmonized accounting standards and disclosure requirements, increasing linkages of the world Stock market indices, and regional integration of stock exchanges.

Adopting International Principles

One of the most recent aspects of integration of the world stock market is the adoption of various principles and standards issued and stated by the international and regional commissions, federations, and associations. Such international standards and principles are supposed to reduce diversity of the world stock markets' laws and practices and to increase the level of integration and improve coordination among the world stock markets regulators. Recently, several institutions recommended the international standards and principles as shown in Table No, 5-3. These groups include global and regional commissions of securities, global and regional federations of stock exchanges, global and regional associations of corporate governance associations.

Table 5-3. Summary of the world organizations and commissions, which have effects on the world stock markets

Major Organizations	Examples of Organizations	Contributions
World Securities Commissions	IOSCO	Statement of objectives and principles Technical reports and public instructions Resolutions concerning major issues Multilateral memorandum of understanding
Regional commissions	Forum of European Securities Commissions	Recommendations, coordination in developing regulations
World Federations	(WFE) World Stock Exchanges	Stock Market principles Best practices for clearing and settlements
Regional Federations	Euro-Asia stock exchanges federations	Stock Market principles Best practices for clearing and settlements
World Corporate associations	OECD	Principles of corporate governance Best practices
	ICGN	Corporate governance guidelines Voting rights principles
	Commonwealth Association for corporate governance	Guidelines and recommendations

First group: the IOSCO commission: It is the worlds' recognized body of the government regulatory commissions. The IOSCO contributions in concurrence with the practices and laws of stock trading ascertained in various aspects: First: It issued 46 resolutions from 1983 to 2003 covering various issues such as clearing and settlements, coordination between cash and derivatives' markets, cross- borders transactions and disclosures standards. Second: It issued 30 principles concerning securities regulations. Third: It issued more than one hundred documentations regarding principles, standards regulations, surveys, and reports about almost all aspects of stock trading. Fourth: It issued multilateral memorandum of understanding among its members, as a response to the increasing international activity in the securities and derivatives markets, and to meet the need of cooperation and consultation amongst IOSCO Members (IOSCO, 2002a and 2002b).

Second: New various regional securities commissions were emerged recently by regional securities commissions: in order to coordinate between the national securities commissions. The Forum of European Securities Commissions and the Committee of European securities regulators are examples of these organizations. In addition, the emerging of the World Federation of Exchanges, it is the world federation of the stock exchanges, located in Paris. It includes 54 exchanges, 22 affiliates, and 35 bourses from all over the world, which forms about 97 % of world stock market capitalization. It issued stock marketing principles and good practices, related surveys of trading practices, regulations, enforcement, trading halts, and other topics (WFE, 2004). The WFE adopted fifteen market principles of stock trading including organization and operation, access to market, listing and disclosure of trading financial products, trading, clearing and settlements, business conducts, investor protection, and transparency. It requires from its members an obligation to adopt their trading activities based on the suggested principles as rapidly as is feasible (WFE, 2002).

Third; there are now various regional stock exchanges which have established recently, and have significant impact on the world stock marketing concerning trading practices, jurisdictions, and interrelationships among stock exchanges. These federations of exchanges include South Asian Federation of Exchanges, Federation of Euro-Asian Exchanges, East Asian and Oceanic stock exchange federation, Union of Arab Exchanges, Ibero-American Federation of Stock Exchanges, and the Federation of European stock Exchanges.

Most of these regional federations issue recommendations and standards to be adopted by their members of stock exchanges. For example the Euro-Asia stock exchanges federations stated 28 best practices to enhance the stock exchanges in transition countries into alignment with global standards. The related best practices include regulating of stock exchanges, institutional framework, operation of stock exchanges, clearing, settlement, custody and registration, issuers listing rules and ongoing disclosures (FEAS, 2000)

Fourth: There are many world and regional corporate governance organizations are now existed in the world economy. This group includes the organization for Economic Co-operation and Development, which issued principles of corporate governance (OECD, 1999) International Corporate Governance Network which issued statements on global corporate governance principles (ICGN, 1999) and statements on global implementation of share voting principles (ICGN, 2000). The Commonwealth Association for corporate governance which issued guidelines and principles in 1997 regarding corporate governance ethics (CACG, 1999).

Adopting Accounting Standards and Disclosure Requirements

Today, the majority of the world jurisdictions adopt harmonized accounting standards and disclosures requirements. The need for generally accepted international accounting standards and disclosures requirements exists in various situations of stock trading, including:

1. Listing or dual listing requirements for secondary stock markets in home stock exchange or in foreign stock exchanges.
2. Primary stock market of international and local public offerings.
3. Annual financial reports of the listed firms in local and international stock markets.
4. Interim reports of listed firms in stock exchanges.
5. The reporting of other disclosure requirements and material changes.

The harmonized accounting standards and disclosures requirements became reality due to the willingness of the related regulators, and the efforts of various international bodies. There are three bodies, which play a critical role in the harmonization and the internationalization of the world accounting standards and other disclosure requirements of stock marketing activities, including the international public offering requirements, the cross listed firms in the case of first listing requirements, and for annual and interim reporting. These major bodies are:

First: the International Accounting Standard Board: This is a generally accepted accounting standards setting body located in London that aims to develop a unified single high quality accounting standards for preparing financial statements of business firms to be applicable and acceptable all over the world. It was established in June, 1973 by the accounting official agencies of nine countries, namely: Australia, Canada, France, Germany, Japan, Mexico, Netherlands, UK, and USA. Today, more than one hundred countries are members with two million accountants. It works in cooperation with the IFAC, IOSCO, Word Bank, UNCTAD, Bank for International Settlements and other national accounting standards boards such as the FASB of USA, ASB of Japan, ASB of UK, and CNC of France. This accounting body was known as the international accounting standards committee during the period from 1973 to 2001, which became known thereafter as the international accounting standards board. It issued the generally accepted international standards named as IASs, then IFRSs for preparing financial statements. About 41 IAS standards were issued from1973 to 2002 (IASC, 2002) and thereafter issued 5 IFRS statements up to 2004. The most recent accounting standards being issued by the IASB were related to business combinations and insurance contracts.

Second: The IFAC, which is the professional accounting national organizations are organized in a federation known as international federation of accountants since 1977. It is located in New York and includes 118 states, 158 organizations and 2.5 million accountants. It works through specialized committees such as public sector, management accounting auditing, ethics and education committees. It published 36 standards regarding ethics and auditing in computerized environment and designated from 100 to 1000 (IFAC, 2000). It also issues international accounting practice statements, international public sector accounting standards and auditing practice statements.

Third: the IOSCO issued various resolutions concerning adopting international accounting standards and auditing, these are:

1. Adoptation of a resolution concerning international standards in auditing (IOSCO Resolution, 1992).
2. Adoptation of a resolution concerning accounting standards IAS 7, and asked its members to prepare cash flow statements in their home jurisdictions according to IAS 7 (IOSCO resolution, 1993).
3. Adoptation of a resolution regarding accepting the International accounting standards for preparing financial statements of listed corporations (IOSCO resolution, 2000).
4. Adoptation of international disclosures standards for cross-border offerings and initial listings.

As a result, the international accounting standards and other disclosure requirements received wide recognition and acceptance in the last few years. Various significant steps have just been implemented recently, which lead to almost harmonized international accounting standards and other disclosures requirements, which may be summarized as following:

- Issuing international disclosure standards for cross-border offering and initial listing for foreign issuers in 1998 by the international organization of securities committees of (IOSCO, 1998) It requires information about directors, selected financial data, capitalization and indebtedness, reasons for the offer and risk factor, history and development of the company, business overview operating results, liquidity and capital resources, trend information, share ownership, major shareholders, related party transactions, plan of distribution, markets, selling shareholders, dilution, expenses of the issue, share capital, memorandum and articles of association.

- A resolution on IASC standards was issued by the IOSCO in 2000. It stated that the Presidents' committee recommended that IOSCO members permit incoming multinational issuers to use the 30 IASC standards to prepare their financial statements for cross boarder offerings and listing with special treatments related to reconciliation, disclosure and interpretation (IOSCO Resolution, 2000). In a survey conducted about the disclosure requirements of 43 stock exchanges indicated that the stock exchanges require on average about 80% of the IOSCO recommended disclosures for listing. In addition, the highest conformity with IOSCO benchmark was for disclosures of financial results. The stock exchanges are now more closely interested in disclosures policies and practices than five years ago in 1998. In addition, about two third of participated stock exchanges implemented changes in disclosures rules during 2001 and 2002 (Frost, 2003).
- The European commission accepted that all listed companies in the European stock markets to apply the international accounting standards issued by the IASB no later than 2005. In addition, Australia which is one of establishing countries of IASB, and one of seven setters attached to the IASB will accept IFRSs as the national accounting standards starting the beginning of 2005. In addition, many developing countries accepted the IASB as their national accounting standards during the last decade such as Malaysia, Malta, Kuwait, Cyprus, Oman, and Thailand.
- Many jurisdictions adopted the international disclosure standards (IDS) stated by the IOSCO. In a survey about the implementation of international disclosures standards, it indicated that 16 jurisdictions out of 17 members were either accepting documents from foreign firms based on IDSs or they have taken steps in this regard. Eight jurisdictions, namely: Australia, Belgium, Germany, Hong Kong, Japan, Luxembourg, Netherlands, and Switzerland indicated that they permit foreign firms to use IDSs without the necessity of changing their laws and rules (IOSCO, 2000). In addition, the SEC of USA permits in some cases foreign issuers to comply with IDSs for non-financial requirements as alternative to US disclosures requirements (Karmel, 2001).

Finally, it may be stated that not like other related laws and regulations of stock trading, the accounting and other disclosures requirements may be in the final process of harmonization at least for standards of preparing financial statements of listed corporations in the world stock exchanges. With the exceptions of the US, Japan, and Canada stock markets, which require reconciliation according to their national accounting standards issued by their own financial reporting standards boards. However, for the US stock market there is an extensive debate to accept the IASB standards, besides the US FASB standards at least for foreign firms that are listed in the US stock markets, instead of keeping foreign listed securities using the form of ADR alternative. The SEC issued recently a concept release about the possibility of accepting international accounting standards in American stock markets.

Regional Integration of Stock Exchanges

Various experiences were implemented or were under debate regarding the integration of national and regional stock exchanges, considering different forms of integrations such as direct mergers, group alliances, group associations, and through cross network connections. Recently, there are many proposals, studies and reports related to integrate stock markets nationally or regionally. Some of these ideas have been implemented such as national and regional integrations including horizontal and vertical merges. For example, the experience of unifying the local stock exchanges in one major national stock exchange happened in Spain and Italy as well as margining of some European stock exchanges under incorporated legal entity and merging cash and derivative markets have undergone.

Some of the benefits of national or regional integration of the stock market exchanges are increasing liquidity in one market, removing jurisdictions' obstacles, diversifications of risk, when products from a geographical area are listed in one integrated stock exchange, and thus reducing the cost of trading. The integration processes among stock market exchanges may have the benefit of economies of scale, reconcile legal differences and trading mechanism and platforms, harmonize clearing and settlement systems attached to the integrated stock exchanges and reduce the home bias practices as well as reduce transactions costs.

For regional stock exchanges integration, three experiences that have been implemented mainly in the European Economic Area in the last decade may be reported:

First: the merger of Amsterdam, Brussels and Paris stock exchange in one holding company incorporated under Dutch law under the name of Euronext N. V in 2000, after two years and in 2002, followed by other two stock exchanges including the London International Financial Futures and options Exchanges and the Portuguese-Lipson- stock exchange. In spite of the fact that these five stock exchanges work independently through local subsidies, their work is based on unified trading platform and single clearing system. The Euronext stock exchange group is now trading in both cash and derivatives, as well as in secondary and primary markets.

Second: The Nordic exchange alliance was singed in 1998 between Copenhagen and Stockholm stock exchanges to work on a joint trading system and consequently joint trading rules (CSE, 1999). Thereafter, this merger process expanded, and witnessed new mergers in Nordic Baltic area. In 2004 this alliance was named as NOREX alliance and includes seven stock exchanges, four clearing agencies, and three central securities depositories. The Alliance currently consists of the Copenhagen Stock Exchange, Helsinki Stock Exchange, Iceland Stock Exchange, Oslo Börs, Riga Stock Exchange, Stockholmsbörsen and Tallinn Stock Exchange. This means that this alliance has integrated the hall Nordic region and two thirds of the Baltic area (NOREX, 2004).

Third: In 1995, the Euro list system started to operate in all European stock exchanges, Switzerland and Norway, but legally organized as a Belgium stock company. It started with 59 European listed securities that were incorporated in the system. The system aims to create blue chip European companies which can be listed in all European stock exchanges beside their home exchanges using a single set of documents, under the condition that the market capitalization value should not be less than one ECU billion (Licht, 1998).

However, it is not clear where such trend will lead to, or to what extent the integration process will continue, how, and what is the best mechanism of stock market integration. In addition, there are no consent about the advantages of integration process of stock markets as compared to the existed market segmentation and diversification, and whether this is the time to move more and more to new experiences of integration in other regions of the world stock markets.

For example, in spite of the above-mentioned experiences, two paradigms for Europe stock market integrations are proposed: a central European stock exchange or a decentralized national exchange linked through European- wide network (Ramos, 2003). While others such as Noia study (1998) suggested implicit mergers and remote accesses through cross-network externalities that increase the profit of European stock exchanges. Other studies related to regional integration of stock exchanges were conducted to examine, if other regions should follow the same movement occurred in the European stock exchanges integrations. For example, El Serafile and Shahed (2002) reported that there is a need to restructure and privatize the Arab stock exchanges before moving to mergers or alliances or moving ttwords integration of Arab stock exchanges in one Arab stock exchange. Pieper and Vogel (1999) found that the Central American securities markets lack the development and depth to realize the Latin stock market integration, at this point of time.

INTERNATIONALIZATION OF STOCK MARKETS

Various aspects of stock market internationalization now exist in the world stock markets and will be explored in this chapter, including four major topics. These are: increasing of the foreign trading in the world stock market, increasing the role of international mutual funds, increasing the number and the value of cross listed firms, and the international public offerings by developed and emerging based firms.

Increasing Foreign Share of Stock Trading

One of the major merits of internationalization of the stock markets is increasing the share of foreign trading and ownership in the world stock markets. The share of foreign trading in the world stock trading used to be limited and immaterial. For example, Cooper and Kaplanis (1994) found that in 1987, 100% of stock equities in Sweden, 98% in US, 91% in Italy, 79% in the UK, 75%, in Germany, and 94% in Spain were owned by residents.

However, this situation has been changing rapidly, just during the last decade. There was a significant increase of the traded value of foreign transactions which reached about $ 5,759,353.2 million in 2005. The value of foreign trading in NASDAQ increased from $ 81 billion in 1995 to $ 712 billion, in NYSE, it increased from $ 260 billion in 1995 to $ 1,829 billion in 2006. While the value of foreign trading in London stock exchange increased from $ 627 billions in 1995 to $ 1,829 billion in 2006. The increasing ratio of the value of foreign trading from 1995 to 2006 reached 7292% in Swiss, and up to 1837% in Germany, as presented in Table 5-4. The foreign trading ratio formed about 77% of total traded value of London stock exchange, and 1166% of Swiss stock exchange, this means that the foreign stock trading is about 12 times of domestic stock trading in Swiss exchange (WFE, 2006). In addition, the share of foreign trading including foreign direct investments has been increased significantly because of expanding practices of using the GDR and ARD instruments in both secondary and international public offerings in both USA and European markets. However, the increase of foreign trading ratio to total traded value of the world stock markets may have some disadvantages regarding stock market stability, which may be summarized as follows:

First: foreign investors may look for firms with special merits only, such as large firms. Kang and Stulz (1997) reported that ownership by foreign investors are strongly biased against small firms, while it is biased in favor of large firms, factory firms, and ADRs firms and those with good accounting performance.

Second: There is a serious criticism against the foreign portfolio capital flow, as a short-term rather than long-term investment.

Third: Various studies blamed foreign speculators and the free flow of equity investments in the instability of stock markets in emerging countries. For example, Froot, et al. (2001) found that there is sensitivity of local stock prices to foreign fund inflows, which is positive and large. Sarno and Taylor (1999) found that the sudden actual or reversal portfolio flows might have played an important part in the East Asian crisis. The World Bank (2000) stated that the increasing of capital flows might be accompanied by continued high volatility and frequent crises as in 1990s. Singh and Weisse (1998) argued that there is some serious criticism against the portfolio capital flow, as a short-term rather than long term investment, which may lead to various problems such as: economic and financial crises, undermining the existing bank and financial systems.

Table 5-4. Top five markets based on value of foreign stock trading (1995 and 2006) in $ millions

Exchange	1995	2006	Increased Ratio (1995-2006)	Percentage to domestic trading
London	626,862.9	3,295,091.2	526%	77%
NYSE	260,643.4	1,828,614.3	702%	9%
Swiss	17,600.8	1,283,454.3	7292%	1166%
Nasdaq	81,353.0	712,045.8	875%	7%
Deutsche Borse	13,801.5	253,518.0	1837%	10%

Source: WFE, 2006 and 2007.

Increasing the Role of International Mutual Funds

One of the new merits of the internationalization of the world stock markets is increasing the value of mutual funds in the world stock markets and extending it to the emerging economies. There are various international funds and investment firms that play a critical role in the world stock markets, including closed-end funds, mutual open-end funds, insurance companies, pension and provident funds, and hedging funds. The role of such funds is increasing in both developed and emerging markets. In spite of the fact that the majority of the world mutual funds are located in USA and Europe, this phenomenon is extending so rapidly to Asian and emerging economies. The world funds with exception of USA funds increased from 52 to 273 funds, during the period from 1991 to 1998, while the net asset value increased from $ 16 billion to $125 billion for the same period (Kaminsky et al. 2001).

The majority of these funds' investments are stocks of firms located mainly in developed countries.

However, reducing risk, through diversification requires holding a variety of portfolios of securities. Accordingly, a substantial part of mutual funds equities are now from emerging markets. The net private portfolio across stock market witnessed high fluctuations during the period from 1995 to 1999 because of Asia financial crises in 1997-1998 (IMF, 2000). The World Bank report (2000) stated that the capital flow of equity portfolio is not able to take full advantage of international portfolio diversification, has unstable structure relation between stock markets and less stable aspects compared to the direct foreign investments flow. Accordingly, increasing linkages of stock markets as a consequence of increasing equity portfolio flows to emerging countries may be considered as a negative aspect, leading to destabilizing of emerging stock markets.

The existed high volatility of equity portfolio flows between stock markets created unstable linkages. Thus, there is serious criticism against the portfolio capital outflow from emerging markets, done by the mutual funds, and is considered only as a short-term rather than long term investment, and mutual fund mangers considering to emerging markets only for a possibility of higher return and run in first opportunity. For example, Grabel (1996) found that international portfolio investments have two negative aspects on developing economies, including the increasing potential risk and macroeconomic instability, which impose constraints on policy autonomy.

This negative aspect may be related to what is known as a home bias practice which means that the majority of mutual funds and local individual investors hold a portfolio of a large share of national equities compared to foreign securities. They include foreign securities only for diversifying purposes and reducing risk or for extra high returns. The home bias concept is related to the fact that equity portfolio is concentrated in local markets and not in international foreign markets in spite of the benefit which may be gained from international diversification. Tesar, (1995) found that there is a strong evidence of a home bias in national investment portfolios despite the potential gains from international diversifications.

Increasing Trading Value of Cross-Listed Firms

The practice of cross listing is the most significant phenomenon that creates linkages among stock exchanges. The idea of cross listing is that a listed firm in a domestic exchange looks for second or more stock exchanges to be listed there simultaneously. The number of dual listed firms has increased significantly during the last decade. Cross listing has started in the late seventies by the large multinational corporations to be listed in two or more of the developed stock exchanges. Today, it is not limited to multinational corporations, but it's extended to many national firms even to firms located in emerging countries. As a consequence of increasing the number and trading size of cross-listed firms in many of stock exchanges, some leading corporations' issues are traded now in foreign stock exchanges almost of the same size or more compared to trading in their home exchanges.

For example, the trading value of the major Dutch corporations' stocks traded in foreign exchanges ranges from 30% to 46% of the total trading value as compared to the traded value of the national stock exchange. The foreign exchanges where the Dutch firms are traded include NYSE, NASDAQ, London, Germany, and Swiss Exchanges (ASE, 2000). The majority of foreign firms listed in second stock exchange have to meet dual requirements of exchanges; other firms which may not meet the second exchange requirements use the so called depository receipts as an alternative for cross listing.

The major factors that have to be considered in selecting the foreign stock exchanges includes cost of trading, accounting requirements and any related laws that protect investors, and other listed requirements. Firms appear less likely to list their shares on foreign stock exchanges with higher disclosure levels than those of their domiciles (Biddle and Saudagaran, 1989). The main obstacle of cross listing is the different requirements of accounting standards that is going to be waved by adopting International Accounting Standards Committee, which will eventually lead to international accounting harmonization, and thus makes cross listing process more beneficial and less costly. Firms which may not meet the second exchange requirements use the so called depository receipts as alternative for cross listing.

There are various possible ways of cross-listed firms including direct cross-listed or using alternative methods, the cross-listed may be second listed in another local stock exchange, or in another foreign exchange, using one currency or multicurrency as presented in Table 5-5. The following section represents a summary of types of cross listed shares.

Table 5-5. Types of cross-listed securities

Types of Cross Listing	Details
Listed in more than local exchanges	Under one jurisdiction One currency, one time, different places in one country
Cross listed in local and foreign exchanges	Under different jurisdiction More than one currency, different times, different places
Dual listed firms with attached derivatives	Derivatives traded under different jurisdiction from the underling shares
Listed in a form of ARD	Foreign security listed in US stock market
Listed in a form of GRD	Global Register depositary shares
Regional listed firm	Euro- listed security in EU stock exchanges

Sabri, 2007.

Direct dual listed firm in local exchanges: in some of the developed countries: there are more than one stock exchange such as in USA, Canada, Japan, Germany and Spain. Accordingly, a firm may have its securities listed in more than national stock exchanges. This process is so simple and has no jurisdictions conflicts, and may be conducted automatically using the same documents for the first listing unless there are some unique or specialized requirements.

Dual listing in national and foreign stock exchange: This occur using one currency, but under different jurisdictions such as a European firm to be listed in more those European stock exchanges.

Dual listing in national and foreign stock exchange using different currencies, such as a European firm to be listed in USA stock exchange using the Dollar. The majority of dual listed firms are using two or more different currencies.

Cross listed regional base: Such as the Euro lists system, a major European company, may be listed in about 27 European stock markets, under the condition that the securities first are listed in three major stock exchanges. Then it may use the same documents to be listed in all European Stock exchanges.

Dual listing in national and foreign stock exchange with attached derivatives listed in different stock exchange: In most of cases, the dual listed firms have attached derivatives which trade in another national or foreign market or in both markets and thus increase the involved stock exchange for one underling security to more than four stock exchanges.

ADR (American depository Receipts) are negotiable certificates that represent a foreign company and be traded mainly in US stock exchanges. The process of offering and selling the ADR is conducted by specialized depositary houses which are mainly major banks, or specialized depository houses. This instrument was created to avoid that foreign security to be traded without satisfying the listed requirements applied to the national securities, the practice of using deposit receipt as a way of trading foreign security started in the early of twenty century, but it is increasing significantly in the last decade. The demand for depositary receipts is increasing by about 30% annually; it reached about 32 billion shares in 002, with a traded value of $ 550 billion (BNY, 2003). The trading value of Mexican, Argentine, and Chilean stocks that were traded in the US was greater than the total value traded in their respective domestic stock markets during the year 1995. In 1995, 87% of Mexican local stock market indices, 54% of Argentine stock market, 62% of Chilean stock markets, 71% of Brazilian stock markets were available for trading in the form of ADRs in US stock market as found by a study (Hargis, 2000). In addition, about 67% of the foreign listed companies in NYSE were using global depositary receipts method as reported by Martell, (1999). The number of cross listing is expected to increase, due to the competitions among the international stock exchanges, to attract other foreign stocks for dual listing.

Another alternative for cross listing of foreign firms is using what is known as the global depositary registered share. Similar to the American depositary receipts, foreign securities may listed as global depositary receipts which issues by foreign depositary house such as that in Euromarkets. GDRs listed at some European Stock exchanges such as Luxemburg stock exchange. Using of ADR and GDR as alternative mean of cross listing in foreign markets has benefits for both possible investors as well as for listed securities. ADR and GDR both may be used in the process of international public offering in the primary market as well as to be traded in the secondary markets as cross listed securities.

The holder of ADR or GDR has no voting rights, and it has a specific system for trading, pricing, and settlings, and usually traded in foreign currency rather than the national currency. There are various types of depositary receipts including un-sponsored which issues without a formal agreement with the related company; the sponsored form which issues by with the related company. The depositary receipts may be traded inside stock exchange or OTC, and may be used in primary or secondary market, and may be listed by initiating from the foreign company or may be initiated by specialized depositary company.

If we considered the size of the above forms of cross listing it may be concluded that it is increasing and expanding to new markets as presented in Table 5-6. Which shows the number of listed foreign firms in the world stock market as it was in 2002. It's clear that there is a significant increase of cross listing in most of the stock exchanges such as NYSE, NASDAQ, London, Tokyo, Paris, Australian, and Luxembourg as compared to a previous decade. In addition, newly developed stock exchanges have started to admit foreign firms only in the ninnies such as Milan, Madrid, and Lisbon. The top ten stock markets as based on the number of foreign listed firms is classified as developed stock markets, and is accounted for 83% of the number of dual listed firms in the world stock markets. These are: NYSE, London, NASDAQ, Frankfurt, Luxembourg, Paris, Amsterdam, Swiss, Brussels, and Singapore.

The cross-listed firms are extended to emerging stock exchanges such as Johannesburg stock exchange. In addition, in the last decade various major firms from emerging countries listed their stocks in developed stock exchanges. For example, the number of cross listings of Latin American firms in Foreign exchanges increased from 2 in 1989 to 106 in 1999, and the traded value of Latin American firms in US exchanges increased from $ 2,669 million in 1990 to $167,990 million in 1996 (Hargis, 2000). On the other side some emerging stock exchanges started to attract foreign listed stocks from both developed and emerging markets. In addition, the concept of cross listing has expanded to even small stock markets classified as frontier stock exchanges, such as Botswana stock exchange, which includes 9 foreign listed firms (IFSE, 2000).

Table 5-6. Number of Foreign listed Shares in International Stock Exchange in December, 2006

Exchanges	Number	Rank
NYSE	451	1
London	343	2
Nasdaq	321	3
Euronext	256	4
Singapore Exchange	247	5
Luxembourg	224	6
Mexican Exchange	203	7
Deutsche Börse	104	8
Swiss Exchange	92	9
Australian Stock Exchange	78	10
Other stock exchanges	478	
Total foreign listed stocks in 2006	2,789	

Source: WFE, Focus, 2007.

Today, the listed foreign firms form more than the domestic listed firms in some stock exchanges such as Luxembourg stock exchange. It forms 42% of the total listed firms in Zurich, and 40% in Amsterdam (IFSE, 2000). In the Toronto stock exchange, about 189 stocks are cross - listed in the US and other stock markets, which accounted for 78% of the total trade volume, while at the same time the Toronto Stock exchange included 66 foreign listed companies (Ahn, et al. 1998). The share of cross-listed stocks in total trade volume in some stock exchange is higher than domestics' shares. For example the trade value of foreign firms listed in London stock exchange has increased up to 58% of the total trade stock value in 1999 (IFSE, 2000). In addition, the majority of the world securities listed in foreign markets is listed in their home exchanges. However, this is changing, many firms listed in foreign securities while not listed in any of their home exchanges. There are many Canadian and European firms listed in NASDAQ without being listed in their home exchanges.

If we look in more details to the geography of the cross listed firms in the world stock markets, we may conclude that these are mainly concentrated in the Northern American and the European stock markets, with less part concerning Latin American, South Africa and some of Asian stock markets. For example the foreign, dual listed firms originated in Netherlands are listed in Europe stock exchanges of about 58 securities, 17 in NASDAQ, 16 in NYEs. The UK dual listed Firms are listed in other European stock exchanges of about 55 securities, other 55 securities listed in NASDAQ, and 46 listed in NYSE. Canadian companies are listed in Europe stock exchanges of about 45, while 40 securities listed in Amex, 165 listed in NASDAQ 165, and 65 listed in NYSE, 65. South African firms are listed in NASDAQ of about 15 securities, in London 55, in Brussels 18, and in Frankfurt 6, (Pagano, et al. 2002)

The cross listing processes is attracting various parties. First, the listed firms look for increasing liquidity and broad base for stockholders. Second, the stock exchange looks for foreign firms to be listed with an intention to increase revenues and more competitions to other stock exchanges. Third, there is a benefit for both, the less developed stock markets and the developed markets as well. There is an opportunity to invest in different markets, different securities and different currencies. Fourth, some emerging stock exchanges also try to attract other foreign firms from both developed and emerging firms. In addition, various empirical studies reported other benefits for cross listing concept. For examples, Claessencs (1995) stated that emerging stock markets have provided attractive investment and diversification opportunities for industrial countries, which became increasingly integrated with the world financial market and reduced their costs of capital. Biddle, and Saudagaran study (1991) indicated the benefits of foreign stock listings, including enhancing name recognition among investors and consumers in the foreign country, building ties and images to the foreign financial community, increasing local ownership and increasing employee relations benefits. Tanzer (1991) reported how an American Apple corporation gained publicity in Japan by getting listed in the Tokyo stock Exchange. Baker (1992) reported that the major benefits of foreign listing are to broaden shareholder base. Foerster and Karolyi (1999) found that non US firms listed in US exchanges as ADR (American Depository Receipts) earn cumulative abnormal return of 19% during the year before listing and an additional 1.2% during the listing week, but they lose 14% during the year following the listing, and referred these changes to market segmentation hypothesis and to the expansion of the shareholder base.

In addition, the cross listing concept may be used to create an association between developed and emerging stock markets. Such adventure increases financial and economic ties and expand the association between different geographical regions, creating awareness of the listed corporations and their products. For example, a study conducted by the author (Sabri, 2002) examined the possibility of introducing stocks in both stock exchanges in developing and emerging markets in a neighboring area, which is the Euro -Arab stock markets (Mediterranean region) and found support to the concept of cross listing of foreign companies, to benefit from diversification of investments, reducing risk, and increasing financial and economic ties. However, the study recommended removing restrictions on foreign investments and transfer of funds from the Arab size, and to increase the awareness of companies and investors regarding to the benefit of cross listing, such as diversifying investments and improve risk sharing for both markets.

On the other side, cross listing may have some disadvantages as related to weakening the local stock exchanges and reducing their annual revenues. In addition, it may increase the volatility of underling shares in the home exchange. Other limitations may exist in certain conditions such as increasing the systemic risk in the home stock exchange and may create price fragmentations. In addition, increasing the share of cross listed securities in all over the world may reduce the benefit from the diversification concept of using multi portfolio from cross economies. Various studies examined the impact of cross listings of firms in more than one exchanges on the volatility of underling stock prices. The majority of these studies indicated that the cross listing of firms may increase price volatility. For example, the high price volatility may come from reducing the domestic market liquidity, because the cross listing may divert order flow to the foreign market, therefore may have a negative impact on the domestic stock market (Ramchand and Susmel,1998; and Domowitz et al. 1998).

International Public Offerings

Besides the cross listing firms, in which national securities are to be sold in foreign secondary markets, there is a possibility for national firms to sell their issues in foreign primary markets upon establishments or in further issues of capital, or when national private companies go public. The practices, regulations and requirements of international public offering is so varied, and mainly depend on the related laws in both the home and the host countries in which securities are to be sold. Other regional institutions also may have various regulations to organize the international public offerings.

However, there are four possible conditions are used for international public offering: First: private companies decide to go public using foreign markets to get more liquidity or to issue shares in foreign currency. A company's decision to go public may occur for various reasons:

1. Technical reason such as the increase of number of stockholders, many jurisdictions state the maximum number of a private company to fifty members. The moment this number exceeds this level, the company has to go public and switch to become a public corporation.
2. Another reason is related to listing the company in the secondary stock market, and makes the transferability of the capital share easier and liquid.
3. Improving the stock price in the market: This is influenced by the news about the decision of going public and is reflected positively in most cases on the price of the company's share, especially, when it goes public using international offering instead of the local market.
4. Companies select international markets for initial offering rather than local offering look for broader base for investments, and thus lowering cost of offering and capital to enhance the future market price of firm. This enables the company for cheap borrowings and helps to rebalance their account after high investments and growth (Pagano et., al. 1998). Another study found that international public offering may be perceived as of better quality and will be diversified and priced compared to domestic market (Khurshed, 2003). Chaplinsky and Ramchand (2000) reported that global equity offerings expand demand and the benefit is associated with increasing foreign stockholders. Miller (1999) concluded that foreign firms that enter US capital markets raise new equity capital in a public offering and experience a positive change in shareholder wealth. However, not all companies can succeed in international offering, but some sectors are more attractive for foreign investment

such as IT and technology sectors. Many European based companies prefer to go public in NASDAQ stock market because of the less costs and relevant requirements.

The process of going public is based on the laws of home, and the market country. However, and generally speaking, the process started by getting the permission from the home country legislation, adjusting the by-laws of the firm, restating the articles of incorporation to fit the corporation status and getting approval of stockholders in a special meeting, and deciding upon the portion or the part of the selling, the selling price, the international offering period, and the closing time and date, and other attached plans for employees or other groups of stockholders. On the other side, certain conditions and requirements should be met regarding the home or market country, especially the audited financial statements and other requirements, permissions and fees.

Second: A public corporation decides to increase its own capital through new subsequent offering by issuing a part of the authorized capital, and decided to offer the share in international market or in both local and foreign markets. The new issue may include a premium in case of par value shares, or based on stated value in case of no- par value shares.

Third: Privatization of public sector: Some countries prefer to implement the privatization process of their state owned companies in international markets. This action may be conducted by some countries that are urgently needed for hard currencies, and or needed to connect their local financial system to international financial systems. In addition, this process aims to attract foreign investors to the national market. However, selling the state enterprises in international markets may not include all types of industries and sectors for political or economic reasons. For example, the Turkish government privatized public banks in international and local markets, through international public offering. The privatization process started with stating the capital value based on special financial statements prepared for this purpose and decided upon the number of outstanding shares, the par value, and the portion to be privatized and to be sold in public offering and the part to be kept for government, employees or other related parties. The period of public offering and the mechanism should consider both laws of home and host countries.

Fourth: In case of establishing a new corporation for the first time through which the initial promoters or investors pay for the expense of underwriting the issuance in foreign markets. The part of capital which should be purchased by the promoters is probably stated by the home country. Many jurisdictions stated that the promoters should cover at least 10% of the new established corporation shares. The ratio between the shares to be sold locally and internationally in the primary market may be stated by promoters. However, in spite of removing the restrictions that are imposed on foreign ownership of the securities, many countries prefer to have the majority of the shares to be owned by national investors, and accordingly, they may request that international public offering should not exceed 49% of the total shares of a newly established corporation.

The international equity offering is one of the most sophisticated procedures compared to other cross border stock trading. Due to the fact that there are lots of contradictory regulations and timetables between the firm's home and host's related rules. In addition ,many firms offer their own primary capital or increase it simultaneously in both local and international capital primary markets. Accordingly, this issue has received an attention lately from the related jurisdictions in order to make the related procedures more accurate, efficient, feasible and easy to implement. In addition, there is a need to reconcile the contradicted rules, frameworks, and timetables which organize the offering process from the first proposed step to the final settlements, and the completion of the process including stating the price, dealing commence, underwriting and settlement processes.

The major issue here is the harmonization between the home country legislation where the issuing company is based, and the host country where the public offering takes place. The Forum of European Securities Commissions issued the European passport report to facilitate public offering of securities within the European economic area by adopting the European passport regulations. This includes leaving the full control of the entire set of documents to the home country authority and having an automatic procedures based on a simple notification to the host country where the initial offerings or listing takes place (FESCO, 2000). The FEAS requires that stock exchanges in transition economies lead investors to offer an assessment of the present and the prospective assets, liabilities, financial position, profits and losses, the commercial prospects of the issuer of the securities that have and to be available before the offer (FEAS, 2000). Finally, some jurisdictions stated other rules to control the price issue of the offered security, definitions of public offering, usually related to percentage of free shares to be traded, or required the issuing process to be conducted through specialized investment firm or by the issuer directly.

CONCLUSION

This chapter explored the major features incorporated in the world stock markets based on the concept of globalization. This book classifies the concept of globalization of the world stock markets into three sub terms including liberalization, internationalization, and integration, and discussed the attached practices for the three major aspects. The liberalization of stock market increases the trading volume of stock markets and liquidity, but may have various negative effects which may be reflected on the stability of the world stock markets. In addition, the linkages between sub-segments of the financial markets also have been increasing, including stock markets, bonds markets, derivatives markets, loans, interest rates and banks, exchange rates and money markets and this is specially when there is a significant increase in the linkage between world stock markets, mainly related to the correlation of stock price movements in high volatility periods.

The positive and adverse effect of the above-mentioned practices such as international public offerings, foreign trading, and cross-listed securities, closed national and international stock price indices and harmonization of accounting and disclosures requirements are not materialized yet. There is a need to indicate what are the effects of the above practices in the world stock markets in the various aspects of information flows between the related parties, the risk factor in both local and host stock markets, the cost of trading in the home and other related markets, the trading volume, price behavior, the volatility of volume and return. Finally, the phenomenon of globalization is more expanding and going in depth in the world stock markets, but it is still far from being integrated or transferred to a harmonized unified market.

REFERENCES

Agenor, Pierre-Richard (2003) "Benefits and costs of international financial integration: theory and facts" *World Economy*, 26; 1089-1118.

Ahn, Hee-Joon, Charles Q. Cao, and Hyuk Choe (1998) "decimalization and competition among stock markets: evidence from the Toronto Stock exchange cross-listed securities" *Journal of Financial Markets* 1; 51-87.

ASE, (2000) Amsterdam stock exchange: facts & figures (July, Amsterdam, Netherlands).

Baker, H Kent (1992) "Why US Companies List on the London, Frankfurt and Tokyo Stock Exchanges" *The Journal of International Securities Markets* 6; 219-227.

Bekaert, Geert, and Campbell R. Harvey (2000) "Foreign speculators and emerging equity markets" *Journal of Finance* 55; 565-613.

Biddle, Gary C. and Shahrakh M. Saudagaran (1989) "The effects of financial disclosure levels on firms' choices among alternative foreign stock exchange listings" *Journal of International Financial Management and Accounting* 1; 56-87.

Biddle, Gary C. and Shahrakh M. Saudagaran, (1991) "Foreign stock listings: benefits, costs and the accounting policy dilemma" *Accounting Horizons* 5 (3); 70-81.

BNY (2003) *The global equity investment guide: the case for investing in depositary receipts* (The Bank of New York, NY).

Chaplinsky, Susan and Latha Ramchand (2000) "The Impact of global equity offerings" *Journal of Finance* 55; 2767-2789.

Claessencs, Stijn (1995) "The emergence of equity investment in developing countries: overview" *The World Bank Economic Review* 9 (1); 1-18.

Cooper, I., Kaplanis, E., (1994) "Home bias in equity portfolios, inflation hedging and international capital market equilibrium". *Review of Financial Studies* 7; 45-60.

Domowitz, Ian, Jack Glen, and Ananth Madhavan, (1998) "International cross listing and order flow migration: Evidence from an emerging market" *Journal of Finance* 53; 2001-2028.

CSE (1999) Rules governing issuers of securities listed on the Copenhagen stock exchange (Copenhagen Stock Exchange, Copenhagen, August).

El-Serafile, Healah and Shahira F. Abdel Sahhid (2002) "World stock exchanges are integrating/consolidating/merging: what could be done by Arab Exchange" (Cairo & Alexandria Exchanges, Working Papers No. 2, available on line; www.feas.org/library).

FEAS (2000) Best practices for the development of stock exchanges in transition economies (Federation of Euro- Asian Stock Exchanges).

FESCO (2000) A "European Passport" for issuers (The Forum of European Securities Commissions, France).

Foerster, Stephen R. and Andrew Karolyi (1999) "The effects of market segmentation and investor recognition on asset prices: Evidence from foreign stocks listing in the United States" *Journal of Finance* 54; 981-1013.

Froot, Kenneth A. Paul G. O'Connell and Mark S. Seasholes (2001) "The portfolio flows of international investors" *Journal of Financial Economics* 59 (1); 189-216.

Frost, Carol Ann (2003) *Disclosure Survey* (World Federation of Exchanges, Paris, March).

Gardiol, Lucien, Rajna Gibson-Asner, Nils S. Tuchshmid (1997) "Are Liquidity and Corporate Control Priced by Shareholders? Empirical Evidence from Swiss Dual Class Shares" *Journal of Corporate Finance* 3; 299-323.

Grabel, Ilene (1996) "Marketing the third world: the contradictions of portfolio investment in the global economy" *World Development* 24 (11); 1761-1776.

Hardouvelis, G., D. Malliaroupoulos and R. Priestley (1999). EMU and European stock market integration. (Center Economic Policy Research, Discussion Paper).

Hargis, Kent (2000) "International cross- listing and stock market development in emerging economics" *International Review of Economics and Finance* 9; 101-122.

Henry, Peter Blair (2000) "Stock market liberalization, economic reform, and emerging market equity prices" *Journal of Finance* 55; 529-564.

IASC (2000) *International Accounting Standards IAS 33* (International Accounting Standards Committee, United Kingdom).

IASC (2002) *International Accounting Standards* (International Accounting Standards Committee, United Kingdom).

ICGN (1998) *Global share voting Principles* (International Corporate governance Network, San Francisco).

ICGN (1999) *Statement on global corporate governance network* (International Corporate governance Network, London).

ICGN (2000) *Statement on global of ICGN voting principles* (International Corporate governance Network, London)

IFAC (2000) *IFAC Handbook 1999; Technical Pronouncements* (IFAC, New York).

IFC (1999) *Emerging Stock Markets Fact Book 1999* (International Finance Corporation, Washington D. C.).

IFSE (2000) *International Federation of Stock Exchanges Database* (Paris, September).

IMF (2000) *International capital markets: development, prospects and key policy issues,* World Economic and Financial Surveys, (Washington, September).

IMF (2003) *Global financial stability report, Market Developments and Issues*, International Monetary Fund, March).

IOSCO (1992) A resolution concerning international standards on auditing (International Organization of securities commissions, October).

IOSCO (1993) A resolution concerning accounting standards 7 (International Organization of securities commissions, October).

IOSCO (1998) International disclosure standards for cross-border offerings and initial listings by foreign issuers (International Organization of Securities Commissions September).

IOSCO (2000) Report on Implementation of International Disclosure Standards (International Organization of securities commissions, October).

IOSCO (2002b) A resolution on IASC Standards (International Organization of securities commissions, May).

IOSCO (2002b) *Multilateral memorandum of understanding concerning consultation and cooperation and the exchange of information* (International Organization Of Securities Commissions, May).

Jayaraman N., K. Shastri, K. Tandon (1993) "The impact of international cross listings on risk and return, the evidence from American depository receipts" *Journal of Banking & Finance* 17; 91-103.

Kaminsky, Graciela Laura, Richard K. Lyons and Sergio Schmkler (2001) "Mutual fund investment in Emerging Markets: An overview" *World Bank Economic Review* 14; 315-340.

Kang, Jun- Koo. and Rene M., Stulz, (1997) Why is there a home bias? An analysis of foreign portfolio equity ownership in Japan. *Journal of Financial Economics* 46; 2-28.

Karmel, Roberta (2001) "Will convergence of financial disclosure standards change SEC regulation of foreign issuers" *Brooklyn Journal of International Law* 26; 485- 525.

Kawakatsu, Hiroyuki and Matthew R. Morey (1999) Financial liberalization and stock market efficiency: an empirical examination of nine emerging market countries *Journal of Multinational financial management* 9; 353-371.

Khurshed, Arif (2003) Initial public offerings: does multinational matter?" *Finance Letters* 1; 24-28.

Kim, Sang W., and John H. Rogers (1995) "International stock price spillovers and market liberalization: Evidence from Korea, Japan and United States" *Journal of Empirical Finance* 2 (2); 117-144.

Lauridsen, Laurids (1998) "The Financial Crisis in Thailand: causes, conduct and consequences?" *World Development* 26; 1575-1591.

Levine, Ross and Sara Zervos (1998) Capital Control Liberalization and Stock Market Development, *World Development* 26; 1169-1183

Licht, Amir N. (1998) Regional stock market integration in Europe" (CAER II, Discussion paper No. 21, Harvard Institute for International Development).

Martell, Terrence F., Luis Rodriguez Jr., and Gwendolyn P. Webb (1999) "The Impact of Listing Latin American ADRs on the Risks and Returns of the Underlying Shares" *Global Finance Journa*l 10 (2); 147-160.

Miller, Darius P. (1999) "The market reaction to international cross-listings: Evidence from Depositary Receipts" *Journal of Financial Economics* 51; 103-123.

Mueller, Gerhard. (1999) "Global financial accounting standards setting at crossroads" *Emerging Issues in International Accounting* (Niagara University, USA); 7-11.

Noia, Carmine Di, (1998) Competition and integration among stock exchanges in Europe: Network Effects, Implicit mergers and remote access (Center of financial Insinuations, University of Pennsylvania).

NORDIX (2004) Press Release: Nordic Integration Continues (NORDIX, available on line www.norex.com/press).

OECD (1999) *Principles of corporate governance* (Organization For Economic Co-operation and Development, France)

Pagano, Marco, Fabio Panetta and Luigi Zingales (1998) "Why do companies go public? An empirical analysis" *Journal of Finance* 53; 2651-2694.

Pagano, Marco, Ailsa A. Roell, and Josef Zechner (2002) "The Geography of Equity Listing: Why do companies List aboard?" *Journal of Finance* 57 (6); 2651-2694.

Pieper, Paul B. and Rober C. Vogel (1999) "Stock market integration in Latin America" (CAER II, Discussion paper No. 21, Harvard Institute for International Development).

Ramchand, L., and R., Susmel (1998). "Volatility and cross correlation across major stock markets" *Journal of Empirical Finance* 5; 397-416.

Ramos, Sofia B. (2003) "Competition between Stock Exchanges: A Survey" (Research No. 77, FAME, International Center for Financial Assets Management and Engineering, Geneva).

Sabri, Nidal Rashid (2002) "Cross listings of stocks among European Arab markets" *Finance India* 16; 205-227.

Sabri, Nidal Rashid (2007) Recent Developments and Stock Market Stability" (Manuscript under publication).

Sarno, Lucio and Mark P. Taylor (1999) "Moral hazard, asset price bubbles, capital flows, and the East Asian crisis: the first tests" *Journal of International Money and Finance*. 18; 647-657.

Shawky, H. A., R., Kuenzel and A. D. Mikhail, (1997) "International portfolio diversification: A synthesis and an update" *Journal of International Financial Markets, Institutions & Money* 7; 303-327.

Singh, Ajit and Bruce Weisse (1998) "emerging stock markets, portfolio capital flows and long- term economic growth micro and macroeconomics perspectives" *World Development* 26; 607-622.

St John, Alexander B. (2001) "The regulation of cross- borders public offerings of securities in the European Union: present and future" *Denver Journal of International Law and Policy* 29 (3); 237-258.

Stulz, Rene M. and Walter Wasserfallen (1995) "Foreign equity investment restrictions, capital flight, and shareholder wealth maximization: theory and evidence" *Review of Financial Studies* 8; 1019-1057.

Tanzer, A. (1991), How Apple Stormed Japan *Fobers* (May, 27) 40-41.

Tesar, Linda L. (1995) "Home bias and high turnover" *Journal of International Money and Finance* 14; 467-492.

Torre, Augusto De La, Eduardo Levy-Yeyati and Sergio L. Schmukler (2002) "Financial globalization: unequal blessings" (The World Bank, Working Paper No. 2903).

UN (2000) *World Investments Report 1999* (United Nations, New York and Geneva).

UNCTAD (2003) *World Investments Report 2003*; FDI Policies for development: National and international Perspectives (United Nations, New York and Geneva).

UNCTAD (2006) *World Investments Report 2006*; FDI Policies for development: National and international Perspectives (United Nations, New York and Geneva).

WFE (2002) *Market Principles* (The World Federation of Exchanges, Paris).

WFE (2004) World Federation of Exchanges: About the organization (Available on line: http://www.world-exchanges.org

WFE, (2006) World Federation of Exchanges Data Base (available on line http://www.world-exchanges.org

WFE, (2007) *Focus* Issue No. 167 (World Federation of Exchanges, Paris, January, 2007.

World Bank (2000) *Global Development Finance 2000* (The World Bank, Washington, D. C).

World Bank (2001) *Global Development Finance 2001* (The World Bank, Washington D. C.).

Chapter 6

EFFICIENCY OF INTERNATIONAL STOCK MARKETS

INTRODUCTION

The question of stock market efficiency arises, each time a national, regional or global stock market crisis occurs or the stock price volatility increases significantly. Efficiency of the stock market may be indicated in the form of a traded security, a group of traded securities, a sector of an industry, a national stock market, a regional stock market, or for the worlds' stock markets. The concept of stock market efficiency has undergone under extensive debate during the last two decades. In addition, substantial features have emerged into the world stock markets which justifies reexamining this concept. Some of the newly emerged features of the world stock market may impair the efficiency of the stock market, and thus leads to a stock market crisis. Accordingly, this chapter aims to discuss this issue, in order to offer a comprehensive theoretical framework based on state of the art. In the next chapter, empirical investigations as well as surveys of experts' opinions regarding stock market stability will be discussed and explores.

The phenomena of stock market inefficiency appears in various cases, such as: changing prices based on non- fundamentals, the sharp decline of stock prices within a short period of time, a long recovery period to get back to normal levels, noise trading and adverse information which leads to overreaction of traders' behaviors in irrational manner, overreaction to introducing new related laws, increasing of extra-ordinary stock return volatility, increasing correlations amongst the world stock markets indices during falling of stock prices, stock prices that are not in accord with fundamentals and transmission of falling prices from one market to others. The issue of stock market crises used to be connected to the developed markets. However, due to the new trading environment, the issue is extending to emerging stock markets. During the last decade, two regional stock market crises were occurred, the Latin American stock crisis in 1994- 1995, which included Argentina, Brazil, and Mexico and the South Asian stock crisis, which occurred in 1997.

The stock market crisis, which is contradictory to the stock market efficiency, means falling of stock price index for a national, regional, or global market to a new record during a short period of time (a day or a week). In spite of the fact that there is no consent in regards to the generally accepted level that determines stock market crisis. Literature states that falling of the stock prices up to 25% during a week trading for a national or a regional index is considered as a stock market crisis. In addition, the period for recovery, restitution and picking-up the stock market prices to normal prices may take one to two years in case of stock market crisis. The stock market crises may be a consequence of global events, such as of 1987 crash, because of local events such as those occurred in Mexico, or may be caused by regional events such as of 1997-1998 in South Asia.

The discussions of stock market efficiency in this chapter have been articulated into four parts as presented in Table 6-1. The first part discusses the efficiency of stock market in a normal situation that reflects the fundamentals for both firms and the national level. The second part will present the traditional classifications of stock market efficiency concept. The third part is devoted to present the different situations that partially impair the efficiency of the stock market, which may lead to high price volatility of stock market during unstable trading periods. The fourth part presents interpretations and models, which impair substantially the efficiency of stock markets that concludes to a stock market crash. This presented classification used in this chapter is just a way to discuss these complicated issues that have so contradictory conclusions and interpretations as empirical, related surveys and official investigations reports found. However, it should be noted that the partial and essential causes of stock market crisis are overlapped and have cross-related conditions.

Table 6-1. Possible situations of stock trading efficiency

Situations	Prices	Features
Normal situation of market efficiency	Prices reflect firm and national fundamentals	Normal growth of security prices reflecting an increase in owners' equity and other firm's fundamentals
Traditional classification	Content efficiency effect Hypothesis levels effects	
Partial impair of efficiency	Extraordinary high volatility of stock prices	Return to normal level prices in a short period
Substantial impair of efficiency	Falling of stock price index to a new record The falling of prices is so fast The long period for recovering and return to normal prices	A market crisis or may be called crash, Flu (Asia), Tequila (Mexico) Regional and global effect

Stock Market Efficiency in a Normal Situation

Stock prices should respond to fundamentals and real economic data. The fundamental data is related to two factors. The first factor is the firms' data, which includes dividends distribution, repurchasing of shares announcements, earning per share, earning announcements and forecasting. The second factor is related to the national economy factors of the home security, such as inflation, national currency exchange rate, employment data, monetary policy and other economic fundamentals as presented in Table 6-2.

Table 6-2. Summary of fundamentals which are supposed to be reflected in stock market prices

	Announced data
Firm fundamentals	Earnings per share and price earning ratio
	Dividend payout ratio
	Repurchasing programs
	Book to market ratio
	Distribution of free shares (split shares)
National fundamentals	National currency exchange rate
	Interest rate
	Inflation rate
	Economic growth (GDP) and other economic indicators

First: Response to earning per share: The most important factor of the firm's fundamentals is the earning per share. The earning per share is supposed to depict the present performance of the firm. Accordingly, the market price should reflect its P/E ratio. Other related measures such as accounting earnings, financial ratios, and forecasting measures are also considered as a part of the firms' fundamentals. Several studies reported positive effect of the firms' fundamentals on stock prices in various stock markets. For example, Chiang et al. 1997 found that changing in earning per share is an important factor in changing stock prices. Maddala and Nimalendran, (1995) found that earning surprises have significant effect on stock prices.

Second: Response to repurchases programs: The announcements and the implementation of repurchasing programs are considered as a fundamental data that has an impact on the stock price changes. The announcement of stocks repurchases leads in general to positive signals regarding stocks' prices, and creates a higher positive response than dividends announcement. Empirical studies in US and other developed markets reported positive responses to repurchasing programs. For example, in the US markets, Ikenberry et al. (1995) examined the long-run of a firms' performance following an open market share repurchase announcement and found that the average abnormal return for four year return after announcement was 12%. Persons (1997) examined the repurchasing share method of tender offer and concluded that a repurchase tender offer is used to signal large information asymmetries, and thus causes larger stock price increase than dividends.

Similar conclusions were reported for other developed and emerging markets. Li and McNally (2000) found that Canadian firms use the share repurchase as a mean for reducing financial slack and the agency costs. A report (CGRK Report, 2000) indicated that about 75 firms that announced to buyback their own shares witnessed a rise by 19.1% in the first 10 days of public announcements as compared to 10% in the Korean stock market price index. Rau and Vermaelen (2000) concluded that the UK firms' activities in repurchasing their own shares are influenced by the tax consequences.

Third: Response to book - market ratio: Book -market ratio, is one of the firms' fundamentals that is reflected in the stock prices. Accordingly, announcing at the end of the fiscal years' book to market ratio may have a positive or a negative impact on stock price movements. Some studies examined the response of stock prices to the book / market ratio and other related measures including fair accounting value and size of the firm (Fama and

French, 1995; Chan et al. 1991; and Bagella, et al. 2000). These studies indicated that the book to market and the size of the firm effect are important factors in the movement of stock market prices. Moreover, Skjeltorp (2000) found a positive relationship between the short-term market impact and the book- market ratio.

Fourth: Response to stock dividends and distribution of shares: Distributions of cash dividends is a positive sign that have positive impact on stock prices. This is also applied to the announcement of distribution shares instead of cash. In many jurisdictions, the corporate laws require the deductions of reserves based on stated ratios (for example 20% of the annual net profit). The accumulated reserve is similar to what is known as retained earnings, which eventually is considered as a part of owners' equity of the firm. It can be distributed to shareholders as additional shares in proportion to current ownership. This practice is known as shares distribution or stock splits, which results in the issuance of additional shares to the shareholders. In spite of the fact, that the distribution of shares to stockholders is not more than an accounting entry that reconcile the changes of the equity accounts including the reserves and the retained earnings, and its no more than an issuance of a memorandum notifying the shareholders about the number of their shares, this announcement creates a significant positive effect on the related stock price in the world stock markets.

Fifth: Response to inflation data: The response of stock prices to the announcement of financial inflation data and consumer price index is considered as one of the fundamentals that can be reflected in the stock prices of the national firms. The inflation rate reflects the changes in currency exchange rates, exports and import factors and price index of commodities and services. Based on the perceptions of foreign owners, an increase in the rate of inflation means devaluation of the held equities in that specific country because higher inflation will put a downward pressure on the value of the home currency in the foreign exchange markets in addition to the possibility of transferring this case into the neighboring countries. Emerging countries suffer from higher inflation rates that are reaching two digits. For example, the annual inflation rate in Turkey exceeded 100%, and in Mexico inflation reached 28% in 2000 (IMF, 2001). Accordingly, in some of stock markets with high inflation rate, the market price of the listed firms fall according to the announcements of inflation rates, especially in the case of countries that have substantial part of foreign trading.

The above conclusions were reported by many researches who investigated the impact of announcing inflation rates on stock prices and on the volatility of stock returns. For example, Ely and Robinson (1997) reported that stock prices are related to the overall movements of consumer price index. Other studies examined the relationship between inflation rates and stock market prices, performance and volatility and concluded that a significant relationship between inflation rates and stock prices exists (Omran and Pointon, 2001 and Morelli 2002).

Sixth: Response to changes in national exchange rates: One of the most critical factors that have direct impact on stock prices is the changes in the national currency exchange rate against other currencies; this issue will be discussed later in this chapter.

Seventh: Response to other economic data: announcing national economic measures may be reflected on the national stock market prices. Kwon and Shin, (1999) indicated that Korean stock market price indices reflect macroeconomic variables such as production index, trade balance and money supply. As for the unemployment factor, Boyd et al. (2005) found that announcing a rise in the unemployment rate is good news for stocks during economic expansions.

CLASSICAL CLASSIFICATIONS OF EFFICIENCY CONCEPT

In the related literature of the concept stock market efficiency has two general prominent classifications. The first classification is known as the efficiency hypothesis, and the second one is related to the content classifications as presented in Table 6-3.

Table 6-3. Summary of classical classification of efficient stock market concept

Classical classification	Sub- types
Hypothesis efficiency levels effect	Week -form efficiency
	Semi- Strong form Efficiency
	Strong form Efficiency
Content Efficiency effect	Informational efficiency
	Operational efficiency
	Allocation efficiency

Hypothesis Efficiency Levels

The next classical classification is the efficient market hypothesis which categorized efficiency into three levels. The weak level is based on the fact that the share prices reflect all historical information, the second level known as the semi-strong level, which is based on the historical data as well as other public information available concerning that share. The strong level reflects historical data, public data, and insider information (Fama, 1970; and 1991). This classification of stock market which is known as efficient market hypothesis (EMH) is considered as the classical classification of the stock market efficiency concept. Fama efficient market hypothesis has been examined extensively, especially at the week level in many developed and emerging stock markets to provide and received criticisms as reported by various studies. However, Fama, (1998) reviewed the majority of such studies and defended his interpretations by stating that the anomalies of stock market prices tend to disappear in long times.

Content Classification

The stock market efficiency may include three parts:

First: Operational efficiency: in efficient stock markets, trading costs should be at as minimum as possible. The cost of trading includes commissions, fees, and market impact, which is the average cost of trading in a country. In spite of the fact that most of the world stock markets have changed, the fixed commission rates to a negotiated system in order to increase competition and reduce cost, but is still far from being at the minimum.

Second: Allocation efficiency: It is related to the way of allocating investments, and distributing portfolio allocations for diversifications in order to reduce market risk.

Third: Informational efficiency: It is known as pricing efficiency, which means that prices of a stock reflects fundamentals, traders act rationality, and they are well informed and profit seeking, all public information are included, and equilibrium price is a function of trading.

PARTIALLY IMPAIRED STOCK MARKET EFFICIENCY

The literature related to the concept of stock market efficiency is so varied and overlapped. It is essential to distinguish between factors and situations were there is a possibility of impairing the concept of the stock market efficiency partially, which will be presented in this section. The other situations which may cause substantial impair to the efficiency concept will be presented in the next section. The partial inefficient situations may be categorized into various groups as presented in Table 6-4. The inefficient partial impair of stock market concept may be explained as that the stock market returns reflect factors which are not related to neither the firm nor national fundamentals. Examples of variables which are reflected in stock market returns are the time trading side effect, or size of the firm, or due to behavioral aspects of investors. For example, trading in special days or even in nice weather such as a sunny day may improve the mode of investors and becomes more optimistic; thus creates positive stock market returns. The effect of non- fundamental factors on stock market returns is reported in various empirical studies, which covers both developed and emerging markets.

Table 6-4. Summary of partially impaired situations of efficiency in stock markets

Inefficient situations	Sub- types
Time trading Effects	January effect
	Monday effect, weekend and holyday effect
	Seasonal Affect disorder (SAD Effect)
Firm efficiency Effects	Size inefficiency (small firm effect)
	Interaction effect of derivatives with underling shares
	Low price earning ratio effect
Behavioral Effects	Traders are not rational all times
	Traders are less rational in most of the times
	Traders are not rational due to some social and psychological factors

Side Effects of Timing in Stock Trading

The Stock Market Efficiency may be impaired due to what is known as time side effect. Trading during specific times such as before and after weekends, beginning and ending of the years, holidays, special seasons and even in different weather days may have side effects that represent abnormal situations and a high price anomalies in specific periods of trading.

- Weekends, and Monday effect: The Monday effect means that trading on Mondays is more negative than trading in other days of the week. Various empirical studies reported that trading in before and after weekend days may have effects on stock market returns, which may impair the stock market efficiency. (Ariel, 1990; Agrawal and Tandon, 1994).

- Seasonal Effect (SAD Effect): Various studies concluded that the inefficient stock market may be impaired and show as seasonal affective disorder, during pre-holidays and at the beginning of the months and found some anomalous of stock markets (Brockman and Michayluk; 1998; and Cadsby and Ratner, 1992).
- January Effect: several studies discussed this anomalies phenomenon of the stock market prices that occurred during trading in January months and reported various reasons for impairment including tax causes, earning announcements, end year information, window dressing, and other announcements (Bhardwaj et al. 1992, and Singal and Chen, 2001).

Firm Efficiency Effect

The inefficiency concept of stock market may be related to a firm or to the exchange market. As for the firm, the efficiency may be the consequence of the size effect, from interaction with derivatives' trading with the underling firm, or from the low ratio of price earring effect. The small- firms' effect is related to the concept that investing in small firms may produce above normal return. Various researches reported different explanations in an attempt to explain this phenomenon. The small firm effect is considered as contrary to the efficient market hypothesis (Fama and French, 1995; and Lee et al. 1998).

Behavioral Classifications

One of the interpretations of impairment of stock market efficiency is to use investors' psychology, and sociology theories to explain the rational or irrational of traders of stock markets. In spite of the fact that this type of analysis is referred to Keynes in the 1930 who pointed out the gambling game of stock traders. Even though this concept has been evolving during the last decade, and it is still in the emerging process.

However, the last decade witnessed a long list of researches that are working in this field, which is became known as behavioral finance, and applying that to stock markets. These studies extracted various psychological concepts such as overconfidence, prospect theory, regret theory, conservatism cognitive dissonance, conformity pressures, mental accounting, and self -esteem, and tried to apply and explain their effect on capital assets pricing theory and stock markets. These researches are aimed to conclude new behavioral interpretations for inefficient stock markets and to explain the causes of high volatility and stock market crises, and the limits of arbitrage, price setting, and investment decisions (Glaser, 2003, Ricciardi and Simon, 2000; Olsen, 1998; Barberis and Huang, 2001; Barberis, et al. 2001; Shleifer, 2000; Hirshleifer, 2001; and Daniel, et al. 2001).

Finally, it is a necessary to distinguish between two situations regarding the behavior of investors. For partial impairment of stock market efficiency, it is assumed that investors generally are not rational all times of stock trading, or they are less irrational in most of the times of stock trading, or they are not rational in short times due to some social and psychological factors. However, the overreaction concept and what is known as noise trading assumes irrational trading is considered in this presentation as one of the substantial factors to impair stock efficiency; thus, it will be discussed in the next section.

Interpretations of High Price Volatility and Stock Markets Crises

There are no clear causes of the stock market inefficiency which may lead to a stock market crisis. The causes of stock market crashes in 1987, 1989, and 1997-1998 are not clear yet and this is applied to even 1929 stock market crisis. Many of the mentioned causes of the 1987 crash are related to US stock market such as introducing a new tax law, increasing the bonds yield and inflation data, although such elements were not existed in other markets but they also were severely hit by the crash such as the Germany stock market (Sabri, 1995 a). A long list of empirical studies reported different causes for stock market inefficiency which have contradictory conclusions. In addition, there are various opinions amongst different groups of experts concerning the total elements that maximize the probability of evolving a stock market crisis (Sabri, 1995b).

Therefore, this section aims to synthesize the causes of stock market crises, which has been articulated and stated based on the state of arts and empirical investigations regarding stock market crises, which have been published in the last fifteen years. The causes of substantial impairment of stock market efficiency can be modeled to reside in eight causes as classified and presented in Table 6-5. However, it is intended to classify models and interpretations of stock markets as if they have been independent causes, it should be noted here that the formulated causes are so interrelated with each other's as well as their interpretations

Devaluation of Currency Exchange Rate Cause

The effect of exchange rate and money market on stock market volatility has received a lot of attentions lately. It is now considered as the most significant factor in the stability of the world stock markets. This is related to the significant increase of foreign shares in the world stock markets. For foreign investors, devaluation of currency in the home country where equities are held means losses in the values of their equities for the same percentage, or even more. National currencies' appreciation or depreciation rates may occur for various reasons, including, inflation rate, currency demand, supply, and money market situation, changing of cash flow of foreign trading in stock markets, gain, or loss of international competition to stock and financial markets, and the adjustment of the balance of trade and for other reasons. A homes' country exchange rate (price) relative to other currencies is determined by inflation, income level, governmental regulations, and expectations. These factors affect the demand and supply schedules and thus cause an evaluation or devaluation of a certain currency relative to other currencies. In addition, the range of changes in currency exchange rate is dependent on the currency system.

Table 6-5. Causes and interpretations of high volatility and stock market crises

Causes	Interpretations
1. Devaluation of currency exchange rate against other currencies	Capital outflow from national stock markets Falling of stock prices more than the devaluation ratio of currency
2. Overreaction causes	To noise trading and adverse information
	To introducing new related laws
	To Political risk
3. Bubble and hazard interpretation	Stock and financial crisis associated with bad loans, which is known as a moral hazard problem.
4. Market Inefficiency cause	Inefficiency of corporate and equities laws
	Inefficiency of Institutional practices
	Inefficiency of volatility control measures
	Inefficiency of trading mechanism
5. Financial Contagion cause	High correlation between the world stock indices
	Volatility spillover between stock market pairs:
	Transmission due to overnight information
	Transmission during sharp declining of prices
6. Econophysics' cause	Changes in stock prices follow crowed effect which lead to a power law statistics distribution
7. Volume volatility cause	Volume volatility leads stock prices volatility
	Size of transactions dissemination information reflects on stock prices
8. Liberalization and foreign trading	Irreversible of flow of equity
	Adverse effect of foreign trading
	Effect of major markets to other stock markets
	Adverse effect of dual listed and multi- currency trading
9. Adverse effect of derivatives markets	Volatility due to changing option index, interaction with underling shares,
	Adverse effect of introducing new options
	Index future and index options: leading cash market and interaction with underling shares
10. Alternative investments	Bonds: changing of bonds yield, volatility in bonds index, interaction with share trading,
	Interest rates: changing of rates and insufficiency of financing intermediates

According to the above fundamentals, and based on supply and demand the national currency exchange rate appreciates or depreciates relative to other currencies which is reflected negatively or positively on the stock markets. In addition, the change of currency rate may come directly from the government during the official devaluation or evaluation of the national currency against other currencies mainly, the USD or a group of currencies.

The fluctuation and volatility of national currency rate against other currencies are significant and prominent in many economies, especially in some emerging countries. For example, the Mexico currency ranged between 7.8 per USD and 10.3 per USD during the period from January 1997 to December 2000, the Korean currency ranged between 864 to 1633 per USD, the Malaysian currency rate ranged between 2.5 to 4.2 per USD, the South African Currency ranged from 4.4 to 7.7 per USD, the Turkish currency rate ranged from 116,150 to 683,705 per USD, formulating more than 600% during the same period (IMF, 1997 to 2001 and WFE, 2006). This is also applied to developed countries, for example, the exchange rate of German currency (DEM) against USD ranged between: 1.6366 to 1.8280 during the period form January 1998 to the end of December 1998. The exchange rate of Italian currency (ITL) against the USD ranged between: 1,618 to 1,803 during the period form January 1998 to the end of December 1998. The exchange rate of Canadian dollar against US dollar ranged between 1.3481 to 1.5786, with monthly changes from a 5% up and 3% down during the period 1997 to 2000. The exchange rate of Swiss Frank (CHF) against USD ranged between 1.3483 to 1.8057, with monthly changes ranged from 5% up to 8% down during the selected period 1997 to 2000 (WFE, 2006).

The devaluation of a national currency against foreign currencies for market reasons or based on a devaluation decision by the government creates serious disruption in the world stock market. First, it may initiate a financial crisis as that happened in the Mexican crisis of 1994, the financial crisis of South Asia of 1997, the Russian crisis in 1998, and in the Brazilian market in 1999. Second: it has a negative effect on the regional context of financial systems, which is known now as the contagion phenomena that may create problems to the neighboring and regional markets. Third, it has a direct effect on increasing stock return volatility which may lead to destabilizing stock trading. Fourth: it increases equity outflows form the national stock markets, which leads to falling of the prices significantly. Fifth: Information about possible devaluation of national currency may have more dramatic effect than the devaluation it self, because in first case investors may find that there is a possibility to avoid losses.

The above findings were reported by a long list of empirical studies. For example, a study found that change in currency rate was ranked as number one in all selected predictive factors which has effect on stock price volatility when compared to other variables in developed stock markets, including Paris, Zurich, Madrid, Milan, Frankfurt, and Toronto stock exchanges (Sabri, 2007). This conclusion was reported for emerging markets also, in which stock trading volume and currency exchange rate respectively represent the highest positive correlation to the emerging stock price changes; thus represent the most predicting variables of increasing price volatility (Sabri, 2004). In addition, Kearney (1998) found that exchange rate volatility is a more significant determinant of stock volatility than interest rate volatility. Phylaktis and Ravazzolo, 2000 discussed the stock prices and exchange rate dynamics and found that the US stock market acts as a conduit through which the foreign exchange market and local stock markets are linked. Bailey et al. (2000) found that news of intraday changes in Mexican currency exchange rate affect prices and trading volumes in Mexican stock markets as well as Latin American equities markets, in which for example the value of pesos dropped from 3.4 per droller to 7 per dollar compared to a drop of Telephones Mexico stock from 63 to 28 USD during the same period.

Overreaction Causes

The overreaction concept is related to the fact that during some periods of stock trading, prices respond to non-fundamentals fully or partially rather than fundamentals. The overreaction of investors may impair the efficiency of stock market substantially and is considered as one of the main causes of stock market crisis. The overreaction of traders may occur due to various causes, including: overreaction to adverse information, noise trading and overreaction for political factors, overreaction to earning information, overreaction for introducing new laws and regulations (Sabri, 2002).

First; overreaction to noise trading: It is considered as the most argument against the efficient stock markets that may initiate a stock market crisis. The noise trading and overreaction are interchangeable terms that represent irrational trading and produce prices that are not based on fundamentals. The overreaction of stock traders phenomenon increases during market declines, recessions, and stock market crashes, and it exists in both developed and emerging stock markets, as reported by various studies in many stock markets. For example, in the US stock market (Chopra et al. 1992). In Spain, (Alonso and Rubio, 1990), in Pacific countries stock markets (Ahmed et al. 1999), in East Asian markets (Ajayi and Mehdian, 1994). The overreaction of stock market mainly exists during periods of declining in stock prices and when here is uncertainty of markets trends.

Second: overreaction to introducing new laws: The overreaction in stock markets may be found as a response to introducing and/ or changing tax laws. Including tax transactions, capital gain tax, income tax and other related taxes. The discussing of a tax bill in American Congress during 1987 was considered as one of the main causes of 1987 stock market crashes. Bolster et al. 1989 indicated that the tax code change in US had a powerful effect on trading behavior of stock market and was significant in January 1987. In UK, Green et al. 2000 reported that changes transactions fees had have a significant effect on share price volatility. Hu (1998) indicated that changes in stock transaction tax in Hong Kong, Japan, Korea, and Taiwan reduced the stock market prices. Similar findings reported in Swedish stock market (Umlauf, 1994).

Third: overreaction to political risk: The political factor also, may be considered as one of the causes of overreactions in stock markets and may increase volatility in stock prices. The negative effect of political situation in stock market prices may occur during normal changes as in new elections or sudden changes in the political systems or due to regional developments. Various studies discussed the effect of political factors in stock market prices and indicated that political news increases the stock volatility. For example, Lobo, (1999) found that US midterm election is a significant source of uncertainty in stock market. Alexakis and Petrakis, (1991) found that the behavior of stock market index is mainly related to social and political factors beside investment opportunities. Brooks, et al. (1997) reported that the stock market volatility in South Africa behaves like that observed in developed stock market after a political change in 1990.

Bubbles and Hazard Causes

One of the interpretations for the sharp fall of stock prices is related to the concept of assets price bubbles. The most recent interpretation of bubble concept is connected with financial crisis and associated with bad loans, which is known as a moral hazard problem. The stock bubbles means over evaluation of stock prices, which existed in various stock markets during some periods of times such as in Japan during late 1980s and in some of Asian countries around the mid of 1990s and found that price shocks primary affect firms relying in bank financing rather than equity financing (Goyal and Yamada, 2004). Some believe that bubbles may be related to institutions and mainly financial institutions and not to fundamentals (Huang and Xu, 1999). Various studies examined the existence of bubbles in stock prices. The majority of these studies reported that stocks' price bubbles exist during some periods and in various markets, mainly in Asia financial markets. Ahmed et al. (1999) reported that stock market prices contain elements of speculative bubbles that are not justified by fundamentals data in ten Pacific countries.

Market Inefficiency Causes

The stock market inefficiency may be produced because of the inefficiency of institutional practices and laws, corporate and equity laws. The efficiency of related laws for stock trading means more developed, more competitive and more relevant to cope with and absorb the stock market crises and extraordinary high price volatility. Various studies were conducted in the majority of developed and emerging stock markets concerning the relevancy of the existing laws and found that the inefficiency of various aspects of the related laws and procedures may affect or increase the possibility of initiating the stock market crises, which support the inefficient model of stock market law environment. The causes of market inefficiency may be related to one of the following aspects:

Corporate Laws Pertaining to Stock Markets

First: The inefficiency of the corporate laws may come from various reasons. First: The legalization of some types and features of corporate shares such as bearer shares, inferior voting shares, and no- par value shares. Second: The poor governance regulations, which organize the management board and supervision of the corporation. Third: The legal constrains to protect shareholders minority. Forth: The legal constraints that are imposed to protect investors. For example, Johnson et al. (2000) reported evidence that the weakness of legal institutions and the poor corporate governance had an important effect on the stock market declines in the Asian crisis in 1997. Becht (1999) reported that legal constraints aimed at strengthening minority protection might destroy liquidity of corporation and voting power concentration through blocks has a negative effect on liquidity.

Second: the inefficiency of institutional market and trading mechanism is one of the possible causes of stock market instability. Since 1987 stock market crash many empirical studies were conducted in various stock markets to investigate the role of institutional features of stock exchanges in stock market crises. This includes trading mechanism, cash settlements, type of orders, trading hours, and computerizing of trading activities. The world stock exchanges use different trading and pricing systems, different settlements cycles ranging from one to seven days. Even though, few of the world stock exchanges are still using floor-trading systems, the majority use various models of computerized systems. The question here is, which mechanism is the most relevant to cope with stock market crises.

Inefficiency of Controlling Volatility Measures

There is a mixed effect of the stated measures to deal with emergencies and to help in managing stock price volatility: The world stock markets use different measures to control the price volatility, including price limits of ups and downs of stock prices' changes from the pervious day, margin requirements and circuit breakers. The aim of imposing such regulations is to freeze or stop stock trading when high- low price movements reach a stated level in one trading day. As it is indicated in chapter four, the majority of the world stock markets used one or more types of controlling measures to work either automatically, or discretionary. However, the question that arises is whether these preventive measures are sufficient to deal with emergency in stock market trading. Various studies reported that such preventive measures are not sufficient or not efficient, and they only delay the rational price movements. For example, Chen (1994) examined the price limits regulations in Taiwan and reported that price limits have not a significant impact on reducing price volatility. Kim and Limpaphayom (2000) found that high trading volume stocks hit price limits more frequently than lower trading volume stocks. In addition, some studies reported that price limits and margin requirements may create volatility rather than reduce it.

Finally, it can be concluded that controlling measures may be sufficient to deal with low or average stock volatility, but it may be difficult to cope with high price volatility or stock crises. This may be due to trading outside stock exchanges, especially for countries, which have bearer shares that are not controllable. However, the perceptions towards using controlling measures received contradictory perceptions from the stock markets experts. Some believe that this is not relevant interference of stock trading mechanism, while others believe that such measures may work in normal conditions and not in emergencies, thus it might be a cause of stock market crisis rather than preventing it.

Contagious Cause

Another reported cause for market instability is increasing linkages between the world stock markets. The increasing linkages may create negative aspects for stock market, due to the fact that increasing linkages reduces stock market segmentation, but not to an extent to create an efficient integrated one. This situation may be considered as a major cause for stock market crisis. In addition, the correlations and integration between the world stock markets have been increasing since 1987 stock crash. The stock markets had become closer to each other. The correlation between stock markets indices has increased significantly since 1987 crash and during high volatility and declining prices periods. Otherwise, they are moving separately based on their own respective fundamentals. Thus, the transmission of high volatility of stock prices and stock crashes from one market to another exists and materializes significantly during periods of sharp fall and high volatility of stock prices.

The above conditions created what is known as the financial contagious, which means crisis spread to other markets based on irrational trading. In spite of the fact that this newly introduced concept to the state of the arts of stock market's stability is not well defined nor the causes are stated, the following observations may be articulated regarding this new possible cause of stock market crisis:

- Fundamentals are not sufficient to protect a country or a financial market from the financial contagion spread by irrational trading. Foreign investors, mutual funds and the existing financial linkages play a critical role in initiating financial contagious crisis.
- The ties of the stock markets indices have increased significantly after 1987 crash, and after 1995 - 1998 crashes. The correlation among stock market indices is intensified during the instable periods, while they go independently during stable periods of stock trading. Thus, financial contagious situation may be materialized only during crises times.
- Transferring of volatility may occur during overlapping hours of trading as well as from closing to opening trading information.
- A significant increase in cross price indices correlations occurs immediately after stock market or financial crisis initiate in a country or in a region.
- There is no clear way in which the contagious concept works or what is the mechanism of transferring crisis from one country to another or from financial market to another. In addition, there is no connection even to the concept of hedging trading. The only general accepted interpretation is related to the irrational trading practice.

Finally, the following factors may lead to initiate the financial contagion:

High Correlation between Stock Market Indices

The high correlation between the world stock markets is considered as one of the most risky environments, especially during periods of high volatility and sharp falling of prices. Sabri (1995a and 1995b) found that the fall of international indices is the most risky element in destabilizing the local stock markets as perceived by the stock market experts. Various empirical studies investigated the correlations between the world stock market indices in different times, using various models. Some studies examined the existing correlation between two or more stock indices, while other studies examined the correlations between stock exchanges within one or more regions, and others covered both developed and emerging stock exchanges.

The high correlation of stock prices exist between the developed stock indices, the emerging stock indices, among many pairs of stock markets, and between both developed and emerging stock indices. Bertero and Mayer (1990) found that the high correlations between markets have persisted since the 1987 crash. Koutmos (1995) found that the linkages and interactions between NY, Tokyo, and London stock markets have increased substantially after the 1987 crash era.

Transmission of Intraday Volatility

Various studies discussed the phenomena of transmission of volatility across markets and the dynamic interactions between stock price co-movements, due to flow of daily information. The studies covered the transmission during overnight to opening trading (sequential trading) as well as during overlapping trading hours. They reported that stock market volatility interactions and spillover exist, reciprocal and transmission from one market to another market. For example Schwert (1990) found that the stock volatility jumped dramatically during and after 1987 stock crash. Kane et al. (2000) found that volatility generally raises after large prices changes, but usually reverts to pre- jump level within a week or two. Ramchand and Susmel (1998) Found that there is evidence that morning volatility originating in New York spills over to the London market. In addition, Christofi and Pericli (1999) found the Latin American stock markets exhibit stronger volatility spillovers than other regions in the world.

Volatility Spillover between Stock Market Pairs

Many empirical studies examined the volatility spillovers between stock market pair's indices. Such as in Sweden, Norway and Finland; (Kinf and Pynnonen, 1999), in Australia and New Zealand (Brailsford, 1996; US, Canada and UK; Jeong, 1999) in US, and Mexican; (Soydrmir, 2000) and reported that there is a significant link, volatility spillovers exists, and the volatility surprises of those pairs affected each others, and volatility surprises of each national market is clearly transmitted to others. Kanas (1998) found the reciprocal stock price volatility spillovers exist between Frankfurt and Paris and between Paris and London.

Econo-physics Model Cause

In the last decade, many statistical physicians have introduced new interpretations for the causes of stock market crashes. The concept is based on statistical physics of financial time series, known as the "econophyisc" interpretation of the causes of stock crises. It is based on the following interpretations:

- The stock market crises are analogous to critical points in statistical physics and assumed that market price movements follow power – law distributions (Stauffer, and Sornette, 1999).
- Stock market crises are related to the existence (or not) of long, medium, short- range power- low correlations in the financial cycles (Ausloos, et al.1999 and Ausloos, 2000).
- Large variations of stock prices are due to a crowd effect with many interacting agents imitating each others' behavior (Bak, et al. 1997; Paljgyi, and Mantegna 1999).
- When interactions among traders become stronger and reach some critical values, a second phase transition and bull and bear market may be observed, and the phase

transition from a bull market phase to a bear market is considered as the stock market crash (Kaizoji, 2000).

- Stock crashes of 1929, 1987, and 1997 have the same origins that are found in the collective crowd behavior of the market traders leading to a critical point (Sornette, and Johansen 1998).
- The stock market becomes highly ordered at crashes, but gradually loses this order during static periods (Poniza, and Aizawa. 2000).
- Stock price fluctuations occur in all magnitudes in analogy to earthquakes with different eight orders of magnitude (Gopikrishnan et al. 2000).

The above empirical studies were conducted in various stock markets, and reported similar conclusions. However, the above concepts and stated interpretations do not provide as assistance to predict future crises or to suggest policies for avoiding and reducing the possibility of evolving future stock crashes.

Volume Volatility Causes

The high volatility of stock prices and crises may be created because of volume volatility. Various studies reported that volume leads stock prices changes and found significant relationships between volume volatility and stock volatility, and reported that trading volume is a source of risk due to the flow of information. For example: Sabri (2004) found that the volatility of trading volume was the first predicted variable of the stock return volatility in the majority of emerging stock markets. It is ranked as number one amongst eight variables in Mexico, Korea, Malaysia, Turkey, and South Africa. In the developed countries, it is ranked as number two among seven predicted variables of stock return volatility after the changing of exchange rate as reported by Sabri, (2007). Saatcioglu and Starks, (1999) found that volume leads stock prices changes in four out of the six emerging markets. Blume, et al. (1989) stated that a portion of the losses on S & P stocks in October, 1987 was related to the magnitude of the trading volume and not to real economic factors. Chan et al. (2000) reported that trading volume for foreign stocks is strongly associated with NYSE opening price volatility. Accordingly, high volatility of trading volume will lead to high volatility of stock returns, and may increase the possibility of emerging stock market crisis. More details for this issue will be discussed in the next chapter.

Liberalization of Stock Market Causes

The liberalization is one of the major reasons for creating close relationships between the world stock exchanges. The liberalization of the world stock market may reduce the cost of trading and increasing liquidity, but may be considered as a major reason for financial crises, increasing price volatility and stock market crisis, such the one occurred in the South Asian stock markets. The liberalization of emerging stock countries has been under strong debate since the 1997 stock market crises. The liberalization of the world stock market is one of the globalization phenomenon as presented and discussed in the previous chapter but is considered as one of the major causes for initiating a stock market crisis, mainly due to adverse effect of foreign trading, reversible flow of funds and the impact of leading stock markets, and due to the effect of trading in multi currencies.

The Adverse Impact of Foreign Trading

In Stock Markets, the volatility of cash flow to equity markets is now considered as major cause of last stock market crash of 1997-1998. The general perception in the world stock markets that foreign speculators are first to withdraw from the stock markets during instable conditions. The published data of equity flows during the 1997 and 1998 supported this argument. For example, the capital outflow of equities from the Asian stock markets as a response to the financial crisis, during the years 1998 and 1999 were 24.5 billion (IMF, 2000). Accordingly, foreign investors were often to be blamed for the Asian financial crisis (Choe et al. 1999). The issue of foreign investments has become more significant as long as the foreign shares of stock trading are increasing in the majority of the world stock exchanges. In some of stock exchanges, such as in the London Stock exchange, the ratio of foreign trade value of stock transactions exceeded the value of the domestic transactions.

The Reversible Flow of Funds

The reversible flow of funds from national stock markets leads to a significant decreased in liquidity of stock trading, and thus may lead to stock market crisis. The equity portfolio flow between developed and emerging stock markets is not working in one direction. During the last decade, some negative political and economic changes in emerging countries lead to a significant cash outflow. For example, during the year 1998, there was a negative cash outflow of about $ 18 billion from Asian emerging markets (IMF, 2000). As the high volatility of equity portfolio flows between developed and emerging markets, it creates instability in emerging stock markets.

Impact of Leading Stock Markets

There are two world leading stock markets including US, and Japan which have an influence on the world stock markets as indicated by several studies. In addition, there are some leading stock markets, which influence their regions or related twins. Many empirical studies reported that the US stock market has significant influence on other markets and not vise versa. Its influence became greater during the 1987 crash period. Other studies reported that Japan might have some influence on other markets. For example: Kearney, (2000) found that the world stock market volatility is caused mainly by Japanese and US stock markets and transmitted to European stock markets. John et al. (1995) found that short-term volatility and price changes spill over from developed to emerging markets, but not vice versa. Arshanapalli and Doukas (1994) found that the US stock market is found to have a considerable impact on the France, German, and UK in post crash period.

Trading in Multi Currencies and Cross Listing Firms

Due to liberalization of trading concept, many stock markets are now trading and pricing the traded stocks in multi currencies. This situation may invites directly the problem of national currency to the stock markets and adds to the adverse effect produced by the dual listed firms in various jurisdictions dealing with various currencies. In addition, the dual listed firms are increasing in numbers, volume, and markets as indicated in the previous chapter. The pricing of a stock in different markets with different currencies, different pricing methods different methods of settlements and other related conditions, increases the fluctuation stock price volatility. Accordingly, the trading of the dual listed firms are have an adverse effect on the price volatility of underlying shares and may initiate a stock market crisis in their one home stock exchanges, specially that the dual listed firms usually present the main traded securities in their home bases.

Derivatives Market Effect

The adverse impact of derivatives on the volatility of underlying stock prices may be considered as one of the major causes of increasing price volatility, which may initiate a stock market crisis. This is valid for all derivatives including, options, futures, index options, and index future markets. The impact of option markets on the volatility of underlying stock prices may come as a result of changing in option share index; interaction with underlying shares, introducing new options in the related stock market. Several reports accused the option market as the reason for the high stock price movements in the major stock international markets. In addition the future markets lead cash markets stock market volatility to increase after introducing index future trading or index equity trading as being presented by many empirical studies. Chan, (1992) found that when more stocks move together, the futures lead the cash index to a greater degree and futures markets are the main source of market wide information.

Alternative Investments Causes

The inefficiency of stock markets may emerge because of volatility or significant changes in other markets. Such markets are considered as alternative investments to stock trading. Most of the related studies found that the volatility linkages between the stock market and related markets are strong. Due to the fact, that such markets form alternatives for stock investments, which may be transferred to bonds, currencies trading or deposits and vice versa in short times. These markets include bond markets, money markets, and short-term deposits. Accordingly, changes in bond yields may have significant influences on stock market.

Changes in Deposit Interest Rate

The monthly changes of interest rate are significant and vary from one country to another and from developed markets to emerging markets. For example during the 1998 and up to the end of 2000, the changes in interest rates ranged in Italy between 1.44% to 3.91%, with monthly changes between 9% up and 13% down. In Spanish ranged between 1.50% to 3.60%, with monthly changes between 21% up and 19% down. In emerging markets, the level of changes in interest rate was so high compared to developed economies. For example, the Mexican interest rate moved from 6.67% as a minimum to 22.7% during the period 1997 to 2000. The interest rate in South Africa extended from 8.75% to 20.25% during the same period (IFC, 1998-2001; IMF, 1997-2001, and WFE, 2006).

The different deposit programs in banks are the major investment vehicles, which compete with investments in stock markets including cash and derivatives markets. Individual investors, mangers of provident and mutual funds, and investment firms are looking for the best opportunity of investment. Accordingly, when the deposit interest rate falls down, it is expected to transfer funds to stock markets and vice versa. Thus increasing deposit interest rate can be reflected negatively in the stock market, as well as increasing volatility of interest rate may be transferred to stock markets. In addition, changing of interest rates in developed countries such as in dollar, and Euro may be reflected in other developed as well as emerging stock markets.

Various empirical studies supported the adverse effect of changing interest rate on the volatility of stock returns. For example, changing interest rate is considered as the most predicting variable of stock return volatility after changing the currency exchange rate, and stock trading volume in the developed markets (Sabri, 2007). In addition, it was found to be the first predicting variable in Malaysian, Turkish, and South African stock markets deposits (Sabri, 2004). In addition, Koch, and Saporoschenko (2001) found that the stock returns of keiretsu financial firms have negative responses to interest rate increases. Nikiforos and Sawhney (2002) found linkages between increases in interest rates and the adversely effect on stock market. Chen et al. (1999) reported that unexpected changes in discount interest rate contributed to higher stock market volatility.

The Effect of Bond Trading

The effect of bond's trading as alternative investment instrument on the volatility of stock prices is due to the changing of bonds yield, and interaction with share trading. The bond market is a strong alternative to investments in stocks. Accordingly, the improvement of bond yield may shift investments and liquidity from stock markets to bonds markets. The bond market includes government bonds, corporate bonds, treasury bills, and government notes. The world bond markets are witnessing significant changes during short periods, which may reflected on increasing volatility of stock markets. For example, the French government bond yields per annum were moved from 3.78% to 5.71%, between 1998 and 2001. The German government bond yield moved from 3.53% to 5.35%, with monthly changes between 10% up and 8% down during the same period. The Spanish treasury bill rate per annum ranged from 2.56% to 5.05%, and the Canadian treasury bill rate per annum ranged between 4.18% and

5.75%, for the same period (IMF, 1997- 2001). Finally, empirical investigation supported the idea that changing of bonds yields may lead to high stock price volatility.

CONCLUSION

This chapter presented the efficiency of stock market concept in four possible situations. First represents the normal situation which reflects both firm and national fundamentals. The second situation represents the traditional classifications of stock market efficiency. The third part allocated to the partial impairment of stock markets efficiency and their related interpretations. While, the fourth part presentd in this chapter is related to the substantial impairment of stock market efficiency and the associated situations that may lead to stock market crisis.

However, the term efficiency is not well defined yet and still considered as controversial issue. It only concentrates on the concept of determining prices based on the best available information of fundamentals for equities. However, the stock market efficiency concept failed in various occasions in the last two decades. The relationship between efficiency and other factors including volatility, risk, liquidity, and return is not articulated yet. In addition, it is more complicated now due to the newly emerged practices to the stock markets. The majority of the mentioned classifications of hypotheses and interpretations need to be examined in light of new practices. The behavior of stock markets in the last fifteen years as well as the effect of the new practices being incorporated to the stock markets as explored in this book, requests that the present interpretations of stock market efficiency has to be re-investigated, in order to suggest new theoretical framework. Finally, it should be noted the above possible causes and interpretations of stock market crisis are applying to both emerging and developed markets.

REFERENCES

Agrawal, A. and K. Tandon (1994) "Anomalies or illusions? Evidence from stock markets in eighteen countries" *Journal of International Money and Finance* 13; 83-106.

Ahmed, Ehsan, J. Barkley Rosser Jr and Jamshed Y. Uppal (1999) "Evidence of nonlinear speculative bubbles in Pacific- Rim stock markets" *The Quarterly Review of Economics and Finance,* 49; 21-46.

Ajayi, R. A. and S. M. Mehdian (1994) "Tests of inventors' reactions to major surprises: the case of emerging markets" *Journal of International Financial Markets, Institutions & Money.* 4; 115-128.

Alexakis, P. and P. Petrakis (1991) "Analysing stock market behavior in a small capital market" *Journal of Banking & Finance* 15 (4); 471-484.

Alonso, A., and G. Rubio (1990) "Overreaction in the Spanish equity market" *Journal of Banking & Finance.* 14; 469- 481.

Ariel, R. A. 1990. "High stock returns before holidays: Existence and evidence on possible causes" *Journal of Finance* 45; 1611-1626.

Arshanapalli, B. and J. Doukas (1994) "International Stock Market Linkages: Evidence from the pre-and post October 1987 period" *Journal of Banking & Finance* 17 (1); 194-208.

Ausloos, M. (2000). "Statistical physics in foreign exchange currency and stock markets" *Physica A,* 285; 48-65.

Ausloos, M., N. Vandewalle, Ph. Boveroux, M. Minguet, K. Ivanova. (1999). Application of Statistical physics to economic and financial topics" *Physica A*, 274; 229-240.

Bagella, Michele, Leonardo Becchetti and Andrea Carpentieri (2000) "The first shall be last. Size and value strategy premia at the London stock exchange" *Journal of Banking & Finance*. 24; 893-919.

Bailey, Warren, Kalok Chan and Y. Peter Chung (2000) "Depositary Receipts, Country Funds, and the Peso Crash: The Intraday Evidence" *Journal of Finance* 55; 2693-2717.

Bak, P., M. Paczuski and M. Shubik (1997) "Price variations in a stock market with many agents" *Physica A,* 246; 440-454.

Barberis, Nicholas, and Ming Huang (2001) Mental accounting, loss aversion, and individual stock return *Journal of Finance* 56; 1247-1292.

Barberis, Nicholas, Ming Huang, and Tano Santos (2001) "Prospect Theory and Asset prices" *Quarterly Journal of Economics* 116; 1-53.

Becht, Marco (1999) European corporate governance: trading off liquidity against control *European Economic Review* 44 (4-6); 1071-1084.

Bertero, Elisabetta and Colin Mayer (1990) "Structure and performance: global interdependence of stock markets around the crash of October 1987" *European Economic Review* 44; 1155-1180.

Bhardwaj R. K. and L. D. Brookw (1992) "The January anomaly: Effects of low share price, transaction cost, and bid-askbias" *Journal of Finance* 47; 553-575.

Blume, M. E. and, A. C. Mackinlay and B. Terker (1989) "Order imbalances and stock movements on October 19 and 20, 1987" *Journal of Finance* 44; 827- 848.

Boyd, John, Jian Hu and Ravi Jagannathan. (2005) "The stock market's reaction to unemployment news: Why bad news is usually good for stocks " *Journal of Finance* 60; 649–672

Brailsford, T. J. (1996) "Volatility spillovers across the Tasman" *Australian Journal of Management* 21; 13-28.

Brockman, P. and S. Michayluk (1998). "The persistent holiday effect: Additional evidence" *Applied Economic Letters* 5; 205-209.

Brooks, Robert, D., Sinclair Davidson, and Robert W. Fatt (1997). "An Examination of the effects of major political change on stock market volatility: the South African experience" *Journal of International Financial Markets, Institutions & Money* 7 (4); 255-275.

Cadsby B. and M. Rather (1992). "Turn- of- month and pre- holiday effects on stock returns: Some international evidence" *Journal of Banking and Finance* 16; 497-509.

CGRK (2000) A LG Securities Report (Korean Economy Daily Report, Consulate General of the Republic of Korea CG No. 450).

Chan, K (1992) "A further analysis of the lead- lag relationship between the cash market and stock index future market" *Review of Financial Studies* 5; 124-152.

Chan, Louis K. C., Yasushi Hamao, and Joser Lakonishok 1991. "Fundamentals and Stock Returns in Japan" *Journal of Finance* 46; 1749-1765.

Chen, Yea- Mow (1994) "Price Limits and Stock market Volatility in Taiwan" *Pacific- Basin Finance Journal* 1(2); 149-154.

Chiang, Raymond, Ian Davidson and John Ckunev (1997) "Some further theoretical and Empirical implications regarding the relationship between earnings, dividends and stock prices" *Journal of Banking & Finance* 21; 17-45.

Choe, Hyuk, Bong- Chan Kho and Rene M. Stulz (1999) "Do Foreign Investors Destabilize Stock Markets? The Korean Experience in 1997" *Journal of Financial Economics* 54 (2); 227-264.

Chopra, Navin, Josef Lakonishok and Jay R. Ritter (1992) "Measuring abnormal performance: Do stocks overreact?" *Journal of Financial Economics* 31; 235-268.

Christofi, A. and A. Pericli (1999) "Correlation in price changes and volatility of major Latin American stock markets" *Journal of Multinational Financial Management* 9; 79-94.

Daniel, Kent, David Hirshleifer, and Avanidhar Subrahmanyam, (2001) 'Overconfidence, arbitrage, and equilibrium asset pricing" *Journal of Finance* 56; 921-965.

Ely, David. P. and Kenneth. J. Robinson (1997). Are stocks a hedge against inflation? International evidence using a long-run approach. *Journal of International Money and Finance*. 16; 141-167.

Fama, Eugene F., (1970). "Efficient Capital Markets: A review of theory and empirical work" *Journal of Finance* 25; 383-417.

Fama, Eugene F. (1991) "Efficient Capital Markets: II" *Journal of Finance* 46; 1575-1616.

Fama, Eugene F. and Kenneth R. French (1995). "Size and book to market factors in earning and returns" *Journal of Finance* 50; 131-155..

Fama, Eugene F., (1998). "Market efficiency, long term returns and behavioral finance" *Journal of Financial Economics* 49; 283-306.

Glaser, Markus, 2003. "Behavioral Finance" (No. 3-14, Sonderforschungsbereich, 504, University of Mannheim).

Gopikrishnan, P., V. Plerou, Y. Liu, L.A. N. Amaral, X. Gabaix, H. E. Stanley (2000) "Scaling and correlation in financial time series" *Physica A* 287; 462-474.

Goyal, Vidhan K. and Takeshi Yamada (2004). "Asset price shocks, financial constrain and Investment: Evidence from Japan" *Journal of Business* 77; 175-200.

Green, Christopher J. Paolo Maggioni and Victor Murinde (2000) "Regulatory lessons for emerging stock markets from a century of evidence on transactions costs and share price volatility in the London Stock Exchange" *Journal of Banking & Finance* 24; 577-601.

Hirshleifer, David (2001) "Investor Psychology and Asset Pricing" *Journal of Finance* 56; 1533-1597.

Hu, Shing-yang, (1998) "The effects of the stock transaction tax on the stock market- Experiences from Asian Markets" *Pacific – Basin Finance Journal* 6; 447-464.

Huang, Haizhou and Chenggang Xu (1999) "East Asia: miracle or bubble? Financial institutions and the financial crisis in East Asia" *European Economic Review* 43; 903-914.

IFC (1998-2001) *Emerging Stock Markets Factbook 1998- 2001* (International Financial Corporation, and Standard & Poor's, Washington, D. C).

Ikenberry, David, Josef Lakonishok, and Theo Vermaelen, (1995) "Market under-reaction to open market share repurchases" *Journal of Financial Economics* 49; 181-208.

IMF (1997-2001) *International Financial Statistics* (International Monetary Fund, Washington, D. C).

IMF (2000) *International Capital Markets: Development, Prospects and Key Policy Issues,* World Economic and Financial Surveys, (Washington, D. C. September).

Jeong, Jin-Gil (1999) "Cross-border transmission of stock price volatility: Evidence from the overlapping trading hours" *Global Finance Journal* 10 (1) 54-70.

John, K.C., Wei; Liu Yu-Jane,Yang Chau-Chen, and Chaung Guey-Shiang (1995) "Volitality and price changes spillover effects across the developed and emerging markets" *Pacific-Basin Finance Journal*. 4 (1); 114-146.

Johnson, Simon, Peter Boone, Alasdair Breach and Eric Friedman (2000) "Corporate governance in the Asian financial crisis" *Journal of Financial Economics* 58; 141-186.

Kaizoji, Taisei (2000) "Speculative bubbles and crashes in stock markets: An interesting – agent model of speculative activity" *Physica A*, 287; 494-506.

Kanas, A. (1998) "Volatility spillover across equity markets: European evidence" *Applied Financial Economics* 8; 245-257.

Kane, Alex, Bruce N. Lehmann and Robert R. Trippi (2000) "Regularities in volatility and the price of risk following large stock market movements in the US and Japan" *Journal of International Money and Finance* 19; 1-42.

Kearney, Colm (2000) "The determination and international transmission of stock market volatility" *Global Finance journal* 11; 41-52.

Kearney, Colm (1998) "The causes of volatility in a small internationally integrated stock markets: Ireland, July 1975- June 1994" *Journal of Financial Research* 21(1); 85-104.

Kim, Kenneth A and Piman Limpaphayom 2000 "Characteristics of stocks that frequently hit price limits: empirical evidence from Taiwan and Thailand" *Journal of Financial Markets* 4; 415-442.

Kinf, Johan and Seppo Pynnonen (1999) "Local and global price memory of international stock markets" *Journal of International Financial Markets, Institutions* & Money 9 (2); 129-147.

Koch, Timothy W. and Andrew Saporoschenko (2001) "The effect of market returns, interest rates and exchange rates on the stock returns of Japanese horizontal Keiretsu financial firms" *Journal of Multinational Financial Management* 11 (2); 165-182.

Koutmos, Gregory (1995) "Asymmetric volatility transmission in international stock markets" *Journal of International Money and Finance* 14 (6); 747-762.

Kwon, Chung S. and Tai S. Shin (1999) Co- integration and causality between macroeconomic variables and stock market returns. *Global Finance Journal.* 10, 71-81.

Lee, Cheng- Few, David C. Porter and Daniel G. Weaver (1998). "Indirect Tests of the Haugen- Lakonishok Small- Firm/ January Effect Hypotheses: Window Dressing versus Performance Hedging" *Financial Review* 33 (2); 177-194.

Li, Kai and William McNally (2000) Information Signaling or Agency Conflicts: What Explains Canadian Open Market Share Repurchases? (The University of British Columbia).

Lobo, Bento J. (1999) "Jump risk in the U. S. stock market: Evidence using political information" *Review of Financial Economics* 8 (2); 149-164.

Maddala, G. S. and M. Nimalendran (1995) "An unobserved component panel data model to study the effect of earnings surprises on stock prices, trading volumes and spreads" *Journal of Econometrics,* 68; 229-242.

Morelli, David (2002) "The relationship between conditional stock market volatility and conditional macroeconomic volatility empirical evidence based on UK data" *International Review of Financial Analysis* 11; 101-110.

Nikiforos, Laopodis and Bansi L. Sawhney (2002) "Dynamic interactions between Main street and Wall street" *The Quarterly Review of Economics and Finance* 42; 803-815.

Olsen, R. A. 1998. "Behavioural finance and its implications for stock- price volatility ?" *Financial Analysts Journal* 54; 10- 19.

Omran, Mohammed Omran and John Pointon (2001). "Does the inflation rate affect the performance of the stock market? The case of Egypt" *Emerging Markets Review* 2; 263-279.

Paljgyi, Zoltjn and Rosario N. Mantegna. (1999) "Empirical investigation of stock price dynamics in an emerging market" *Physica A.* 269; 142-149.

Persons, John C. (1997) "Heterogeneous Shareholders and Signaling with Share repurchases" *Journal of Corporate Finance* 3; 221-249.

Phylaktis, Kate and Fabiola Ravazzolo (2000) "Stock Prices and exchange rate dynamics" (Working Paper, EFMA Conference, Athens).

Poniza, A. and Y. Aizawa. (2000) "Evolutionary financial market models" *Physica A,* 287; 507-524.

Ramchand, L., and R., Susmel (1998). "Volatility and cross correlation across major stock markets" *Journal of Empirical Finance* 5; 397-416.

Rau, Raghavendra P. and Theo Vermaelen (2000) Regulation, Taxes and Share Repurchases in the UK (November, working Paper).

Ricciardi, Victor and Helen K. Simon. (2000). "What is Behavioral Finance?" *Business, Education & Technology* 2;

Saatccioglu, Kemal and Laura T. Starks (1999)." The stock price- volume relationship in emerging stock markets: the case of Latin America" *International Journal of Forecasting* 14 (2); 215-225.

Sabri, Nidal Rashid (1995a) "Stabilization of Stock Markets; the Case of the Frankfurt Exchange" *Journal of Multinational Financial Management* 5; 23- 32.

Sabri, Nidal Rashid (1995b) "Experts' Opinions Toward Price Stability During the Stock Market Crisis" *International Journal of Commerce & Management* 5; 130-146

Sabri, Nidal Rashid (2002). "Roots of stock market volatility and crises: a synthesis and suggested remedies" *International Review of Comparative Public Policy* 13; 1-53.

Sabri, Nidal Rashid (2004). "Stock Return Volatility and Market Crisis In Emerging Economies" *Review of Accounting and Finance* ; 3 (3); 59-83.

Sabri, Nidal Rashid (2007) "High volatility and stock market crises in developed economies" (Manuscript under publication).

Schwert, G W., (1990). "Stock volatility and the crash of '87" *Review of Financial Studies* 4 (1); 77-102.

Shleifer, Andrei (2000). *Inefficient Markets- An introduction to behavioral finance* (Clarendon Lectures in Economics, Oxford University Press).

Singal, Vijay and Honghui Chen (2001) "What Drives the January Effect?" (Virginia Tech Working Paper).

Skjeltorp, Johannes Alte (2000) Market Impact of Open Market Share Repurchases in Norway (Research Department, Central Bank of Norway).

Sornette, Didier and Anders Johansen. (1998) "A hierarchical model of financial crashes" *Physica A,* 261; 581-598.

Soydrmir, G. (2000) "International transmission mechanism of stock market movements: evidence from emerging equity markets." *Journal of Forecasting* 19 (4); 149- 177.

Stauffer, Dietrich and Didier Sornette. (1999) "Self-organized percolation model for stock market fluctuations" *Physica A*; 271; 496-506.

Umlauf, S. R. (1994) "Transaction taxes and the behavior of the Swedish stock market." *Journal of Financial Economics* 44; 227-240.

WFE (2006) *World Federation of Exchanges Database* (Paris, France). Available on line www.world-exchanges.org.

Chapter 7

STABILIZING AND DESTABILIZING FACTORS OF STOCK MARKETS

INTRODUCTION

In the previous chapters, we discussed the various aspects of new developments in the stock markets, including recent legal, trading, and globalization aspects that have been taking place in the last decade, and that have an effect on the stock market stability. In addition, we explored the issue of stock market crisis and the stock market efficiency concept, and their theoretical framework as presented in the state of the arts in the last decade. However, up to this point, the question of stock market stability has not been tackled exclusively in this book. Accordingly, there is a need to devote this chapter to discuss this issue.

The stability of stock market has two folds:

First, to keep the stock return volatility at a low or moderate level, volatility means uncertainty of stock price changes in short periods of trading. The low or moderate level of return volatility is acceptable and even preferable, which may accomplish extra returns to investors and speculators, but when it increases to high levels it might lead to destabilize stock markets.

Second, to minimize the conditions that might initiate a stock market crisis. The stock market crisis is defined by three elements; the falling of stock prices to a new record, the long period of trading in which stock price index is falling, and the long time to recover to the previous level of prices. There is no clear theoretical framework to point out the possible conditions, which may lead to a stock market crisis. However, one of the main conditions is increasing the level of stock price volatility in stock markets.

The stock market instability comes from either internal or external factors. The internal factors are related to one of the following:

- Information related to security fundamentals such as dividends, earning ratios, repurchasing plans, and merging plans.
- Information related to instruments attached to a security such as changing in bond's yield or a new rating issued by a credit rating agency, or in case of derivatives attached to the underlying of the share.

- Information related to a sector of industry at the national level, such as falling stock prices in communication industry in national or global context.
- Economic national fundamentals such as devaluation of a national currency or changing the prime interest rate by the central bank.

The external factors are related to conditions occurred outside the national economy, and may be found in one of the following causes:

- Changes in other stock markets such as sharp changes in stock prices in the leading world or regional stock markets
- Changes in an industrial sector at international level, which may be reflected on the stock price index to the national industry.
- Changes in one of the fundamentals in the world leading economies such as changing the prime interest rate in the USA by the US Federal bank, or in the LIBOR market.

In order to explore the above factors of the world stock market instability, both descriptive and empirical analysis will be presented in this chapter. The descriptive analysis will include survey of perceptions of the stock market experts in two developed stock markets. While the empirical analysis will cover two studies, one is related to the developed stock markets, while the next one is regarding to the emerging stock markets.

Stability of Stock Trading as Perceived by Stock Market Experts

The stock markets experts may express their attitudes towards factors, which may enhance stability of the stock market, based on their experiences and perceptions. The Frankfurt stock market experts were asked to rank a list of stated situations which may enhance stability of the stock markets (Sabri, 1995a). Summary of their responses is presented in Table 7-1. It shows that the Frankfurt stock market experts perceived the conditions that represent the safest factors to stabilize the stock markets, including:

Table 7-1. Rank of factors which enhance atability of stock market conditions as perceived by stock market experts

Conditions (Rank No. 1 as the Safest)	Rank
An increasing share of banks and pension funds	1
The short cash settlement system	2
The relevant dealing system	3
The relevant standard price system	4
The relatively small portion of foreign investment as un-loyal clients	5
The relevant stock exchange admission regulations	6
The price limits system	7
The loyalty of stockholders to their companies	8

- Increasing the share of financial institutions including banks and pensions funds in the stock markets.
- The cash settlement system
- The dealing system

In addition, the Amsterdam stock experts reported similar findings, in which considered the following factors as the safest conditions in stabilizing stock markets:

- Increasing the share of Dutch banks and pension funds in Amsterdam stock exchange.
- The present dealer system, which permits exchange members to act as agents and as principals.
- The present pricing system.

Accordingly, the stock market experts believe that to have solid stockholders is the most stabilizing factor in the world stock market, besides having a good market mechanism including dealing, pricing, and settlements systems. This view is built on the perception that institutional participations in stock market will reduce the noise trading, and irrational reactions accompanied by individual and foreign investors in stock markets.

Corporate Ownership Structure

Accordingly, the ownership structure is a significant issue concerning the stability of prices in stock markets. Thus, family controlled, control chains, public holding, residents' ownership, and institutional firms have positive impact in case of noise, and irrational trading compared to widely held firms, individual investors and foreign ownership. Thus, we may conclude that the world corporate structure is moving to be less solid concerning the stability of the stock markets. As long as shares owned by individuals, foreign investors, private ownership, and minority control groups are moving ahead against shares held by the public, residents, institutional and majority control groups of corporate ownership.

For example, in a recent survey indicated (FESE, 2002) that the non- resident investors have become the driving force of European markets. In addition, Parrino et al. (2003) study found that there is an increase in shareholdings of individual investors and a decrease in institutional investors. Ownership construction has direct impact on liquidity and stability of stock markets, and may create differentials between ownership and control rights. For efficiency and stability of stock markets local, institutional and public owners have advantages compared to individuals, foreigners, and private ownerships in this regards. Considering the structures of the world stockholders, it is found that four significant changes may have direct impact on the stock market stability. Theses changes are:

From Institutional to Individual Ownership

In general, the institutional to individual ratio of ownership is considered as a measure for presenting the possibility of increasing high return volatility in stock markets. The reaction of individual inventors during unstable periods of trading or during the high volatility of stock trading, is considered to be less rational than the reaction of institutions such as the mutual funds, banks and other financial organizations. Accordingly, the increasing share of individual investors in the world stock market which is now about one third of the total market may be considered as a negative aspect. The individuals' ownership of corporate stocks represents 49% in US, 50% in Italy, and 34% in Korea (OECD, 2003).

From Public to Private Ownership

Due to the privatization movement of public sector that occurred in the old socialists' states and in the majority of the emerging countries in the last two decades, many countries abandoned their ownership in many sectors and sold them to the private sector. Accordingly, the public share in the world corporations has been reduced to the minimum. For example, the survey of the Federation of European Securities exchanges (FESE, 2002) indicated that the public sector owns between 0% in London Stock exchange, to less than 10% in Stockholm, Copenhagen, Paris, Deutsche Brose, and Madrid. In spite of the idea that liberalization and privatization are the generally accepted concepts in the world economy, the public sector may act as a stabilizer factor in case of falling prices, or during unstable periods of trading.

From Residents' to Foreign Ownership

Up to the nineteen eighties, the majority of ownership of equity portfolio in the major stock markets was mainly owned by domestic residents as reported by Cooper and Kaplanis (1994). The home bias concept is related to the fact that equity portfolio is concentrated in local markets and not in international foreign markets in spite of the benefits which may be gained from diversification. However, this situation has been changing gradually. For example, the foreign ownership of US stock equities has increased from $11,240 million in 1995 to $107,522 million in 1999, with an increase of about 957% in five years (IMF, 2000). For other stock markets, the share of foreign ownership is increasing rapidly as presented in Table 7-2. It constitutes more than 50% of total ownership in London, Amsterdam and Helsinki Exchanges, and more than one third of the total ownership in other five stock exchanges.

Foreign investors are considered by several studies and official reports as less loyal stockholders and they are the first to run out from the market. In addition, they were often blamed for the Asian financial crisis (Choe et al. 1999). The World Bank report (2004) found that about sixteen emerging countries witnessed negative inward portfolio equity flow from financial markets between 1999 and 2003, especially in the years 1997, 1998 and 2002. For example, the Argentina stock market witnessed about $10.8 billion negative portfolio equities out flow in 1999, and $3.2 Billion in 2000. The Malaysian stock market witnessed outflow of portfolio equity from 1997 to 2003 of a total of $10.4 Billion. The Indonesian stock market witnessed outflow of about $10.7 billion between 1997 and 2000. However, some distinguish between foreign investments in form of direct investments from portfolio equity investments, and they consider first one as more favorable in case of stock market stability.

Control by Minority Ownership

Some corporate laws permit that a minority may control the firm by the dual class voting rights, or through other systems such as the cross-ownership structure. The trend to differentiate between common stock holders based on voting rights still existing in various jurisdictions, and may increase, especially after removing the restriction from foreign ownership. Thus, corporations may protect themselves by issuing special stock classes for foreigners or other groups of owners with less voting rights.

Accordingly, the concept of controlling the corporation still exists in spite of liberalizations and globalization effect on the world stock market. The control of the company comes mainly from founders, promoters, and families. Faccio and Lang (2002) found that the 44% of the Western European corporations are family controlled, while state controlled is a significant factor in large firms in certain European countries, and reported a discrepancy between ownership and control. Other studies discussed the issue of ownership and voting rights, such as: Lemmon and Lins (2003) found that large separation between cash flow ownership and control rights indicates that insiders have the motivation and the ability to be engaged in expropriation. In addition the control rights does not mean that the controlling company should own 51% of the votes, due to the fact that there are passive shareholders who do not vote at all, which allow a group to control a company with 30% or less as reported by the OECD survey (2004). This situation may lead to increasing the size of less loyal stockholders; thus lead to the risk of irrational trading during stock market crisis.

Table 7-2. Foreign ownership of total equities for selected developed and emerging stock exchanges (1995-2000)

Stock Market Exchanges	Foreign Ownership of total Equities
Copenhagen Stock Exchange	24%
Helsinki Exchanges Groups	60%
Amman Stock Market	44%
London Stock Exchange	66%
Amsterdam Stock Exchange	50%
Egypt Stock Exchange	23%
New Zealand	40%

Sources: Based on: Fact books of the respective stock exchanges (1999- 2000).

Instability of Stock Trading as Perceived by Market Experts

In spite of the fact that so many empirical studies examined the issue of stability of stock markets, a limited opinion surveys were conducted to address the same issue far from analysis of historical data. The reactions of stock markets come first from the related experts as brokers, specialist, and dealers working for their accounts or for their customers. Their rational or less rational reactions to news and developments are mainly based on their experiences and behaviors. Accordingly, there is a need to investigate their opinions, attitudes, and perceptions in this regard. Therefore, this chapter will report two opinion surveys that were conducted by the author in two developed markets, namely are related to perceptions of stock market experts in Frankfurt and Amsterdam stock exchanges (Sabri, 1995a, and Sabri, 1995b).

For the first study, the stock market experts including banks representatives (brokers) and *maklers* (specialist) as the decision makers who perform the stock trading functions of selling and buying as well as determining the stock prices and quotations. Banks are the only institutions permitted to deal in the German exchanges through their representatives, who bring buying and selling stock orders. The *maklers* work as specialists or mediators and execute orders, conclude deals, and to determine the official daily stock prices. The survey aimed to indicate the most possible factors that increase the instability situations of the stock markets based on stock market experts' experiences and perceptions.

In addition, to find if there is a significant difference between the perceptions of the two groups (the bankers as brokers and the *maklers* as specialists) concerning each of the selected possible factors which may lead to de-stabilizing conditions of the stock market. The related experts were asked to rank eight listed statements, which may contribute to the market disability at certain events. The list of situations was selected as based on the reported causes of stock crises mentioned in the official reports and various empirical studies. The opinions of Frankfurt stock experts regarding factors, which may decrease the stability of the stock market (Sabri, 1995a), are presented in Table 7-3.

Table 7-3. Rank of de-stabilizing factors as perceived by stock market experts (Rank 1 as the most risky)

Merits and Conditions	Rank
Other major international share indices fall down	1
Using the computer terminals	2
Increasing the shares trading outside the stock exchange	3
To close down or/and reduce the daily work hours (to trade-hold in certain events)	4
Increasing the foreign investment	5
Using bearer share certificates by corporations (instead of named certificate)	6
Increasing the listed foreign companies in national exchange	7
Increasing the listed national companies in foreign stock exchanges	8

It shows that the most possible de-stabilizing factors as perceived by Frankfurt stock market experts are:

- Falling of other major international share indices
- Using the computerized system in stock trading
- Increasing the share of trading outside the stock exchanges
- Using systematic and judgmental control measures by the exchange management

The second study, examined the opinion of the Amsterdam stock experts including bankers, specialists known as *hoekmen* and brokers. The bankers and brokers are the members who have to bring under an obligation all orders from their customers to the specialists; however, the broker member needs a banker to complete the deals and to handle the financial matters. The specialists work as intermediaries on the exchange between the bankers and brokers and fix the official prices of the shares. The total number of Amsterdam stock market experts participated in this survey was about 65 experts.

The ASE market experts considered the following situations as the most possible risky factors regarding stability of the stock market:

- Falling of the other major international share price indices,
- Effect of option market
- Trading outside the stock exchange
- Using the computerized system in stock trading

Both experts in Amsterdam and Frankfurt stock exchanges perceived the falling of other major international stock price indices, trading outside the stock exchanges, and automation of stock trading as the most possible risky situations that may lead to instability in stock trading at certain events.

Finally, at the end of this section which presented the stock market opinions regarding to stock market stability, we would like to report that the stock market experts of Frankfurt stock exchange show significant differences between the two group members (bank representatives as brokers and the *maklers* as the specialists) concerning the ranks of each of the listed stabilizing conditions of the stock market for five out of the eight listed conditions as merits which may help in stabilizing the stock market. This is also applied to the perceptions of the Amsterdam Stock Exchange experts, which reported different opinions among the three groups of experts regarding six stated conditions out of ten listed situations that minimize the probability of initiating a stock market crisis.

EMPIRICAL INVESTIGATION IN EMERGING STOCK MARKETS

This section is reporting the finding of a study conducted by the author (Sabri, 2004) intended to examine the stock market crisis using a sample of five emerging markets, in order to determine the most influential factors to initiating stock price volatility and crisis in emerging stock markets. Five emerging countries were selected from regions of Latin America, South Asia, East Asia, Europe, and Africa. The study used data from the World Federation of Exchanges Database, Paris, The IMF International Financial Statistics monthly books (1997-2001) and the annual Factbooks (1997-2001) published by the International Financial Corporation.

The end monthly changes of stock price indices for each of the selected five emerging stock markets were used in this study covering 48 months from January 1997 to December 2000 as a dependent factor. In addition, the associated monthly changes of the stated predicting measures for each of the respective stock emerging markets used as the independent factor, which includes stock trading volume, bond trading volume, inflation rate, deposit interest rate, currency exchange rate, and international price indices. The backward multiple regression procedure was used in this study based on the relationship between the monthly changes of stock price indices as the dependent variable (Y), and the stated predicting causes as the independent variable (x_1, x_2,..).

The study found that local as well as international factors are possible factors for increasing price volatility in emerging stock markets. Concerning the national factors, the volume of stock trading and exchange rates were found to be the most common predicting factors. The volatility of stock volume is changing based on local firm and national economic fundamentals as well as foreign trading, and other international factors. However, the exchange rate was found to be less significant than stock trading volume as a predicting factor for stock price volatility of emerging stock markets. On the other hand, changing of inflation rate was the least predicting factor for the volatility of emerging stock markets. This result is applied to Turkey, which is considered as a country with high inflation. In spite of the fact, that changing or accelerating inflation rate, or unexpected increase of inflation has a significant impact on stock prices and volatility of stock markets. Table 7-4 represents the summary of the predictive factors for high volatility and possible crises in emerging stock markets as found in this study.

It is revealed that trading stock volume is the most predicting factor compared to all other used variables in emerging stock markets, as showed to be the most associated positive correlation to the volatility of stock price index. The currency exchange rate was the second important factor for predicting stock price volatility in emerging markets. The international price indices, deposit interest rate, and bond trading volume were found as moderate predicting variables for volatility of stock prices in emerging economies, while the inflation rate was the least predicting factor It indicates that the deposit interest rate, bond trading volume, and international price indices have varied impact on stock price volatility for the five emerging stock markets. In addition, changing of deposit interest rate was one of the most predicting factors for stock price volatility in Malaysia, Turkey, and South African stock markets, while it was the least predicting factor in case of Mexican and Korean stock markets. It also, concluded that NYSE stock price index has an impact only on Malaysian stock market, while it has no impact on the other four emerging markets.

The study also reported that there are significant differences regarding the adopted regression models for emerging markets as presented in Table 7-5. It shows that the changing of stock trading volume is the only common factor in all of the five stock markets, and the deposit interest rate is a common factor of predicting stock return volatility in four stock markets out of five. This is also applied to the international stock prices indices, which were included in the adopted model of four emerging markets out of the selected five markets. Finally, changing in currency exchange rate of national currency against USD has a significant impact on stock volatility. It is included in the adopted regression model in three out of five emerging economies.

Accordingly, it may be concluded that changes in stock volumes, interest rate, and international price indices have significant impact on stock market volatility in the emerging markets. However, it should be noted that both stock trading and deposit interest rates are so volatile, which are reflected on stock volatility very deeply.

Table 7-4. Ranking of predicting factors for high return volatility and possible crises in emerging stock markets

Variables	Mexico	Korea	Malaysia	Turkey	South Africa	Average Rank
Stock volume	1	1	1	1	1	1
Exchange rate to USD	1	3	5	1	1	2
Tokyo price index	4	1	6			3
London price index				1	1	
Deposit interest rate	7	6	1	1	1	4
Bond volume	1	5	1	5	6	5
NYSE price index	5	4	1	6	7	6
Inflation rate	6	7	7	7	5	7

Source: Sabri, 2004.

Table 7-5. Summary of the adopted regression models in the selected emerging stock exchanges

Stock Exchanges	Adopted regression models for predicting stock return volatility
Mexico	Stock volume, currency exchange rate, bond volume
Korean	Stock trading volume, Tokyo stock price index
Malaysia	Stock volume, deposit interest rate, bond volume NYSE stock price index
Turkey	Stock volume, deposit interest rate, currency exchange rate and London stock price index
South Africa	Stock volume, deposit interest rate, currency exchange rate, and London stock price index

Source: Sabri, 2004.

Empirical Investigation in Developed Stock Markets

Another empirical investigation that was conducted by the author (Sabri, 2007) to state possible causes of high return volatility and stock markets' crises in developed economies, using a sample of seven stock developed markets, and covering a period of thirty-six months (1998 to 2000). In order to determine the most predicting variables that have significant influence on increasing stock volatility and in initiating a stock market crisis compared to other factors. The selected causes are the most reported causes of increasing stock volatility and may be expressed in quantitative data. They include the monthly changes in: stock trading volume, national inflation rate, the government bond yield, the trade value of bonds, the national currency exchange rate to USD, the treasury bill rate, and the national deposit interest rate.

The developed stock markets include thirty stock markets and formed 91% of the world value traded. The selected sample will include the top developed stock market, but it excludes the first three markets including USA, UK, and Japan. The first three markets are reported by various studies as the most influential to other markets during high price volatility and crises periods. Accordingly, including such markets makes the analysis too complicated; therefore, this study includes seven developed markets.

The backward multiple-regression analysis technique was used, to examine the relationship between monthly changes of stock price indices as dependent variable and the associated selected seven predicting measures as independent variables. These are: the monthly changes of national stock volume as expressed in percentages, deposit interest rates for national currency as expressed in percentages, bond market volume as expressed in percentages, government bond yield as expressed in percentages, national exchange rates against US dollar as expressed in percentages, treasury bill rates as expressed in percentages, and national inflation rate as expressed in percentages. The time serial data is related to the monthly changes during the 1998, 1999, and 2000 years. The used data for this research was based on two groups of sources: the World Federation of Exchanges Database, Paris (2003), and the IMF International Financial Statistics monthly books (1998-2001) which are related to national inflation rates, deposit interest rates, government bond yield, and treasury bill rates. Summary of the findings of the study (Sabri 2007) is presented in Table 7-6.

Table 7-6. Rank of predictive variables in the weighted average of selected developed stock exchanges

Variables	Average Rank
Stock volume	2
Bond volume	7
Exchange rate to USD	1
Deposit interest rate	3
Government bond yield	4
Inflation rate	6
Treasury bill rate	5
Rank *1* is the most predictive variable	

To compare between the adopted regression models related to the most predictive variables, Table 7-7 presents a summary of the forecasting variables based on the adopted models as concluded in this study. This indicates that exchange rate was included in the adopted predicting models for six out of the seven selected developed markets. Other models included stock trading volume, bond trading volume and deposit interest.

To look into the overall view, this study shows that the currency exchanges rate, stock volume and deposit interest rate respectively are found as the most predictive variables as reported by the majority of the selected stock developed markets economies. These three variables were the least to be removed among the seven predictive factors during the regression analysis models in the majority of developed stock markets. In addition, the currency exchange rate was ranked as number one in all selected predictive factors to stock price volatility. It is found to be the most forecasting variable in six developed stock markets. Followed by stock volume and deposit interest rate which were ranked as number two and three respectively. On the other side, changes in bond volume, inflation rate, and treasury bill rate were the least predictive factors in which their average ranks were the least (from five to seven) among the total used variables in the majority of stock markets.

Table 7-7. Summary of the adopted regression models for stock market volatility in the selected developed stock exchanges

Stock Exchanges	Adopted regression models for predicting stock return volatility
Amsterdam	Deposit interest rate, stock volume and bond volume
Toronto	Exchange rate and deposit interest rate
Milan	Exchange rate and stock volume
Frankfurt	Exchange rate and stock volume
Madrid	Exchange rate
Zurich	Exchange rate
Paris	Exchange rate

Source: Sabri, 2007.

COMPARISON BETWEEN OPINION SURVEYS AND EMPIRICAL STUDIES

It is relevant to make a comparison between the opinion of experts and empirical investigation regarding stock market stability. Summary of the four presented studies are shown in Table 7-8, which reported the most possible factors of initiating instability in the world stock markets during certain trading events.

Table 7-8. The possible adverse factors on stock market stability as reported by Opinion surveys and empirical investigations

	The most effective factor	Rank
Opinion surveys about developed markets	Falling of the major stock price indices	1
	Trading out side stock exchanges	2
	Using computerized system in trading	3
	Effect of derivatives market on cash market	4
Empirical study about developed markets	Changing of exchange rate	1
	Changing of trading volume volatility	2
	Changing in interest rate	3
	Changing in bond yields	4
Empirical study about emerging markets	Changing of trading volume volatility	1
	Changing of exchange rate	2
	Changing in international price indices	3
	Changing in interest rate	4

It indicates that the experts believe that the most risky factors that related to the negative effect of falling stock price indices in major markets, trading outside stock exchanges, switching to computerized trading system and the possible adverse effect of derivatives markets. Finally, it may be stated that for both developed and emerging stock market stability, there are three major factors which have a significant effect on the stability of the world markets, including the exchange rate of currency, the volume of trading, and the national interest rate. Both empirical studies and opinion surveys presented the significant role of falling stock price indices in the leading stock markets to other stock markets. The rest of this chapter will be devoted to explore such factors that have possible effect in the world stock market stability in more details.

Falling of Major Stock Price Indexes

The national stock exchanges are moving towards increasing linkages to other international stock exchanges. The increasing linkages have extended from developed stock markets to other emerging stock markets, as well as from stock markets to other financial and banking systems. Various studies examined the stock market linkages and the majority of these related studies were intended to report whether there is a positive or a negative correlation among stock price volatility, cross-markets in different times and under different conditions, and discussed the stability of the stock volatility over time. Other studies discussed the issue between stock markets in various times, periods and conditions, before, after and around the 1987 stock market crash.

The majority of the related studies found that there is an increasing correlation of the world stock market indices. In addition, correlations increase sharply in the case of falling prices and in periods of market crisis. Examples of these studies: Wu and Su (1998) found that there is significant dynamic relation that exists among four major stock markets including US, Japan, Britain, and Hong Kong, in addition, the correlation among stock markets has been increased considerably after 1987 and it has been increasing in the recent years. Bracker and Koch (1999) reported that international equity markets move together more when the market is volatile or falling. Janakiramanan and Lamba, (1998) found that the US markets influences all other Pacific- Basin Stock markets except the market of Indonesia. Longin and Solnik (2001) found that the correlation among stock markets increases in bear markets, but not in bull markets.

However, it should be mentioned here that the issue of increasing linkages among stock price indices has become more significant in the last few years. This finding was reported by a recent study conducted by the author (Sabri, 2002) who indicated that there were significant changes during the nineties arising from introducing liberal regulatory rules, increasing foreign trading, increasing in number of cross listed firms and equity portfolio flows. The study found that there were significant positive increases from 1994 to 1998, in the degree of correlation between the majorities of the associated markets from 38 associations to 116 associations in the selected sample of the study as presented in Table 7-9.

The study also indicated that the situation had significantly changed from 1994 to 1998 and there was a significant correlation between the stock market indices. A significant correlation was also found between the majority of both developed and emerging stock markets. This includes Malaysia, Taiwan, Argentine, Mexico, Greece and Turkey had significant correlation with other emerging and developing stock markets. In addition, the correlation between each pairs of the selected stock markets had increased significantly as shown in Table 7-10.

Table 7-9. Number of associated markets between stock price indices

Stock Exchanges Indices	Significant Correlation in 1994	Significant Correlation in 1998
Australia	6	11
Japan	2	4
Hong Kong	5	7
Singapore	2	8
Toronto	3	11
London	2	8
New York	6	13
Germany	0	5
South Africa	2	8
Korea	0	0
Turkey	0	4
Greece	0	2
Malaysia	2	8
Taiwan	0	10
Argentina	5	9
Mexico	3	9
Total	38	116

Source: Sabri, 2002.

Table 7-10. List of stock market pairs that witnessed increase more than 100% in the degree of Correlation between the year 1994 and 1998

Stock Market Pairs	Correlation in 1994	Correlation in 1998
Australia - South Africa	.135	.791
London - South Africa	.377	.744
New York - South Africa	.102	.854
Australia – Malaysia	.154	.736
Hong Kong – Malaysia	.378	.727
New York – Malaysia	.194	.712
Singapore – Mexico	.121	.667
Singapore – Taiwan	.227	.683
Singapore – Argentine	.321	.748
Australia-Singapore	.280	.639
Hong Kong-Singapore	.402	.909
Toronto- London	.457	.832
Singapore- New York	.328	.743
Japan- Germany	.119	.739
South Africa- Turkey	.063	.536
Malaysia- Taiwan	.290	.859
South Africa- Argentine	.021	.834
Argentine – Malaysia	.121	.633
Malaysia- Mexico	.032	.620
Mexico- Taiwan	.330	.659

Source: Sabri, 2002.

It indicated an increase in about 30 pairs of stock market of more than 100% in the degree of correlation of price index movement between the year 1994 and the year 1998. Many of the stock market pairs showed negative correlation in 1994 such as Toronto- South Africa, Germany- Toronto, Germany- New York, Turkey- Greece, South Africa- Mexico, and South Africa- Greece that had significant correlation of the stock price movements during 1998. However, increasing linkages is supposed to increase data dissemination and thus increase stock market efficiency. But with the existing cross-markets volatility transmission phenomenon, increasing linkages should be scrutinized carefully. Accordingly, the increase of linkages provides some disadvantages such as a mistake or volatility surprises in one market may be transferred to other stock markets (King, 1990). The free capital flow and increasing linkages may transfer the volatility of inflation and exchange rate from one market to another as that happened to the financial markets in Mexico during 1994 and East Asian region during the years 1997-1998. In addition, other studies found that there are world-leading stock markets such as US, and Japan, which have significant influence on the world stock markets during periods of volatility. In addition, some leading stock markets may have an impact on a specific region or twins. Accordingly, it may be concluded that increasing linkages of the world stock market prices will be more serious in the next coming crises of stock trading.

Automation of the World Stock Market

The second aspect, which was considered as a risky factor, is the automation of stock exchanges. In the last decade, the majority of the world stock exchanges adopted in one way or another electronic trading system as follows.

First: switching the world stock exchanges from floor trading to partially automate trading system. The partially automated systems refer to the system by which orders are processed electronically, while the conclusion is completed through personnel interferences of brokers or dealers to wrap the deals.

Second: switching the world stock exchanges from partially automated to fully automated screen system, in which the various processes of stock trading are implemented electronically.

Third: Using internet services, receiving orders from customers by brokers, but ending in the traditional stock exchanges to conclude the trade.

Forth: Using alternative trading system in which matching for orders implemented based on a computerized system, which will do the match electronically, as non- discretionary action.

The fear of experts from computerizing the world stock market as presented here is coming from their experiences that the personnel handling process of stock trading and judgment in emergencies may be better than automation, which has less control or interfering. This perception of the necessity of judgment and interference, in case of stock trading emergencies, is built on some experiences when the computerized stock system could not process orders during panic trading. As what happened in some European stock exchanges, when the computerized system had been broken down during some severe falling price periods due to the heavily received selling and buying orders. The fears of the world stock experts dealing in the stock markets from automation is supported by some empirical studies which reported that automation of stock trading may increases price volatility of stock markets during periods of instable trading.

Trading Outside Stock Exchanges

Another possible risky factor is the trading outside of stock exchanges, which is considered as one of the most risky factors at a certain event by both surveys. Trading outside the stock exchanges occurred in the following cases:

- In case of trading bearer shares: many investors and banks usually send a part of their trading orders that received from their customers to the stock exchange to be traded their, while keeping the other part to be executive outside based on the stated price in the exchange, in order to save the cost of trading, and they may use the own portfolios to carry out buying orders.
- There are several legislations, permitting listed securities to be traded outside the stock exchange, either over the OTC market or even over non-regular markets.
- In case of using alternative trading system through special electronic networks as supplementary to the stock exchange, where the buying and selling orders matched in non-discretionary manner.

Trading outside exchanges will defuse the automatic or judgmental measures used in the world stock markets to control price volatility such as price limits, safe-harbor rules, margin requirements of settlements, circuit breakers, and trading halts, inside the stock exchanges. The fear of experts that the moment that the traditional stock exchange is closes, it will continue outside the exchange. This issue is going to be more critical, after the fact that some major countries accepted and organized other alternatives for trading outside the exchanges as presented in a pervious chapter. This method trades in stocks by bringing buying and selling orders to the system by means of non-discretionary rules set by the system operator. It is considered a further step in relying more and more on non- discretionary instruments, compared to stock trading in the automated stock exchanges.

High Volatility of National Exchange Rate

The fluctuation of the national exchange currency rates is increasing significantly in the majority of the world economies. This is due to many factors including removing of restrictions used to be imposed on transfer of funds cross boarders, and due to advancement of technology, which led to use electronic transferring of funds cross-countries. In addition, due to the existed significant differences of interest rates for different currencies. To consider the period from1997 to 2000, which witnessed the Asian financial market, it may found that there was a movement of national currency exchange rate against USD up and down within a large range. However, the emerging countries witnessed higher volatility regarding exchange rates than developed countries. For example, the changes in exchange rates of all emerging countries moved more than 75%. In case of national currency of Turkey, it moved more than six times against the USD. For developed countries the exchange rates against USD moved up and down from 13% to 35% during the period (WFE, 2006).

In the previous chapter, we discussed how changing or devaluation of national currency exchange rate against other currencies might initiate a national or regional stock market crisis. In this chapter we reported that changing of currency exchange rate not only affected the emerging stock market, but it is the first predicted variable of stock return in the majority of the world stock markets, and mainly for developed markets. In spite of the fact that the role of national currency may be different between developed and emerging markets. In addition, recent studies indicated that not only there is a significant effect of exchange rate on stock prices volatility, but also, vise versa; which means that a market may lead the another market.

However, it should be noted that changes of currency rate may have a negative or positive effect on stock prices and volatility. In addition, changes of national exchange rate against a foreign currency may have a positive effect on stock prices and volatility, while it may have a negative effect in case of changing national exchange rate against another foreign currency (Wu, 2001). The relationship between stock prices and currency exchange rate has been increasing significantly in the last decade and became more materialized in the majority of the world stock markets, especially after the financial crisis in South Asia in 1997. Changes in exchange rate against other currencies may reflect various fundamental values. This includes official devaluation, inflation rate, currency demand and supply, changing of cash flow of foreign portfolios, and gain or loss of international competition to stock and financial markets.

For examples: Nieh and Lee (2001) reported that currency depreciation drags stock return in German market. Granger et al. (2000) found that exchange rates lead stock prices in South Korean market. Ajayi, et al. (1998) concluded that stock and currency markets are integrated in the developed economies. Mahajan and Futrado (1996) reported that listed firms during fixed exchange regime reported greater abnormal returns compared to listed firms during floating exchange rate regime.

High Volatility of Stock Trading Volume

The impact of volume volatility on stock returns is based on the concept that changing prices need volume to move. It works based on the interpretation that the dissemination of information about trading of stock markets as expressed by volume and size of transactions create the positive aspect, thus receive reactions from speculators. Accordingly, the high volatility of stock prices and crises may be created as a consequence of volume volatility and trading activities. Both developed and emerging stock markets witnessed a high percentage of volatility with average monthly changes in trading value up to 50% for developed stock markets as presented in Table 7-11. While this ratio is so higher in many emerging stock markets with monthly changes up or down more than 100%. The high volatility of trading volume is a significant factor that may create instability in certain trade periods; thus leading to a stock market crisis.

The impacts of volatility volume on stock return volatility are supported by many studies. Such studies reported that stock-trading volume leads to stock price changes and found significant relationships between volume and stock volatility. For example: Jones, et. al, (1994) found that the positive volatility-volume relation documented by numerous researchers reflects the positive relation between volatility and number of transactions. Basci et al.(1996) reported that stock price levels and trading volume in Turkish stock markets are co-integrated. In addition Saatcioglu and Starks (1998) reported in their study that volume leads stock prices volatility in Latin American stock markets.

Table 7-11. Monthly Changes of Traded Value in selected Developed and Emerging Stock Markets. Between November and December 2006

Exchange	%Change
American SE	-11.5%
Bermuda SE	-44.1%
Buenos Aires SE	35.8%
NYSE	-14.9%
Irish	- 30.5%
Australian SE	-21.8%
Colombo SE	-70.4%
Korea Exchange	-13.8%
New Zealand Exchange	-29.4%
Osaka SE	-8.0%
Cyprus Stock Exchange	125%
Shanghai SE	49.4%
Athens Exchange	-17.9%
Borsa Italiana	-28.3%
Cairo & Alexandria	37.4%
Deutsche Börse	-26.8%
Mauritius SE	226.1%
Tehran SE	117.2%

Source: WFE, 2006.

High Volatility of National Interest Rate

As indicated in the above studies the interest rate is considered as one of the major factors affecting stock market returns. The world economy witnessed a high volatility of interest rate during the last decade before falling to its minimum level. The monthly changes percentages of interest rate based on the previous month ranged between 9% and 105% for various countries. The minimum- maximum interest rate during the period from 1998 to the end of 2000 ranged between 0.38% to 3.11 in case of Switzerland for example, which represents a deep falling of interest rates, for other developed countries the interest rate was dropped but not to the same level like Switzerland. For all mentioned emerging countries the interest rates dropped sharply during the period. For example, the interest rate in Turkey ranged between 38% and 106% during the period from 1997 to 2000 (IMF, 1997-2001). However, dropping of interest rates may be considered as a stabilizing factor regarding stock market, but the volatility of interest rates may be reflected significantly on the stock market, which increases the volatility of stock returns.

The above conclusions accord with several empirical studies, which reported the significant effect of interest rate on the volatility of stock market prices. They found that an increase in official discount rates are associated with negative abnormal returns on stock market and vise versa, and reported significant linkages between increases in interest rates and adversely affect on stock market as well between the volatility of both interest rate and stock market prices (Nikiforos and Sawhney, 2002; Kaen et al. 1997; and Kearney and Daly, 1998).

CONCLUSION

Empirical investigations as well as experts' opinions regarding causes of stock market crises and high volatility raise more questions rather than find clear-cut answers. The main causes of irrational movements of stock market prices, and why the world stock market indices move so closely during falling prices periods have not been clarified yet. However, based on both surveys of stock market experts as well as empirical investigation studies of developed and emerging markets regarding factors of stock market stability the following conclusion may be drown out:

- There are common factors as well as unique factors in the different stock markets that have significant influence on stock return volatility, which may initiate a stock market crisis.
- The common factors include national exchange rate, deposit interest rates and stock volume are the most common predictive factors compared to other factors.
- The international possible causes are due to the phenomena of volatility spillovers and to the impact of international leading markets on other national markets.
- Foreign trading is a cause of stock market crisis in emerging markets as reported by various empirical reports and official reports, but it is not the case regarding the developed stock markets as perceived by the stock market experts.
- The stock market experts agreed on conditions that may lead to a stock market crisis in certain events, while they disagreed on the elements, which may minimize the probability of evolving a stock market crises
- The order of predicting factors of stock market volatility concerning emerging economies is different from that related to developed markets, with the exception of inflation rate, which was considered as the least predicting factor in both emerging and developed markets.
- Stock trading volume, interest rate and currency exchange rate were the most common predicting variables for both emerging and developed stock markets. However, stock volume was more significant in the case of emerging markets compared to developed markets, while it was the opposite for exchange rate.
- The impact of stock volume volatility on stock returns is based on local fundament data as well as foreign trading, and other international factors.
- The exchange rate was found to be less significant than stock trading volume as a predicting factor in emerging stock markets in emerging economies compared to the developing economies. This is because that currency exchange rate in some emerging

markets is controlled by government policies during certain periods. However, the devaluation of national currency or falling of the exchange rate against foreign currency may cause a stock market crisis in emerging economies during certain events.

REFERENCES

Ajayi, Richard A., Josepg Friedman and Seyed M. Mehdian (1998). "On the relationship between stock returns and exchange rates: tests of Granger causality" *Global Finance Journal* 9 (2); 241-251.

Basci, Erdem, Suheyla Ozyildinm and Kursat Aydogan (1996) "A note on price-volume dynamics in an emerging stock market" *Journal of Banking & Finance* 20; 389-400.

Bracker, Kevin and Paul D. Koch (1999) "Economic Determinants of the Correlation Structure Across International Equity Markets" *Journal of Economic and Business* 51; 444-471.

Choe, Hyuk, Bong- Chan Kho and Rene M. Stulz (1999) "Do Foreign Investors Destabilize Stock Markets? The Korean Experience in 1997" *Journal of Financial Economics* 54; 227-264.

Cooper, I., and E. Kaplanis, (1994) "Home bias in equity portfolios, inflation hedging and international capital market equilibrium" *Review of Financial Studies* 7; 45-60.

Faccio, Mara and Larry H. P. Lang (2002) "The ultimate ownership of Western European corporations: *Journal of Financial Economics* 65; 356-395.

FESE (2002) Share Ownership Structure in Europe (Federation of European Securities Exchanges, Economics & Statistics Subcommittee).

Granger, Clive W. J., Bwo-Nung Huang and Chin-Wei Yang (2000) "A bivariate causality between stock prices and exchange rates: evidence from recent Asian flu" *The Quarterly Review of Economics and finance* 40; 337-354.

IMF (1997-2001) *International Financial Statistics* (International Monetary Fund, Washington, D. C).

IMF, (2000). *International Capital Markets: Development, Prospects and Key Policy Issues,* (World Economic and Financial Surveys, Washington, D. C., September).

Janakiramanan Sundaram, and Asjeet S., Lamba (1998) "An empirical examination of linkages between Pacific-Basin stock markets" *Journal of International Markets, Institutions and Money* 8; 155-173.

Jones, Charles M., Gautam Kaul and Marc L. Lipson (1994). "Transactions, Volume, and Volatility" *Review of Financial Studies* 7 (4); 641-651.

Kaen, Fred R., Heidemarie C. Sherman and Hassan Tehranian (1997). "The effects of Bundesbank discount and Lombard rate changes on German bank stocks" *Journal of Multinational Financial Management* 7 (1); 1-25.

Kearney C. and K. Daly (1998). "The causes of stock volatility in Australia" *Applied Financial Economics* 8; 597-608.

King, Mervyn A. (1990) "Transmission of Volatility between Stock Markets" *The Review of Financial Studies* 4, (1); 5-44.

Lemmon, Michael L. and Karl V. Lins (2003) "Ownership structure, corporate governance and firm value; evidence from the East Asian Financial Crisis" *Journal of Finance* 58; 1445-1468.

Longin, Francois and Bruno Solink (2001) "Extreme Correlation of International Equity Markets" *Journal of Finance.* 56; 649-676.

Mahajan, Arvind and Eugene P. Furtado (1996) "Exchange rate regimes and international market segmentation: evidence from pricing effects of international listing" *Global Finance Journal* 7 (2); 153-168.

Nieh, Chien- Chung and Cheng- Few Lee (2001) "Dynamic relationship between stock prices and exchange rates for G-7 countries" *The Quarterly Review of Economics and Finance* 41; 477-490.

Nikiforos, Laopodis and Bansi L. Sawhney (2002). "Dynamic interactions between Main Street and Wall street" *The Quarterly Review of Economics and Finance* 42; 803-815.

OECD (2003) *Survey of corporate governance developments in OECD countries* (December, Organization For Economic Co-operation and Development, France).

OECD (2004) *Experience from the regional corporate governance roundtables* (January, Organization For Economic Co-operation and Development, France).

Parrino, Robert, Richard W. Sias and Laura T. Starks (2003) "Voting with their feet: institutional ownership changes around forced CEO turnover" *Journal of Financial Economics* 68; 3-46.

Saatcioglu, Kemal and Laura T. Starks (1999) "The stock price- volume relationship in emerging stock markets: the case of Latin America *International Journal of Forecasting* 14; 215-225.

Sabri, Nidal Rashid (1995a) "Stabilization of Stock Markets; the Case of the Frankfurt Exchange" *Journal of Multinational Financial Management* 5 (3) ; 23-32.

Sabri, Nidal Rashid (1995b) "Experts' opinions towards the stock market stability during the stock market crisis" *International Journal of Commerce and Management* 5 (2); 130-146.

Sabri, Nidal Rashid (2002) "Increasing linkages between global stock markets and price volatility" *Research in International Business & Finance* 16; 349-373.

Sabri, Nidal Rashid (2004). "Stock returns volatility and market crisis in emerging economies" *Review of Accounting and Finance* 3, No. 3; 59-83.

Sabri, Nidal Rashid (2007) "Causes of high volatility and stock market crises in the developed economies" (Manuscript under publication).

WFE (2006) World Federation of Exchanges Data Base (available on line http://www.world-exchanges.org).

World Bank (2004) *Global Development Finance: Analysis and summary tables* (World Bank, Washington D. C.).

Wu, Chunchi and Yong- Chern Su (1998) "Dynamic Relations among International Stock Markets" *International Review of Economics and Finance* 7; 64-84.

Wu, Ying (2001) "Exchange rates, stock prices, and money markets: evidence from Singapore" *Journal of Asian Economics* 12; 445-458.

Chapter 8

EPILOGUE

INTRODUCTION

The international stock market became more and more important, and witnessed significant changes during the last decade. The stock market may be considered as the most important sector in the world economy. It has been connected with almost all social security provident, and pension funds and programs, which cover the majority of the world employees and became a giant sector in the world economy. It is also, connected to the wealth of hundred million of stockholders all over the world. Bearing in mind that the world stock markets include about 50,000 securities, thousands of brokers and dealers, and intermediate agencies, hundreds of million of stockholders with an annual trading value of about $ 71 trillion. The price index of the world stock markets of the WFE members increased about four times in the last ten years between 1995 and 2005 (S&P, 2003 and WFE, 2006). This is also applied to the stock exchanges as trading places, which are witnessing the most prosperity period, as an industry with a new record of annual revenues, net income, with a total owner equity of about $ 18 billion as accomplished in 2004 (WFE, 2005). This is done after moving the stock exchange legal entity from being a public or not for profit organization to be a profit oriented company, which listed itself in the national stock exchange for the majority of the world stock markets. Finally, it became a sophisticated trading process, in which a security may be traded in different ways with different instruments and derivatives, with multi currencies, and under different jurisdictions and cross borders.

These new developments created new challenges reflected in the stability, liquidity, and efficiency of the world stock markets. To face such challenges; regulators, economists, related officials, regional, and global commissions, and academics started to examine the related issues and propose many principles, regulations, standards, best practices and resolutions. To avoid the adverse affects that might accompany these developments, several practices and laws in the world stock markets have been introduced, through conducting research studies, technical reports, and opinion surveys. So many empirical studies have been conducted during the last decade, in the majority of the world stock markets, covering most of the related issues of stock trading. The number of empirical research conducted about various aspects of the stock markets is more than number of studies conducted in any economic issue. However, the majority of these empirical studies produce no conclusive findings concerning the majority of the world stock markets issues, which mainly raised questions rather than found answers or practical solutions.

Regardless of the new practices introduced to the world stock markets, an individual stock market is supposed to work under relevant and efficient conditions and merits. The relevant merits and conditions include:

- Low cost of trading and transactions, this may be measured in basis points.
- High level of liquidity: the liquidity of stock market may be measured as a percentage increase or decrease of stock price based on changes in trading volume.
- High level of transparency
- Protecting inventors' interests
- Protecting other related parties' interests.
- Simplicity of processing and regulations.
- Relevant level of efficiency with less control measures and formal interruptions.
- Working under relevant laws and regulations to meet the stated objectives of the stock markets.
- Increasing information sharing between all concerned parties, to assure a fair pricing mechanism.
- Stability of stock trading with moderate level of volatility and risk. This may be measured by intraday volatility of up and down prices. The average normal stock price volatility is below 5%.

This chapter discusses and synthesis the major issues: positive and negative aspects of the world stock markets, based on the above stated measures and presents suggestions to improve the efficiency and stability of the world stock markets.

Positive Aspects of the World Stock Trading

The new practices and developments in the areas of laws, regulations, methods, environment and trading activities as well as working in a global context have positive, as well negative influences on the merits of the world stock markets, which may be summarized in the next two sections.

It Became a Global Mature Market

Today, the world stock market reached a new level of maturity and development as expressed by various measures including:

- Increasing the capitalization value of stock markets to the GDP ratio in the majority of the world emerging and developed economies.
- There are new records of the size of stock trading as expressed by the annual trading values, the turnover ratio, the numbers of listed companies and securities, in the majority of the world stock markets.

- Increasing of liberalizations, globalization and integration aspects cross boarders and in the majority of the world stock markets.
- There is a rapid increasing in size, and types of cross boarder stock trading in the last few years.
- Migration of many local firms from both developed and emerging countries, to be traded in foreign stock markets looking for less cost of trading and more liquidity.
- Increasing number of securities listed in foreign stock exchanges.
- There are now many national securities which are traded more in foreign stock exchanges than in their home exchanges as expressed by trade value.
- There is an increased in types of traded products, derivatives, indexed products and funds, which make stock market more sophisticated and volatile.

Moreover, there is a significant change in the mechanism of stock trading due to the advancement in technology, communications, and asset management industry which changed the major features of stock markets. For example, the trading of stocks is no longer exercised in an exclusive stock exchange under one jurisdiction. The stock markets have been witnessing major developments in legal, marketing, financial, and management aspects. Various new practices were incorporated to meet the new challenges of the world stock markets, and to face the incoming era of dissolving the jurisdiction and political borders.

Low Cost of Trading

The world stock market has been witnessing a reduction in the cost of trading. Reducing transaction costs of trading has a positive impact on stock trading volume. This is due to the high competition between the world stock exchanges. The competition is also existed between the traditional stock exchanges and the alternative ways of trading using the network electronic systems. Moreover, the competition is increasing rapidly between the developed and emerging stock exchanges to attract foreign securities to be cross listed in their exchanges and for foreign international public offerings. This situation creates high pressures on national stock exchanges as well as on legislations to reduce the cost components of stock trading.

The total transactions costs of stock trading consists of two parts: First; explicit costs, such as taxes, commissions of brokers, fees collected by stock exchanges for listing and trading, custodial and depository fees, and transfer fees. These components of transaction cost may be reduced to increase competitions by regulators. Accordingly, many jurisdictions reduced or eliminated taxes that have been imposed on stock trading recently. The majority of the world jurisdictions reduced the fees and commissions of stock trading. The USA removed the stated commissions and lifted for negotiations. Second; the implicit costs, which includes execution and opportunity costs, these are known as indirect cost, or as market impact cost. It is the average cost of trading in a specific stock exchange. It may be calculated in different ways using benchmarks of post traded prices, opening, closing and high and low price limits.

The cost of trading in stock markets now is lower than that in previous periods, but it still varies among the world stock markets. For example, the total trading cost, which includes the commissions, fees, and market impact cost ranged between 26.60 basis points in case of France, which represents the lowest cost of stock trading, and 179.59 basis points as in case of the Czech Republic which recorded the highest cost based on the Elkins/ McSherry survey. In addition, the average world cost of stock commission decreased from 35.26 BP in 1997 to 25.5 BP in 1999, the average world stock fees also decreased from 9.02 BP to 3.94 BP for the same period (IFC, 1998 and S&P 2000). The cost of transactions in developed and leading stock markets is much lower than that of the emerging and small stock exchanges. However, the majority of the emerging stock markets have a cost of trading of 75 BP or above, while the majority of developed stock exchanges have a trading cost of 50 BP or below (Standard & Poor's, 2000). Another factor participated in the reduction of the cost of trading is the automation of the world stock exchange. The majority of the world stock exchanges switched to automated screen trading instead of floor trading, this leads to cost efficiency and reduces the cost of trading (Jain, 2003; and Hasan et al. 2003). In addition, the cost of trading is expected to be even lower due to accepting alternative trading methods by many jurisdictions.

Low Return of Alternative Investments

There are four types of investors in the world stock market: the financial institutions, non-financial institutions, public sector, and individual investors. Financial institutions include the pension funds, mutual funds, insurance companies, banks and any other forms of financial institutions. The non- financial institutions include all business firms which hold financial assets as long-term investments or as marketable securities. The public sector includes central, local, and independent semi-government agencies holding financial assets mainly for permanent purposes. The individual investors may be connected through direct investment in stock markets, or through mutual and investments firms such as mutual open and closed end funds. The individual, who invests directly in financial assets, follows the prices and trends aiming to improve return, represents the fourth group of investors. The investment share of particpants in the world financial systems may be estimated roughly as 40% for financial institutions, 40% for individual investors, and 20% for public sector and non- financial firms.

Financial institutions and individual investors are changing the components of their portfolios of investments more than public and non-financial institutions, in order to achieve maximum returns with moderate risk. The majority of the two groups are diversifying their portfolios by investing in national as well as foreign markets using various instruments of securities. Both groups are watching the financial markets and stay ready to sell or buy when it is appropriate; thus moving their financial assets among the alternative list of financial assets. The list of financial assets includes the stock groups (cash market, warrants, options and futures, indexed options and futures, and exchange-traded funds) bonds market (government treasury, notes, and bonds, corporate bonds, and forms of foreign bonds) and various types of saving and long term deposit accounts in banks.

Mutual funds as well as individual investors, usually diversify their portfolios, including home stocks and their attached derivatives and warrants products, international based stocks, home government bonds, home corporate bonds, and foreign government and corporate bonds. However, the majority of these two groups are investing mainly in stocks rather than bonds. For example, 86% of the world mutual fund assets, 92% of Asian Pacific mutual funds, and 83% of emerging mutual funds are investing in stocks (Kaminsky, et al. 2001). The stock markets are supposed to give high return but with high risk, and visa verse for other alternatives such as bonds and deposits in banks. Some believe that an investment of pension funds and retirements plans in stock markets is too risky; therefore, investments in various forms of bonds should be included.

Accordingly, significant competition exists among such alternatives of stock, bonds, and bank saving programs, at least for individual investors and various financial institutions that are looking for moderate risk, but with acceptable level of return. Fortunately, it has been for the benefit of stock market, in the last few years that the bond markets and savings in banks offer the least returns and yields. Accordingly, it is unlikely to shift investments from stock markets to other alternative markets. This situation may keep the stock markets improving with moderate stability and less shocks compared to the last decade. However, this situation may change the moment that interest rates increase significantly.

Reforming Corporate Governance and Laws

During the last decade, the majority of the world countries implemented reforms in one or more aspects of corporate governance regulations as presented in a previous chapter. They were mainly concerned with modernizing corporate governance codes and regulations. These changes were implemented in both developed and emerging countries, which adopted guidelines or code of best practices. In addition, there is an international acceptance for the common principles of corporate governance including rights of shareholders, and their role in corporate governance, disclosure and transparency requirements, and responsibility of the board of directors. (OECD, 1999 and 2004).

In spite of the fact that there is no direct relationship between a good organized corporate governance and the performance of the respective corporation in the stock market, there is a general perception that good governance will be reflected in stock prices and trading volume. A McKinsey's Survey reported that investors would pay a premium for a well governed company up to 30% in some emerging countries. In addition, companies with a high score of corporate governance index enjoy higher market price to book ratio, and a firm market value may increase up to 12% by moving from worse to best in elements of good corporate governance (Campos, et, al, 2002). Moreover, a global investor opinion survey conducted in 2002 reported that the majority of investors are ready to pay a premium for a company with good governance standard, the premiums averaged between 12% to 14% in North America and Western European, 20% to 25% in Asia and Latin America, and 30% in Eastern Europe and Africa (GCGF survey, 2002).

Beside that, the majority of the world jurisdictions witnessed significant changes in their corporate laws concerning other aspects of corporate laws. An extensive debate in both developed and emerging jurisdictions regarding many corporate issues and aspects is being under way. The aim of modernizing laws is to create the balance between related parties, including management (the agency), stockholders, creditors, investors, and between liquidity and protection of investors. Other issues also are considered in adopting and modernizing the corporate laws, including the issue of competitions with other markets, facilitating their access to the international markets, the disclosure requirements, the minimum share capital requirements, the issue of controlled companies by minority stakeholders, the market abuse concerning trading in securities.

NEGATIVE ASPECTS OF THE WORLD STOCK MARKETS

On the other side, various negative aspects may be attached to the new incorporated practices in the world stock markets. The negative aspects include the inefficient global integration, impairment of market efficiency, less stable market, market fragmentation, adverse effects of new legal changes, adverse effects of new introduced practices. However, these negative aspects do not exist in all periods of stock trading, but they may be materialized and have adverse impact during periods of deep falling prices and unstable periods of trading, such as in the case of extreme high return volatility. The following paragraphs will explore more about these issues.

Inefficient Integration

It may be concluded that there are various globalization aspects which existed currently in the world stock markets. Such aspects are becoming a reality due to the advancements of technology, and communications, and after series of changes in the world jurisdictions regarding liberalization of stock trading. The aspects of globalizations include removing the majority of restrictions imposed on foreign trading, the integration of regional stock exchanges and settlements agencies, the increasing size of cross- boarder stock market transactions, increasing the share of foreign trading, and increasing the size and value of the cross-listed securities and international public offerings.

Nevertheless, the integration process of the world stock markets is far from being completed or even efficient, as observed by stock market behavior in the last decade. Accordingly, the question here is whether increasing linkages and integration of the world markets is considered a blessing or cress. Other questions may also arise in this regards, such as: What is the benefit of liberalization of emerging stock markets which justifies the high risk placed on their financial systems ?, Is the liberalization of emerging stock markets came too early or implemented too fast ?. Finally, what is the benefit of integration and liberalization as long as it has serious negative aspects?. Such negative aspects may be summarized as follows:

- Increasing the possibility of transmitting high volatility and market crises between stock markets.
- Weakening the internal factors which shape the national stock markets, in favor of external factors, in which national governments and related authorities have no control whatsoever.
- Stock trading process has become more and more controlled by markets rather than by official national agencies.
- Foreign investors share the locals in playing the critical role in the stability of stock market.
- External factors may be more considerable than internal factors in case of weak fundamentals, which may have adverse influence on directing stock market prices and stability.

- Increasing the risk of contagion phenomenon through transferring mistakes from one market to others.
- A high competitive pressure may be produced on local stock exchange due transferring national securities to be listed and traded abroad.
- The process of regionalization may be considered as a step towards globalization from one side, but it may lead to discrimination against economies outside the region, and thus leading to add new restrictions rather than remove them.
- The integration aspects that occurred in the world stock market did not eliminate the fact that any traded security has a home base and is supposed to work under specific national jurisdiction regulations; this home base reality applies to all related parties involved in the world stock markets as well as the to new alternative trading methods of stock trading.
- Integration of the world stock markets decreases the geographical, currency and customers' behavior bases of market segmentation, and thus reduces the benefit of the diversification to the minimum level, without creating an efficient integrated market. For example, more than 70% of the world stock trading is traded in either USD or the Euro. This situation may lead to enhance the home bias phenomenon, which will lead to insignificant integration process.

Impairment of Stock Market Efficiency

The term efficiency has not been well defined yet, and is still considered as a controversial issue, it concentrates on determining fair stock prices based on the best available information for a security which is supposed to stabilize the stock market. However, it failed in various occasions in the last two decades. Also, the relationship between efficiency and other factors including volatility, risk, liquidity and return has not been articulated yet, especially in periods of sharp falling of prices or in case of extreme high price volatility.

The researcher found that the behavior of stock markets in the last fifteen years as well the present interpretations of stock market inefficiency need to be re-investigated, in order to suggest new theoretical framework. This means that the efficiency of stock market concept does not apply to the trading periods of high return volatility and sharp falling of stock prices. The different bases of laws may explain, the different effect of stock market crises on the world stock markets, including the period for recovery.

A Less Stable Market

The instability, high risk and stock market crises doesn't affect only millions of investors and shareholders, but also hurts millions of employees who are depending on their pensions programs. Social security programs in many countries are questioning the high level of risk in investing in stock markets, which is reflected in the ability to pay their obligations. The stability of stock market means less volatility, while in the last two decades, there were various global, regional, and national stock market crises occurred.

So far, there are no clear causes for the instability of the world stock markets, and no stated conditions in which a stock market crisis may evolve or ended. The long list of empirical studies reported more than twenty interpretations and causes for increasing volatility or evolving a stock market crisis (Sabri, 2002). Such as overreactions to noise trading, adverse information to negative earning announcements, political risk, and introducing new related laws. Limitations of basic laws, corporate laws, and stock trading mechanism may lead to stock market crisis at certain events. Liberalization of stock markets and attached foreign trading and volatility of cash flow to equity markets may also be considered a stock market crisis under specific conditions of trading. The impact of cross listed shares, which may lead to high correlation between the world stock indices and increasing the effect of major markets on other stock markets, is also one of the reported causes of stock market crisis. Other causes may be related to transmission of volatility due to overnight information, or during sharp declining of prices. The interactions between option and future markets and cash market including underlying shares, as well as interactions between bond market and stocks markets are considered causes of initiating stock market crisis. Finally, volatility of interest rates, currency rate, and trading volume volatility may lead to stock market crisis.

Table 8-1. The most reported causes of stock market crises

Geographical levels of the crisis	The most causes of stock market crisis
National Level crisis	Devaluation of national currency
	Extreme volatility of equity flows
	Foreign trading attached to liberalization
Regional levels	Financial Contagion:
	Volatility volume cause
	Impact of leading markets on other markets
Global level	Adverse effect of derivative markets
	Overreaction and noise trading
	Increasing correlations between the world stock market indices

In addition, it may be concluded that the factors lead to initiate a stock market crisis in national level may be different in regional or global levels as presented in Table 8-1. The devaluation of national currency and changing in the currency exchange rate against foreign currencies is the most possible cause of initiating a stock market crisis at the national level, followed by the adverse impact of foreign trading and irreversible equity flow accompanied by the liberalization of national economy. However, it may be noted that the above possible causes may have different adverse impact based on the level of the crisis, and the period to cover.

The degree of the stock market crisis may be different from one economy to another based on merits of national economies and other related laws. The high volatility of trading volume, the financial contagion phenomenon, and the impact of leading stock markets are the most important factors in evolving a stock market crisis at the regional level. While the adverse effect of derivatives market, the overreactions and noise trading and increasing linkages between the world stock price indices are the most effective factors in initiating a stock market crisis at a global level.

Market Fragmentation

As presented in this book, the monopoly of stock exchange no longer exists in most developed stock markets such as in USA and European markets. Today, a security may be traded in different times, different currencies, and different stock exchanges through cross-listed securities, along with attached derivatives, in secondary as well as over the counter markets, using two or more possible trading platforms. The national stock market today is a hybrid stock market using exchange and non-exchange markets through ATSs. This new existing situation in the world stock market creates price differences for a single security, due to various causes:

1. Discrepancy in cost of trading from one market to another.
2. Differences due to currency exchange rates in case of trading, and pricing a security in two or more currencies.
3. Differences due to a lack of information regarding the fundamentals of a security in case of limited quotation announcements.
4. Differences due to market fragmentations, where the orders of a security received by various markets and are not matched or interacted.

The above factors may impair the substantiality of the pricing discovery system in the world stock exchanges; which is supposes to be determined by interaction between orders assigned to a security. Accordingly, the question arise here, how the price discovery works among the different systems, in order to find the equilibrium prices, and to what extend does this situation lead to a market fragmentation. The fragmentation may be found not only in price differences, but also in the volatility and bid ask spreads. The stock market fragmentation of the world stock markets may be divided into two parts as presented in Table 8-2.

Table 8-2. Types of stock market fragmentation

Parts of Fragmentations	Cases of Fragmentations
External Fragmentations	Trading thought ATSs or stock exchange
	Cross listed firms trading under one jurisdiction or different jurisdictions
	Multi- currency trading
Internal fragmentation	Block trading and special deals
	Bearer shares' trading outside the stock exchange
	OTC trading for the listed securities

Sabri, 2007.

The market fragmentation may be produced for external factors or internal ones, which lead to various situations of market fragmentations. The most important factor of creating fragmentation is the cross listed securities, especially when working under different jurisdictions. The market fragmentation occurred between the price behavior of a security traded in local and foreign stock exchanges, when there are no interactions or co- movements among the price discovery systems in both markets. The second major external factor, which creates market fragmentation, is trading a security using the alternative trading system besides the traditional stock exchange. The market fragmentation occurred in cross-listed firms might be more significant in case of trading in exchange and non-exchange venues in both local and foreign markets. Internal factors may also produce market fragmentation such as in case of block trading and special deals, where a special price may be agreed upon outside the price discovery system. In addition, bearer shares may be traded out of any stock trading regulated systems through transferring certificates according to the prices that contractors agreed upon. This part of trading is conducted mainly to avoid cost of trading.

The degree of stock market fragmentation is different based on the various discussed internal and external factors. The market fragmentation may increase price volatility and has an adverse impact in case of deep falling prices. However, it should be noted that, there is no agreement between regulators and market experts how to deal with this issue in the world stock markets, and what is the best way to connect the related markets dealing with the same securities.

Adverse Impact of New Introduced Practices

The previous mentioned new practices were introduced to stock markets for different reasons and conditions, For example, the majority of such practices were used mainly due to advanced technology, communications, and internet uses. Other practices incorporated to meet the market demand such as in case of introducing the index fund vehicles, credit rating, varieties of price indices. Other measures were related to liberalization policies, and the spreading of globalization concept. Finally, the new practices incorporated to the trading and settlement system aimed to increase efficiency, liquidity and to reduce the cost of trading in stock markets. The effect of such new practices may not materialize yet due to the short period, and because the last regional stock market crisis was occurred in 1997. However, based on the published various empirical research, previous official reports, and observed evidences occurred in the world stock market, the possible impact of recent developments might be summarized as presented in Table 8-3.

The internet advising and trading in stock markets may lead to a trade abuse, due to lack of relevant information. A control problem may be appear during the processes of stock trading from requesting orders up to cash settlements, due to solving boarders. It is not clear where the transactions initiated or ended and implemented, which may lead to difficulties of implementing laws as well as the need for reconciliations of contradicted regulations. In addition, the internet customers of stock trading may considered as less loyal stockholders. The new practices introduced to the world trading may also have an adverse effect on stock market stability, such as switching from floor trading to computerized trading, which may reduce the possibility of using the human judgment to control the stock trading, and may close the system during instability periods of trading. In addition reducing of the cash settlement period may decrease the liquidity in the world stock markets.

Table 8-3. Summary of recent introduced practices and stock market stability

Recent Developments in	Possible Adverse Situations
Internet trading for advising and trading	Possibility of trade abuse Dissolving of boarders Less loyal stockholders Difficulty of enforcing laws
Shifting from floor to electronics Trading	Breaking down of the system during instability periods of trading
Trading in multi currency	Interaction with the volatility of currency exchange rate
Reducing the settlement cycle	Less liquidity which may produce trade disruption
Changing of the world corporate ownership	Less loyalty stockholders of the individual inventories which may lead to irrational trades Cash outflow of foreign investments Less loyalty of the majority of stockholders in case of minority control corporations.
Expanding markets of derivatives and Index based products and funds	Possibility of market front running Possibility of disconnection between cash and index derivatives markets Adverse effect on underlying in falling prices periods
Increasing the role of credit rating agencies	Conflict of interest Timing of rating may not be relevant Adverse effect on equity market of respective firms
Increasing volatility of foreign cash flow	Less liquidity which may produce trade disruption and regional contagion crisis

The new phenomenon of changing the structure of the world corporate ownership from public to private, and from institutional to individual investors, from resident ownership to foreign ownership, from majority control corporate to minority control is also may be considered as risky factor.

It will lead to less loyalty stockholders, irrational trading and cash flow out of foreign investments; thus creating the possibility of marketing front running. The increasing size of derivatives markets and extending it to emerging markets may have negative aspects on stability of both developing and emerging markets, due to the possibility of disconnection between cash and derivatives markets, and the adverse effect on the underlying assets during the falling prices periods. The increasing role of credit rating agencies may have serious adverse effect on respective securities, in case of irrelevant timing of changing credit rating of bonds issued by listed firms.

Adverse Impact of New Legal Changes

The expected negative effect of introducing new legal changes may emerge during the unstable coming periods of trading. Considering the interpretations of the extraordinary high price volatility and the causes of stock market crises, the new incorporated laws and regulations may have the possibility of producing adverse situations during instable periods of trading as presented in Table 8-4. The changing of economic statues, structure, and legal entity of stock exchanges creates a new trading management with different targets and perceptions, which is not tested yet to cope with stock market crisis. Adopting regulations for more protection to investors may lead to reduction of liquidity and thus destabilizing the world stock markets. Issuing of both no- par and par value shares at once may increase price volatility of the respective security and create significant different prices. Issuing dual class shares continues to create inferior holders thus less loyal stockholders, who may be the first to sell in periods of declining prices. Finally, voting rights and inferior holders are significant issues in stock market stability.

Table 8-4. Summary of recent incorporated legal changes and stock market stability

Recent Developments	Possible Adverse - Positive Situations
Changing legal entity of stock exchange	Stock exchange industry no longer a monopoly market
Modernizing of corporate laws	Protection of investors may lead to reduction of liquidity
Trends towards issuing par value and no- par value at once	Increase price volatility of the respective security and may impair price discovery mechanism
Trend of adopting share repurchases	Interfering in stock trading to influence stock prices
Trends toward dual class share	Impair the mechanism of price discovery, Less loyalty of inferior holders
Extending the inside trading laws to new markets	Decreasing liquidity when it is needed Preventing insiders from trading in critical trading periods
Trading interruptions' regulations	Adverse effects on dual listed firms in other exchanges May delay the falling prices but not prevented
Regulations for cross border transactions	Increasing the routine procedures and cost of trading, Fragmentation of orders
Regulations of alternative trading systems	Fragmentation of orders Impair the mechanism of price discovery No effect of price control regulations

In addition, other legal changes may have additional adverse effect on stock market during unstable periods or through deep falling of prices. For examples, authorizing and regulating alternative trading systems and cross border transactions are considered as the most risky factors compared to other changes. The risky factors are related to fragmentation of orders, impairment the price discovery mechanism, and there will be no possibility of imposing price control measures on the trading process. Imposing the insider trading regulations may also create serious lack of liquidity by preventing the most significant and interested investors to interfere, which may lead to falling prices significantly.

Negative Impact of Globalization

It may be concluded that the major aspects of the world stock market globalization have been incorporated significantly, including integration, liberalization, and internationalization of stock trading process. However, the question arises here about the adverse effect of globalization on the stability of stock market. It is clear from many empirical studies, that there is a possible adverse effect, especially on emerging stock markets, which may be summarized as shown in Table 8-5.

Table 8-5. The side effect of globalization on stock market Stability

Aspects of stock market globalization	The side effect of globalization
I: Liberalization	Increasing volatility of stock prices
	Increases volatility spillovers among stock markets
	Possible national currency problems
	Less national policies to control emergencies
	Transferring of government power to marketing mechanism
	High competition facing national stock exchange
II: Integration	High risk in short term for national financial institutions
	Less diversification which increases risk of investments
	Financial Contagion of crisis
	Reducing segmentation but not emerging efficient integration
	Integration with little harmonization of related laws
III: Internationalization trading	Fragmentation of prices
	Less regulatory measures to control volatility
	Spillovers of stock market high volatility among stock markets

The liberalization of the world stock market may lead in certain events to an increase in the volatility of stock markets, especially in case of transmissions from other stock exchanges, which may lead to reversible cash flow and thus a national currency problem. In addition, the liberalization of the related laws may weaken the national authority in controlling and protecting the national stock market activities during the period of unstable conditions. The integration process of the world stock markets may increase risk for the whole economy especially in the short run, and create national currency problems for emerging economies. In addition, it increases the phenomenon of financial contagion of financial crisis. Internationalization of the world stock markets will increase the possibility of market fragmentations, and leaving the related authorities of less control measures to interfere in stock trading when it is needed.

REMEDIES AND SUGGESTED SOLUTIONS

To consider the mentioned issues in this book, based on the reviewing of state of the arts, considering the new practices, and based on the surveys and related empirical studies, several reforms and solutions may be suggested to enhance the stock market stability. In other words, as long as the concept of stock market efficiency has been impaired fully or partially during certain periods of stock trading, remedies are urgently needed in order to sustain the efficiency of stock markets and to keep stocks trading as rational as possible. Accordingly, the following sections present suggestions which aim at curbing the possible causes of the stock market instability and may help in stabilizing stock prices during instable trading periods as well as during deep falling of prices. However, some of these suggestions need to be tested empirically in further studies.

Adjusted Stock Efficient Hypothesis

The stock efficient hypothesis may be restated based on the stock market behavior in the last two decades and considering the new introduced practices as follows:

1. Generally, stock market is an efficient market in most of trading times, but it includes a segment of inefficiency as shown in the last two decades.
2. The inefficiency segment of stock market moves to be a large and a dominate factor at certain events and conditions.
3. The inefficient segment of stock markets increased significantly in the last two decades.
4. The level of inefficient segment varies from one market to another in normal conditions of trading, but it becomes identical in case of stock crises and during transmission of high volatility periods between the world and regional major stock markets.
5. The causes of increasing inefficient segment of stock markets vary between the world stock markets.
6. It is not known when, where, and to what extent the inefficient segment of stock market increases significantly during instable stock trading periods.

The general proof of the above elements of the suggested model may be found in the long list of the literature conducted in the last two decades. However, various empirical tests need to be conducted, considering the above new assumptions in various national and regional markets and during different periods of trading.

Adopting a World Consolidated Quotation System

Today, about 2000 dual listed securities are traded in the world stock markets are located in different jurisdictions. In addition, many international public offerings have been introduced to the world primary stock markets. In addition, new methods of trading which uses electronic communication networks besides traditional stock exchange are working together in the major world stock markets. Accordingly, the stock trading decisions are spreading all over the world websites, rather than being concentrated around the stock exchange. In the last five years, the number of investors including sellers and buyers using the internet services has been increasing rapidly. For example, the NASDAQ report (2001) found that there are about 28 million on line brokerage accounts in 2001.

The question arises here is how to solve the problem of information to be available for all concerned parties who are located cross-boarders and cross different trading systems?. In addition, how can we assure the flow of stock trading information among the concerned parties. Accordingly, we suggest having a global consolidated quotation system for the majority of the world cross-listed firms traded in different jurisdictions or in different locations and using different methods. This system may be established by one of the world stock market organizations such as the International Organization of Securities Commissions (IOSCO), the World Federations of Exchanges Association, or other related bodies. The system may include the world blue chip securities, based on stated requirements related to the capitalization, traded value, turnover, and the number of stock exchanges in which a security is being cross-listed. The suggested consolidated quotation system may offer the needed information besides the quotation information, types and number of buying and selling orders, as well as the clearing and settlement obligations for transactions.

Reforms Concerning the Bearer Share

The world stock markets concerning the bearer shares may be classified into four groups:

1. There are markets include both registered shares and bearers share issued by the same corporation.
2. There are markets include both registered shares and bearers share issued by differnt corporations.
3. There are markets nclude only registered shares for all classes and types.
4. There are markets nclude registered shares mainly, while bearer shares are connected to special types, classes, or owners.

However, trading in bearer shares is one of the most contradicting issues in the corporate laws. Various legislations support the concept of bearer shares and consider it as a symbol for liberalization of stock markets, while others consider bearer share as a way for tax evasion and money laundering. Accordingly, some countries prevented bearer shares in the last decade such as Brazil and Australia, while we find some counties are introducing it (Sabri, 2005). Trading in bearer shares means no control over the share trading of the listed securities outside the stock exchanges as long as it requires only handling certificates.

Observers recognize that the volume of the outside trading for the listed shares may be estimated to be as much more than the trade volume conducted in inside stock exchanges, mainly to reduce or avoid the cost of trading. This situation creates various share prices beside the exchange stock prices, and may increase the overreaction of stock traders and noise trading in certain events. The bearer share certificate and stock trading outside the stock exchanges make the job of controlling stock market unmanageable, in case of crises.

Therefore, the effect of stock trading outside stock exchanges should be examined thoroughly in case of a market crisis, and to confine the stock trading for the listed firms to inside exchanges. Accordingly, there is a need to change the related corporation laws to replace the bearer share with registered share.

Reviewing Preventive Measures of Controlling Prices

As presented in chapter three, the majority of the world stock markets apply preventive regulations related to freeze or stop stock trading when high- low price movements when reach a stated level in a trading day. The preventive measures may be imposed on a security, group of securities or the whole market, through discretionary instruments including trading halts, and market disclosures, or automatic measures such as stated price limits, and circuit break for the entire market. Preventive measures are used mainly to control the high price volatility For example; the cause of trading suspension of the world stock markets was due to extraordinary fluctuations in stock prices in 2001, which represents 86% of the total trading suspensions (IOSCO, 2002).

The question arises here, are these preventive measures sufficient to deal with the emergencies in stock market trading. Various studies reported that such preventive measures are not sufficient or not efficient, and they only delay the rational price movements. Kupiec (1998) found that margin requirements cannot be used to manage market volatility, but they may reduce the open interest of future contracts. Kim (2001) found that price limits are made more restrictive, and stock market volatility is not lowered. The inefficiency of using such policies, especially the price limits that are imposed now in the majority of European stock exchanges, Asian, and some of emerging stock exchanges are now debatable. Such measures may be sufficient to deal with low or an average price stock volatility, but it may be difficult to cope with high volatility or stock market crises. This may be due to trading outside stock exchanges, especially for countries which have bearer shares which are not controllable. Accordingly, there is a need to examine preventive price volatility measures carefully in order to develop and advance such measures, because automatic preventive measures may create adverse interruptions in the stock trading process, which may initiate a stock market crisis.

Using Treasury Shares as a Stability Instrument

During the stock market crises and sharp declining of stock prices, there was a significant need to increase liquidity in the market. This may occur by the company interfering to buy its own shares, to be held in treasury until market recovery. This is prohibited in all of the world stock markets. In USA recently, the SEC issued a new rule stated that "events following the market breaks in October 1987 and October 1997 have underscored the significant role of issuer repurchases during market downturns and the need for clarity as the applicability of Rule 10b-18 in periods of extreme downturns. On those occasions issuer repurchases provided an important source of liquidity that helped ease market stress" (SEC, 1999). Thus there is a need to consider the firm interference in the stock market to buy its' own shares if the share prices fall to a certain level, and to hold the repurchased shares as long as the market situation requires so.

Accordingly, we suggest that treasury stocks to be used as a way of stabilizing stock market (Sabri, 2003). The basic elements of the suggested concept may be articulated as follows:

- Using this model should be exclusive for corporations listed in the stock exchange, in case of dual or cross listing in more than stock exchanges; this privilege should work only in the home stock exchange.
- The daily stock repurchasing transactions should not exceed 50% of the trading volume for that day.
- In any situation, the holding shares should not exceed 25% of the total outstanding shares.
- To implement repurchasing programs by authorized corporations' laws or by a resolution of the majority of stockholders as well as by the home stock exchange.
- The authorization of repurchasing programs is limited for one year and to be renewing annually, after a careful audit of previous activities.
- The approval and announcement of share repurchasing programs for this model should not be used as a substitute to paying dividends.
- The interference time on stock market is bounded by certain levels of prices or stock exchange performance index, and not by corporate management decisions, to the extent that there is a fund available in the special free reserve.
- The level of interference for repurchase may be set at the share book value, or at par value or at levels in between.
- The market value of a share in stock market is supposed to reflect the earned capital beside the par value, the present and future expectation of the firm. Accordingly, there is justification for interference if market price falls below the book value assuming the fundamentals data of the firm is true. In some states and due to differences in corporate laws and reserve requirements, the level of interference may be set between book value and par value of the share.
- To hold the repurchased shares as long as the market situation requires so. In order to be ready for reselling at a convenient time when the share prices rise to a stated level or when the performance index of the home stock exchange improves to a certain level.
- The stated level of interference may be when the market share value falls below the par value, the book value, or a point in between. Thus, timing and volume of reselling and repurchasing transactions is bounded by the stated ratios of market prices, to par value of the share, or performance index of the home stock exchange were the company is listed.
- The stock repurchasing transactions may be regarded as stock transfers among shareholders rather than dividend distributions. The treasury shares should be presented as an asset under the caption of long-term investments in the asset side of the balance sheet statement.
- The net profits and losses from reselling repurchased shares may be considered as costs or revenues of that period, thus they are to be recognized in income statements as other profits or losses accomplished from other portfolios.

- Disclosure notes should be attached to financial statements to indicate the balance, reselling and repurchasing of treasury shares by dates, numbers, and values.
- The free reserves are the only source of funds to be used for repurchasing transactions for holding treasury shares.
- A corporation should not interfere as a buyer for its own shares in the stock market based on this model to hinder a hostile takeover attempt or to serve other purposes such as employee option plans or for tax advantages.

Reconciling Different Laws and Regulations

This book argues that in spite of significant changes occurred in the related laws, concerning the stock trading towards harmonization and integration; there is still a significant diversification of the related laws, which have direct impact on the issue of stock trading stability. Such recent changes may not be enough to deal with rapid increasing of linkages, and integration occurring in the world stock exchanges. Accordingly, further efforts should be conducted by the world specialized institutions in order to reduce diversity in the related corporate, securities and exchange laws. With new practices taking place, this issue is becoming so urgent, especially with increasing the size of cross-border trading including cross listed firms, international public offerings, internet trading and stock trading consultations, alternative stock trading and cross border clearing and settlements. To cope with this issue, various ways and means were implemented in the last two decades, but none of them were enough to offer the relevant solutions. Examples of theses ways and means are:

- To use alternative methods such as what is, known as global depositary receipts, and American depositary receipts as alternatives to direct cross listings and international public offerings and offshore corporate entities.
- Using mutual recognition approach among twin and regional countries to accept each other, regulations regarding stock trading transactions.
- Relaxing of the related regulations in the national jurisdictions regarding cross borders stock market transactions.
- Developing, and adopting accepted international regulations, principles, practices and codes regarding major issues of stock trading.
- Harmonization of the related laws, which is still in the very beginning and it, seems it is not going to be completed, even in the regional level, especially concerning corporate and securities laws.

However, none of the above approaches led to harmonizing regulations regarding the cross border stock trading. Accordingly, it is recommended to work in a project of reconciling the related laws and regulations in order to avoid the contradicting issues, which now exist in the different laws and regulations, and to develop systemic regulatory benchmarks for the majority of the world jurisdictions.

CONCLUSION

This book meant to discuss the issue of international stock markets stability. In order to accomplish this, the majority of the world new introduced practices were thoroughly examined, the legal aspects of about one hundred countries including both developed and emerging jurisdictions were considered, and the state of the arts regarding efficiency, and stability of stock markets were reviewed intensively. In addition, opinion surveys of stock markets' experts were incorporated, as well as empirical studies which examined the related issues of the world stock market stability.

The main target of the stock markets is to have a relevant trading system and environment to contain one of the most important trading sectors in the world economy. The general merits of the relevant stock market may be a feature of the following: To have a low cost of trading, to offer a high level of liquidity and transparency, to assure protecting of investors' interests and other related parties. To simplify processes and regulations of trading, to work under a relevant level of efficiency and stability with less control measure and formal interruptions, based on relevant regulations, which offers the needed information, and to avoid contagious nature of crisis transmission.

The question here which arises, is to what extent the recent trading and legal practices introduced to the world stock markets satisfy or impair such merits especially that related to efficiency and stability?. This book discussed the positive and negative aspects attached to the recent developments. However, the impact of such developments is not fully visible yet, and as a matter of fact, the moderate stability environment of the world stock trading existed at the beginning of twenty-one century, might be due to the low interest rate of bank deposits and the relatively low yields of both government and corporate bonds which are still existing at the beginning of 2007.

REFERENCES

Campos, Calos E. Roberto E. Newell and Gregory Wilson (2002) "Corporate governance develops in emerging markets" *McKinsey on Finance* (Winter) 15-18.

GCGF (2002) Global Investor Opinion Survey (Global Corporate Government Forum, McKinsey & Company) available on line www.gcgf.org

Hasan, Iftekhar, Markku Malkamäki and Heiko Schmiedel (2003) "Technology, automation, and productivity of stock exchanges: international evidence" *Journal of Banking & Finance* 27 (9); 1743-1773.

IFC, (1998). *Emerging Stock Markets Factbook 1998,* (International Financial Corporation, Washington, D. C.).

IOSCO (2002). "*Report on Trading Halts and Market Closures*" (Technical committee, International Organization of Securities Commissions, October).

Jain, Pankaj, (2003) "Financial Market Design and Equity Premium: Electronic versus Floor Trading" (February. AFA 2004 San Diego Meetings).

Kaminsky, Graciela Laura, Richard K. Lyons and Sergio Schmkler (2001) "Mutual fund investment in Emerging Markets: An overview" *The World Bank Economic Review* 14; 315- 340.

Kim, Kenneth A. (2001). “Price limits and stock market volatility” *Economics Letters.* 71, (1); 141-146.

Kupiec, P. H. (1998) "Margin requirements, volatility, and market integrity: What have we learned since the crash?" *Journal of Financial Services Research* 14, (4); 241-256.

NASDAQ, (2001) *The Globalization of the World Stock Markets* (NASDAQ, USA November, 14).

OECD (1999) *Principles of corporate governance* (Organization For Economic Co-operation and Development, France)

OECD (2004) *OECD Principles of corporate governance; Draft Revised Text* (Organization For Economic Co-operation and Development, France)

S&P (2000) *Emerging Stock Markets Factbook, 2000* (Standard & Poor's, McGraw- Hill Company, New York, USA).

S&P (2003) *Global Stock markets Factbook, 2003* (Standard &Poor's, McGraw- Hill Company, New York, USA).

Sabri, Nidal Rashid (2002) “Roots of stock market volatility and crises: a synthesis and suggested remedies" *International Review of Comparative Public Policy* 13; 1-53.

Sabri, Nidal Rashid (2003). "Using treasury “repurchase” stocks to stabilize stock markets" *International Journal of Business* 8, (4); 426-450.

Sabri, Nidal Rashid (2005). "Legal features of traded securities and high price volatility" *Advances in Financial Economics* 11, 237- 249.

Sabri, Nidal Rashid (2007) Recent developments and stock market stability" (Manuscript under publication).

SEC (1999) *Final Rule: Purchases of Certain Equity Securities by the Issuer and others* (Release No.34-41905 (SEC, New York).

Standard & Poor’s (2000) *Emerging Stock Markets Fact Book, 2000* (Standard & Poor's, McGraw- Hill Company, New York, USA).

WFE, (2005) *Annual Report and Statistics, 2005* (World Federation of Exchanges, Paris).

WFE, (2006) World Federation of Exchanges Data Base (available on line http://www.world-exchanges.org).

INDEX

A

B

E

F

G

H

I

J

K

L

P

Q

R

S

T

U

V

W

Y

Z